Schools
CAN
Change

Schools CAN Change

A Step-by-Step Change Creation System for Building Innovative Schools and Increasing Student Learning

Dale W. **LICK** | Karl H. **CLAUSET** | Carlene U. **MURPHY**

A Joint Publication

CORWIN
A SAGE Company

learningforward

CORWIN
A SAGE Company

FOR INFORMATION:

Corwin

A SAGE Company

2455 Teller Road

Thousand Oaks, California 91320

(800) 233-9936

www.corwin.com

SAGE Publications Ltd.

1 Oliver's Yard

55 City Road

London EC1Y 1SP

United Kingdom

SAGE Publications India Pvt. Ltd.

B 1/I 1 Mohan Cooperative Industrial Area

Mathura Road, New Delhi 110 044

India

SAGE Publications Asia-Pacific Pte. Ltd.

3 Church Street

#10-04 Samsung Hub

Singapore 049483

Acquisitions Editor: Dan Alpert

Associate Editor: Megan Bedell

Editorial Assistant: Heidi Arndt

Production Editor: Cassandra Margaret Seibel

Copy Editor: Lana Todorovic-Arndt

Typesetter: C&M Digitals (P) Ltd.

Proofreader: Rae-Ann Goodwin

Indexer: Kathy Paparchontis

Cover Designer: Candice Harman

Permissions Editor: Karen Ehrmann

Copyright © 2013 by Corwin

Printed in the United States of America.

A catalog record of this book is available from the Library of Congress.

ISBN 978-1-4129-9874-1

This book is printed on acid-free paper.

SUSTAINABLE FORESTRY INITIATIVE
Certified Chain of Custody
Promoting Sustainable Forestry
www.sfiprogram.org
SFI-01268
SFI label applies to text stock

12 13 14 15 16 10 9 8 7 6 5 4 3 2 1

Contents

List of Figures and Tables   ix

Online Resources   xi

Foreword   xiii

Preface   xvii
    Purpose and Need   xvii
    Who Should Read and Use This Book?   xviii
    Organization and Contents   xix

Acknowledgments   xxiii

About the Authors   xxv

1. The Change Creation System   1
    School Improvement   1
    School Reforms   2
    The Roots of the Change Creation System   4
    No Silver Bullet, One Brick at a Time   5
    Standards for Professional Learning and Practice   6
    The Change Creation System   7
    Summary   10

Part I. Fundamentals of Effectiveness   11

2. Fundamentals of Effectiveness for School Improvement   13
    Understanding the Culture   14
    Culture of Discipline   17
    Culture of Change Creation   19
    Culture of Relationships and Collaboration   21
    Culture of Transformational Leadership   22
    Cultural Change   28
    Summary   29

3. Fundamentals of Vision and Successful Change   31
    Vision   31
    Change   37

Success and Failure of Change		38
Effective Sponsorship in Schools		44
Change and Resistance in Schools		46
Universal Change Principle for Schools		51
Summary		54

4. Fundamentals for Creating Learning Teams and Professional Learning Communities — **55**

Collaboration and Teamwork		56
Action Teams and Professional Learning Communities		58
Authentic Teams and Synergy		58
Comentoring Teams		63
Learning Teams		64
Professional Learning Communities		69
Summary		75

Part II: The Process of the Change Creation System — **77**

5. Introducing the Decision-Making Cycle — **79**

Action Teams Decision-Making Cycle		79
Preparing to Start the Decision-Making Cycle		84
Summary		90

6. Identifying Student Learning Needs and Forming Action Teams — **91**

Student Learning Needs That Action Teams Address		92
How to Identify Student Learning Needs		93
Form Action Teams and Select Student Needs to Address		96
Selecting Student Needs to Address		99
Support for Identifying Student Needs and Forming Action Teams		99
Summary		102

7. Introducing Action Teams — **103**

Action Teams in the Change Creation System		103
The Work of Action Teams		104
Purposes of Action Teams		106
Action Team Principles		110
Action Team Process Guidelines		111
Effective Action Team Meetings		114
Action Teams as a Bundle of Changes		116
Summary		117

8. Support for Action Teams — **119**

Keep the Focus on Student Learning		119
Protect Time for Action Team Meetings		120
Establish Routines		120
Provide Regular, Frequent, and Constructive Feedback to Action Teams		121

Understand the Developmental Stages of Action Teams 122
Help Struggling Teams Move Forward 127
Develop Communication Networks and
    Strategies to Share Action Teams' Work and Results 130
Form Administrator Action Teams 131
Summary 132

9. Creating Team Action Plans **133**

Team Action Plan 133
Creating Team Action Plans 143
Support for Action Teams on Their Team Action Plans and Logs 148
Summary 152

**10. Implementing Learning and Inquiry Cycles for Innovation
and Improving Student Learning: Parts 1 and 2** **153**

Implementing Learning and Inquiry Cycles 154
Supporting Learning and Inquiry Cycles for
    Innovation and Student Learning 171
Summary 174

**11. Implementing Learning and Inquiry Cycles for Innovation
and Improving Student Learning: Parts 3 and 4** **177**

Implementing Learning and Inquiry Cycles 177
Supporting Learning and Inquiry Cycles for
    Innovation and Student Learning 187
Summary 189

**12. Assessing the Impact of Action Teams and
Sharing Results and Best Practices** **191**

Assessing the Impact of Action Teams on Teacher
    Practice and Student Learning 192
Sharing Results and Best Practices and Applying
    Lessons Learned 198
Repeating the Decision-Making Cycle Each Year 202
Supporting Assessing the Impact of Action Teams and
    Sharing Results and Best Practices 202
Summary 208

Epilogue **209**

References **213**

Index **221**

Additional materials and resources related to
Schools Can Change: *A Step-by-Step Change Creation
System for Building Innovative Schools and Increasing
Student Learning* can be found at www.corwin.com/
schoolscanchange.

List of Figures and Tables

Chapter 1

Figure 1.1 The Change Creation System   9

Chapter 2

Figure 2.1 Cultural Change–Student Learning Loop   16

Figure 2.2 What Transformational Leaders Do   24

Chapter 3

None

Chapter 4

Figure 4.1 The Desired Evolution of an Action Team   56

Figure 4.2 Building Team Synergy   60

Figure 4.3 Norms for Synergistic/Authentic Teams   60

Figure 4.4 A Synergy/Authentic Teamwork Checklist for Teams   62

Figure 4.5 Learning Team Capacities   65

Figure 4.6 Building Learning Teams   66

Table 4.1 Comparing Elements of Professional
Learning Communities and the Change Creation System   73

Chapter 5

Figure 5.1 Annual Decision-Making Cycles Support
Multiyear Improvement Efforts   80

Figure 5.2 Action Teams Decision-Making Cycle   81

Figure 5.3 Action Teams Drive Plans for Improvement   85

Chapter 6

None

Chapter 7

Figure 7.1 Action Teams Hold Everything Together   109

Figure 7.2 Action Teams—Why They Work:
Strong Process Holds Strong Content   113

Chapter 8

Figure 8.1 Developmental Stages for Action Teams   123

Figure 8.2 Eight-Step Plan to Help Struggling Action Teams   128

Chapter 9

Figure 9.1 Team Action Plan Template   135

Figure 9.2 Team Action Plan Example   137

Figure 9.3 Action Team Meeting Log Template   147

Table 9.1 "Strong" Student Learning Needs—Typical
Problems and Solution Options   150

Chapter 10

Figure 10.1 The Learning and Inquiry Cycle for Action Teams   155

Chapter 11

Figure 11.1 The Action Team Learn-Plan-Act-Reflect Cycle   179

Chapter 12

None

Online Resources

A. Vision Creation

B. Learning Forward Standards for Professional Learning

C. Checklist for Team Synergy

D. Action Teams Decision-Making Cycle

E. A Comparison of the Whole-Faculty Study Groups and Action Teams Decision-Making Cycles

F. Finding Time for Action Team Meetings

G. Illustrative Student Learning Needs

H. Process for Selecting Student Needs by Consensus in an Action Team

I. The Action Teams Process Guidelines

J. Change Creation System Roles and Responsibilities

K. Helping Struggling Action Teams

L. Team Action Plan Template

M. Steps for Creating a Team Action Plan

N. Checklist for Team Action Plans

O. Team Meeting Log Template

P. Checklist for Team Meeting Logs

Q. "Strong" Student Learning Needs—Typical Problems and Solution Options

R. Protocol for Tuning Team Action Plans

S. The Learning and Inquiry Cycle for Action Teams

T. Looking at Student Work Report

U. Action Teams Assessment Forms

V. Action Teams Rubric

W. Action Teams System Survey

Foreword

A revolution took place in staff development in the late 1980s and continued into the 1990s. It was not reported on the evening news. Very few knew it was happening. I was a rebel, along with others I had not yet met, in the rebellion that resulted in the dominant form of professional development today—learning communities.

In 1978, I was approached by the superintendent in Augusta, Georgia, to fill a new position he would be recommending to the board of education. The position was director of staff development. I asked the superintendent, "What would I do?" His response was, "You have the opportunity to determine the scope of the job." I was awed with the prospects yet questioned if "staff development" could be justified to the board as a full-time position. I could not google the term. I found few books as resources. Professional publications heavily favored curriculum development. There was not another position in Georgia with the title. There were no academies to provide support. There were individuals at the Georgia Department of Education who were developing staff development guidelines for local leaders that I found helpful. It would be 1980 before I attended an event sponsored by the National Staff Development Council. By some leap of faith, the position was approved, and I began a personal and professional journey into discovering what I needed to know to be skillful in doing my job.

I view the fourteen years I served as the lead staff developer in Augusta in three stages. The first few years, I was a logistics organizer, designer of credit activities, registrar, and contractor for speakers and presenters. The second stage was the push for school-based staff development, not to be confused with establishing learning communities. Principals requested funding for motivational speakers and workshop presenters. I then added *critiquer* of plans and banker to my repertoire. As the state moved to paying stipends for credits earned, I became a more accomplished accountant and bookkeeper. As the state mandated specific courses teachers were to take to renew certificates and local boards mandated credit hours for maintaining tenure, I found the #1 concern of teachers coming to my office was whether or not they were in compliance with regulations. I saw a dullness in teachers' eyes as they stood before me with papers in hand to register for both district and school offerings. My reports for numbers of teachers and administrators involved in department activities were impressive. The district received accolades from state leaders and national organizations. Yet, I knew something was missing, something wasn't working. I knew student achievement in the district, at best, was stagnant. As I visited classrooms and observed teachers preparing materials in the district's Teacher Center, I saw that all the resources we were putting into training were not improving teacher practice and increasing student learning.

The third stage began in 1986 when my frustration with the status quo was at its highest and, lucky for me, I was in the right place at the right time. Georgia was increasing its staff development funds to local districts at the same time I was chairperson of the National Staff Development Council's 1986 annual conference. Feeling the pressure of accountability mounting, I made the most of my personal connections to leaders in the field who would be presenting at the national conference. Two leaders, Bruce Joyce and Beverly Showers, spoke to the need of increasing student achievement through staff development (Joyce & Showers, 2002). I had to change how I worked. With this realization, I became a staff development rebel. I rebelled against the traditional role I had fulfilled since 1978. Thankfully, I had a superintendent who was willing to hire Joyce and Showers as consultants for a three-year period and to allow me to spend at least 50% of my time with three faculties for one year, adding additional schools in years 2 and 3 (Murphy, 1992). We wanted to document how teacher learning is tied to student learning, how changing teaching behaviors change student behaviors. At the time, I had no idea that we had set our eyes on climbing the Mt. Everest of professional development. I had a new purpose, and plans for my senior years took a sharp turn in a new direction. The years I had left as a working professional would be spent assisting district and school leaders in developing strategies for organizing whole faculties into learning units focusing on what students need for teachers to do. I became a rebel with a cause.

In 1986, *professional learning communities* (PLCs) was not a term used within the staff development community. In our district, in specific schools we targeted, we broke new ground in expecting every faculty member to be in a study group (Murphy, 1992) with no more than five members using student achievement as their measure of effectiveness. We called the groups *study groups* because it seemed a familiar term that did not sound threatening and, building on the staff development Joyce and Showers were providing to teachers on *Models of Teaching* (Joyce & Weil, 1986), I focused on groups studying the research on several models of teaching and practicing those strategies when they met as well as designing lessons they would teach using the strategies.

The six years before I retired from my home district were years of learning how to work with whole faculties in small groups working on student instructional needs. We did not find any schools in the United States doing what we were doing in our district in 1987. We had no model to follow. As I left the district in 1992 and moved into the role of consultant working with faculties in many different parts of the country, I found that few knew what to do to make the connection between staff development and student achievement. *How* was still fuzzy to me, especially when leaving the comfort of my hometown district. For those who called me for help, I said, "We'll learn more together." As it had been with me, school and district leaders everywhere were struggling to meet the needs of teachers and students through archaic staff development systems. More funding brought pressure and high expectations from local boards of education, state departments, and federal agencies.

I share this look into my past because I think it mirrors how the field of professional learning has evolved over the past thirty years. We experienced a staff development revolution in the mid-1980s through 1990s. Every issue of the *Journal of Staff Development* brought news of new "discoveries." Staff developers were explorers. We were exploring new ways of working and were trying what we heard others were doing successfully. We had little research to guide us. We were doing the research ourselves, working researchers. We were doing what had not yet been written. Administrators wanted research to comfort their decision making, and we had little to give them, except what we had just done. We did have studies in training that Joyce and Showers had done with teachers attending summer institutes at the university level (Joyce & Showers, 1983). When we began in 1987, I was asked by an assistant superintendent in my district, "Where has what you are proposing been proven to increase student achievement?" I said, "California." He didn't push for more. Dare I have said, "Nowhere"? We confronted disbelievers. Why should every teacher at a school participate in a study group? Isn't this un-American? Teachers wondered why they were expected to share their secrets of good teaching with other teachers. I recall sitting in a session with a nationally known leader who challenged me on the point of "whole faculty." Another challenged me on the idea that staff developers should be accountable for student learning. How can that be, we don't work with students. Yes, those of us in the middle of the revolution often felt attacked and defensive. However, we prevailed, and new leaders in professional learning today have volumes of research to wade through, maybe too many books telling them what to do and too many consultants anxious to give guidance.

After retiring from my hometown district in 1992, I continued the work for fifteen years in San Diego, CA; Round Rock, TX; Cobb County, GA; Greeley, CO; Seattle, WA; Lake County, IL; Brooklyn, NY; Philadelphia, PA; Franklin County, NC; Baton Rouge, LA; and Kearney, NE; to name a few of the places where I worked with faculties eager to take control of their own learning. I called the work Whole-Faculty Study Groups (WFSG) (Murphy & Lick, 2005).

As I became more experienced and more observant of group work, I stressed the need for members to be more active in their group meetings and to focus on the actions they would take in their classrooms. I began to see that the term *study group* had a passive feel to it. I have said to faculties that if I had known more about what the work of groups would be when I began, I would have called the groups *action groups*. Now, in this book, we are calling the groups *action teams*. Admittedly, I use the word *team* with caution because it seems to me to infer some form of competition. I recall the phrase, "a rose by any other name would smell as sweet." Teachers who work together for the benefit of their students can be called any name and still be effective. What is important is what the three or four teachers do (action) when they are together and what they do (action) in their classrooms as a result of the time spent in a meeting. The inquiry and learning cycle is a series of actions that create changes in teacher practice, and thereby, it creates changes in student learning. If there is no change in how teachers teach or in how students learn, we cannot justify the time spent in meetings.

In consideration of this belief, we are now putting the emphasis on *change* by calling the WFSG system, the Change Creation system. We believe this name is a truer representation of the purpose of the study groups or action teams. Over the past twenty-five years of working with faculties implementing WFSG, my colleagues and I have learned a great deal. Each faculty taught us how to do our work better. We have used what faculties have taught us and the research over the past twenty years to transform the WFSG system into the Change Creation system. We have made substantial improvements to the WFSG design. Just as we expect teachers to make changes in their practices, we should be expected to make changes in our practices.

We are not asking faculties who currently call their learning communities *study groups* and refer to their professional learning model as Whole-Faculty Study Groups to change to the new terms, but we do urge them to consider the changes we have made in the system and whether these changes might help them to improve their work in learning communities and the outcomes of that work.

Once implementation of any process begins, changes naturally happen in how the process is used. The longer a process is used, the more adjustments or modifications occur. Users are the owners. A visitor to a school in Louisiana that began WFSG ten years ago may not recognize WFSG at the school today. However, the faculty is in learning communities; groups have plans and keep logs they designed and groups assess results using tools they developed. The school has made the process invisible. This is what we want faculties to do. Referring to the Concerns Based Adoption Model's Levels of Use (Hord, Rutherford, Huling-Austin, & Hall, 1987), the highest level is Renewal or making an innovation your own. However, to reach the Renewal level, individuals and groups must go through the lower levels of use, that is, Routine, to develop mastery of the innovation to know what to modify.

Now, I am an observer. I see *professional learning community* in every professional publication I receive. Catalogs and advertisements are full of references. Today, believing in the merits of learning communities is like believing in the American way. If asked, any principal is likely to say, "Yes, of course, we have learning communities in our school." Pressed for more descriptive information, we would hear a variety of responses that reflect a wide range in both what learning communities are doing and the likelihood that students are going to benefit from what the teachers are doing. I believe the Change Creation system and this book offer a helpful roadmap and effective approach for greatly improving schools, learning communities, and teaching and for increasing student learning performance.

What will be the next revolution in our profession? Will it be Learning Forward's standards? Will it be the federal government's new "save education" plan? Who will be the rebels? Will it be teachers tired of wasting their time and energy in nonproductive PLCs? Let's hope whatever it is and whoever are the initiators, our country's children will be the benefactors.

Carlene U. Murphy

Preface

This book, *Schools Can Change: A Step-By-Step Change Creation System for Building Innovative Schools and Increasing Student Learning*, provides a change creation process that enables schools to develop significant schoolwide improvements. It lays out step-by-step the necessary concepts and approaches for building innovative schools and increased student learning. If the concepts and processes outlined in this book are fully and effectively implemented, the "school improvement" results can be remarkable.

The Change Creation system has its roots in the schoolwide change system referred to as Whole-Faculty Study Groups (WFSG), which has been widely implemented based on a series of the five books published by Corwin Press, *Whole-Faculty Study Groups: A Powerful Way to Change Schools and Enhance Learning* (1998), *Whole-Faculty Study Groups: Creating Student-Based Professional Development* (2001), *Whole-Faculty Study Groups: Creating Professional Learning Communities That Target Student Learning* (2005), *The Whole-Faculty Study Groups Fieldbook: Lessons Learned and Best Practices From Classrooms, Districts, and Schools* (2007), and *Schoolwide Action Research for Professional Learning Communities: Improving Student Learning Through the Whole-Faculty Study Groups Approach* (2008) by the authors of this book, Carlene U. Murphy, Dale W. Lick, and Karl H. Clauset. Over the years, these books have laid the foundation for the WFSG movement to become one of the successful whole-school improvement processes available to schools across North America.

Research by the authors on school improvement and the WFSG system has continued during recent years. They have examined new approaches to the various processes of school improvement and how current processes, including the WFSG system, could be improved to make the system more effective. Specifically, the Change Creation system, relative to the WFSG system, has been simplified and streamlined to make it easier to use and to provide critical new materials and approaches. The result of all these efforts, the Change Creation system, goes well beyond the WFSG system in substance and practice and, we believe, in total effectiveness.

PURPOSE AND NEED

In an overview and review of the environment relating to school reform and school improvement and a wide range of perspectives on their successes, we and other researchers discovered that most of the major, general initiatives (e.g., A Nation at Risk; National Education Summit, President and Governors; Charter Schools; Goals 2000, Educate America Act; and No Child Left Behind) were, overall, disappointingly ineffective. As we compared these various general school improvement initiatives, we found that they were inconsistent and often at odds with the various professional standards for school learning and practice, including the Standards for Professional Learning by Learning Forward (formerly the National Staff Development Council), 2011; Educational Leadership Policy Standards: ISLLC 2008 by The Council of Chief State School Officers; and The National Board for Professional Teaching Standards.

What this all meant was that there was no "silver bullet" for improving our schools effectively. Instead, these standards pointed out that genuine effective school improvement requires leaders and teachers intimately and creatively involved in a broad-based, creative change system that builds on the professional standards mentioned above.

This approach is precisely the one taken in this book. The first chapter introduces the essence of the book, the Change Creation system, and its foundation being established on the above learning, leadership, and teaching standards. The next three chapters present the critical fundamentals of effectiveness that are required for schools to become successful professional learning communities, significantly improve teaching, and increase student learning. And in the final eight chapters, the book explains, in detail, how the process of the Change Creation system helps schools become and function as professional learning communities by action teams of school personnel.

WHO SHOULD READ AND USE THIS BOOK?

This book should be read and used by anyone who is interested in facilitating staff development, school innovation, and increasing student learning. A primary audience for the book should be the personnel in K–12 schools—all teachers, administrators, and staff—and the district staff who guide and support them. The book is written so that it can serve as a stand-alone guide for the effective initiation, comprehensive implementation, and successful completion of the Change Creation system approach to crucial staff development, major school innovation and schoolwide improvements, and as a textbook or detailed reference book.

For schools that choose to introduce the Change Creation system, all school personnel will be involved in their schoolwide effort. Consequently, in such schools, each faculty member, administrator, and staff member should have a copy, or many copies should be shared with school personnel, allowing full and convenient access across the school.

In addition, the book holds special potential for individual teacher leaders and administrators, school leadership teams, and groups of teachers and administrators who are considering new options for seriously improving their schools.

Other important audiences for this book include the following:

- Central office personnel in school systems, especially for consideration and possible implementation of action teams of school personnel in their school system
- College of Education faculty in colleges and universities, for understanding this new and successful process for schoolwide change and enhanced student learning, as well as for possible use as a textbook or reference book in classes relating to teacher training and school improvement. Preservice teacher training needs to ensure that new teachers have experience working collaboratively in learning teams.
- Community college faculty and administrators for consideration of action teams of college personnel and their application in their institution for collegewide change and improving student learning
- School, community college, college, and university libraries
- Individuals and groups in national and international workshops on action teams and their application in education, from small seminars to large groups
- Individuals and groups in corporate, community, and governmental organizations involved with schools, education, and training

ORGANIZATION AND CONTENTS

The book has an introduction to the Change Creation system, two parts, Fundamentals of Effectiveness and The Process of the Change Creation System, and a large and rich array of important and helpful online resources (available for copying and use by going to www.corwin.com/schoolscanchange).

Chapter 1 gives an overview of the environment relating to school reforms and school improvement and perspectives on their success. It shows that the major, general education initiatives, mentioned earlier, were disappointingly ineffective and were inconsistent and often at odds with the various professional standards for school learning and practice referenced above. The chapter ends with an overview of the Change Creation system, including its new approaches for improving teaching and learning and an outline of the framework for the Change Creation system.

Part I: Fundamentals of Effectiveness

This part of the book addresses the critical fundamentals of effectiveness for understanding and dealing with school culture and cultural change, school vision and change, and authentic teams, learning teams, and professional learning communities. These fundamentals are *required* for schools to be successful in becoming professional learning communities, improving teaching, and increasing student learning. Our focus is on creating the right leadership, vision, culture, and relationships in schools to support and sustain the Change Creation system.

Chapter 2, "Fundamentals of Effectiveness for School Improvement," explains the essentials relating to, dealing with, and creating cultures of discipline, change creation, collaboration, transformational leadership, and school change.

Chapter 3, "Fundamentals of Vision and Successful Change," provides the change concepts necessary for leaders, teachers, and their schools to effectively apply the Change Creation system and move the people and the school toward innovation and increased student learning. In particular, it discusses the directional and inspirational foundation for school change, the *school vision;* the nature and feelings of change; a process for school change; the roles of change; the sponsorship of change; resistance to change; and the most important principle relating to change, the Universal Change Principle.

Chapter 4, "Fundamentals for Creating Learning Teams and Professional Learning Communities," covers authentic teams, learning teams, and professional learning communities, groups of school personnel such as action teams becoming learning teams, and schools developing into professional learning communities.

Part II: The Process of the Change Creation System

Part II of this book discusses and unfolds the process for the Change Creation system through what is termed the Decision-Making Cycle (DMC). The steps of the DMC build on the Fundamentals of Effectiveness given in Chapters 2–4.

Chapter 5, "Introducing the Decision-Making Cycle," provides an overview of the DMC, which is the process of the Change Creation system. It also discusses in detail the preparation that schools need to make before beginning the DMC.

Chapter 6, "Identifying Student Learning Needs and Forming Action Teams," focuses on Step 1 in the Action Teams DMC and offers strategies that the principal and the school leadership team can use to identify specific school-wide student learning needs, form action teams, and help each action team reach agreement on the specific learning needs it will address.

Chapter 7, "Introducing Action Teams," and Chapter 8, "Supporting Action Teams," describe, in depth, action teams and the critical support required for their success, with action teams being the primary vehicles for effectively implementing the Change Creation system. These chapters present action teams in the Change Creation system as designated teams of school personnel who work together to help the school move toward accomplishing the school vision and illustrate the importance of school and district leaders in leading and supporting action teams. Action teams lead the effort to respond to the overarching question that educators need to constantly keep in mind: *What are students learning and achieving as a result of what educators are learning and doing in their action teams?* The Change Creation system has at its core a job-embedded, self-directed, student-driven professional learning system of action teams.

Chapters 9–12 discuss the remaining four steps in the DMC process and its application in detail. Chapter 9, "Creating Team Action Plans," introduces the action plan template that action teams use, explains the task in Step 2 of the Action Teams DMC, how teams use their action plan, the companion to the team action plan, the team meeting log, and it illustrates the importance of school and district leaders in leading and supporting action teams as they create and begin to use their team action plans.

Chapter 10, "Implementing Learning and Inquiry Cycles for Innovation and Improving Student Learning: Parts 1 and 2," and Chapter 11, "Implementing Learning and Inquiry Cycles for Innovation and Improving Student Learning: Parts 3 and 4," address Step 3 in the Action Teams DMC and examine each part of the learning and inquiry cycle. Step 3 is the cycle of learn-plan-act-reflect and the heart of the learning and inquiry cycle that action teams follow—it is the *action* in action teams. This step focuses on what teams need to do for each part of the cycle and how the principal and the school leadership team can ensure that the work of action teams in their learning and inquiry cycles leads to learning and innovation.

Chapter 12, "Assessing the Impact of Action Teams and Sharing Results and Best Practices," details the last two steps in the Action Teams DMC—Step 4, assessing the impact of action teams on teacher practice and student learning, and Step 5, sharing results and best practices and applying lessons learned. The chapter focuses on what each team needs to do to assess its own impact on teacher practice and student learning and how the principal and the school leadership team can assess the schoolwide impact on teacher practice and student learning. It also focuses on the importance of sharing results and best practices at the end of learning and inquiry cycles and at the end of the year, as well as on creating mechanisms to ensure that teams learn from each other and that lessons learned are applied throughout the school. Both of these steps are critical for the school if it is to become a genuine professional learning community.

The book concludes with a brief epilogue by Carlene Murphy, the founder of the WFSG system, on the transformation of WFSG into the Change Creation system and the future for school innovation and improved student learning.

Resources

As indicated in the list of online resources on page xi, a large and rich array of important and helpful resources for this book have been created and are provided online for copying and ease of use. These resources are immediately available by going to www.corwin.com/schoolscanchange.

Acknowledgments

First and foremost, we acknowledge the individuals in schools, districts, state departments of education, and other organizations in the United States and Canada who have been engaged in the implementation of the WFSG system over the past twenty years. It is their work that has enabled us to refine our thinking about the WFSG system and transform it into the Change Creation system that is the focus of this book.

In 2011, Karl Clauset traveled to a number of districts that have been implementing the WFSG system. He was able to visit schools and meet with teachers and school and district leaders to learn about their successes and challenges with WFSG and their lessons learned. The information they shared has enriched this book.

- Franklin County Schools, NC
- Springfield Public Schools R–12, Springfield, MO
- Carthage R–9 School District, Carthage, MO
- Hawthorn School District 73, Vernon Hills, IL
- Wauconda Community Unit School District 118, Wauconda, IL
- Holdrege Public Schools, Holdrege, NE
- Kearney Public Schools, Kearney, NE
- Osborne Unified School District 392, Osborne, KS

We acknowledge our editor at Corwin Press, Dan Alpert, for his encouragement of us to write this book and his guidance and support during the entire process from idea to publication.

We thank our reviewers for taking time from their busy schedules to read our draft manuscript and to provide detailed and thoughtful feedback to us. We have incorporated many of their suggestions into the final version of the manuscript. Their thoughtful feedback has made this a better book. Our reviewers included

Jessica Antosz
Principal
Nanoose Bay Elementary School
Nanoose Bay, BC, Canada

Don Boyd
Principal
Ballenas Secondary School
Parksville, BC, Canada

About the Authors

**Dale W. Lick** is president and professor emeritus at Florida State University, a former president of Georgia Southern University, University of Maine, and Florida State University, and most recently, a university professor at Florida State University, where he did research in the Learning Systems Institute, taught and directed doctoral students in the Department of Educational Leadership and Policy Studies, and worked on educational and organizational projects involving transformational leadership, change creation, learning organizations, distance learning, school improvement, enhanced student performance, educational technology, new learning systems, strategic planning, and visioning.

Included in over fifty national and international biographical listings, Dr. Lick is the author or coauthor of eight books and more than 100 professional articles, chapters and proceedings, and 285 original newspaper columns. His recent books are *Whole-Faculty Study Groups: A Powerful Way to Change Schools and Enhance Learning* (1998); *Whole-Faculty Study Groups: Creating Student-Based Professional Development* (2001); *Whole-Faculty Study Groups: Creating Professional Learning Communities That Target Student Learning* (2005); and *The Whole-Faculty Study Groups Fieldbook: Lessons Learned and Best Practices From Classrooms, Districts, and Schools* (2007), Corwin Press, all with Carlene U. Murphy; *Schoolwide Action Research for Professional Learning Communities: Improving Student Learning Through The Whole-Faculty Study Groups Approach* (2008), and *Schools Can Change: A Step-By-Step Change Creation System for Building Innovative Schools and Increasing Student Learning* (2013), Corwin Press, with Karl H. Clauset and Carlene U. Murphy; and *New Directions in Mentoring: Creating a Culture of Synergy* (1999), Falmer Press (London, UK), with Carol A. Mullen.

Dr. Lick received BS and MS degrees from Michigan State University, and a PhD degree from the University of California, Riverside, all in mathematics, and has three levels of certification in Leading and Managing Change from Conner Partners, Atlanta, Georgia. His alma maters have honored him with the Michigan State University 2006 Distinguished Alumni Award, and on its 40th anniversary in 1994, the University of California, Riverside, honored him with the designation as One of 40 Alumni Who Make a Difference.

Karl H. Clauset is director of the National WFSG Center. He is an experienced school improvement coach and WFSG trainer. Since 1999, he has helped more than ninety elementary, middle, and high schools launch WFSG and has supported the schools through the implementation phase. He was the lead author with Dale Lick and Carlene Murphy for *Schoolwide Action Research for Professional Learning Communities: Improving Student Learning Through the Whole-Faculty Study Groups Approach* (2008), which focuses on the collaborative work teacher teams do to improve their teaching and increase student learning. He is also a senior consultant with Focus on Results and works with principals, school leadership teams, and central office staff to help them align and strengthen efforts to improve teaching and learning.

Previously, he worked as a site developer with ATLAS Learning Communities, a nationally recognized school reform program, and in standards-based reform and international education development at the Education Development Center. In his earlier careers in education, he was a teacher and administrator at the Jakarta International School in Indonesia and taught in secondary schools in Philadelphia, Zambia, and Tanzania. He received a national award from ASCD for the outstanding dissertation in supervision for his doctoral dissertation on the dynamics of effective schooling. As a faculty member at the Boston University School of Education, he taught graduate courses in educational policy analysis, organizational analysis, and planning. Before moving to western Washington in 2003, he served as an elected school board member and board chair for six years in his Massachusetts community.

Carlene U. Murphy is founder and executive director of the National WFSG Center and the principal developer of the WFSG system of professional development. In August 2007, she began her fiftieth year of work in public schools. She started her teaching career in 1957 as a fourth-grade teacher in her hometown of Augusta, Georgia. The next year, she moved to Memphis, Tennessee, where she taught for thirteen years, returning to Augusta in 1972 and retiring from the district in 1993 as its director of staff development. During her fifteen years as the district's chief staff developer, the district received many accolades, including the Award for Outstanding Achievement in Professional Development from the American Association of School Administrators and Georgia's Outstanding Staff Development Program Award for two consecutive years. She was awarded the National Staff Development Council's Contributions to Staff Development Award and served as the National Staff Development Council's chair of the annual national conference in Atlanta in 1986, president in 1988, and board member from 1984 to 1990. The friendships she formed and cemented during the over thirty years of her close relationship with National Staff Development Council were life changing.

After retiring from the Augusta schools, she has worked with schools throughout the United States implementing WFSG. She has written extensively about her work in *Educational Leadership* and *Journal of Staff Development*, and with Dale Lick, she has written *Whole-Faculty Study Groups: Creating Professional Learning Communities That Target Student Learning* (2005) and coedited *The Whole-Faculty Study Groups Fieldbook: Lessons Learned and Best Practices From Classrooms, Districts, and Schools* (2007). Another book with Karl Clauset and Dale Lick, *Schoolwide Action Research for Professional Learning Communities: Improving Student Learning Through the Whole-Faculty Study Groups Approach* (2008), focuses on the work of study groups and gives descriptive data from schools implementing WFSG.

She now lives on a small horse farm just outside of Augusta in a four generational home, which includes her husband Joe, daughter, three grandchildren, and a great-granddaughter. Even with all the activities in such a home, she still finds time to write about her work, correspond with colleagues, and read about the latest developments in education.

The Change Creation System 1

Can you imagine a school where the school board and the superintendent support the principal in deliberately creating an environment that nurtures excellence, trust, risk taking, and creativity? Where faculty and staff develop meaningful relationships, build collaboration and action teams for solving priority learning issues, and share findings across the school toward becoming an authentic learning community? Where members see the big learning improvement picture, create shared values and vision, and empower and inspire each other? Where all personnel are committed to learning, sharing, and relearning to improve learning for all students? Where time and preparation are provided to help everyone understand the essentials of change, share them collectively, and execute them effectively to create learning innovations?

This book is all about providing a process that helps schools create the above environment with effective learning results. In particular, it lays out step-by-step the necessary concepts and the transitional approach for a change creation system for building innovative schools and increasing student learning. If the concepts and processes outlined in the remaining chapters of this book are fully and effectively implemented, the school improvement results can be remarkable.

SCHOOL IMPROVEMENT

High expectations for school improvement are and will continue to be a priority in the minds and thinking of people and organizations across the country. Consider the following illustration of this statement.

A teacher from the late nineteenth or early twentieth century visiting a typical classroom today would find many things quite familiar: teacher lectures; chalk or similar boards; and desks, chairs, and textbooks. However, this same teacher would be surprised at the demands placed on teachers and schools today. For example, a century ago, relatively little was expected of high school students. It was anticipated that high school students could recite from prescribed texts, relate simple scientific facts, and be able to handle basic arithmetic problems. Today, high school students are expected to be able to read and discuss a wide variety of texts and complex materials, understand the nature of science and scientific inquiry, write meaningfully, use computers and basic technologies, and develop serious mathematical skills.

During the twenty-first century, as information and knowledge continue to grow rapidly and become even-increasingly more complex and as the demands of the workplace increase significantly, the expectations for an effective and more relevant school education will become the societal norm. Simply put, schools of the future will face growing demands to provide an education for their graduates who are well prepared to successfully enter the workforce and to deal with a more sophisticated and technological world.

SCHOOL REFORMS

If school improvement is going to be the order of the day for the future, what has come about from all of the school reform efforts that schools have had to endure?

Over the last several decades, there have been many and varied reform movements, including the following:

- A Nation at Risk
- National Education Summit (1989, President and Governors)
- Charter Schools
- Goals 2000: Educate America Act
- No Child Left Behind
- Common Core
- Race to the Top

In his presentation, "School Reform: Yesterday, Today, and Tomorrow," at the 2010 Dean's Symposium at Florida State University, Thomas Good, professor and head of the Department of Educational Psychology, University of Arizona, said, "Reform efforts have uniformly failed. . . . Teachers are responsible for too many things. If you want reforms to be successful you must give teachers time and support to be creative and develop new ways of doing it." Furthermore, he asked, "Will 'Race to the Top' also suffer the same fate?"

In his article in the *Washington Post*, "Five Myths About America's Schools," Paul Farhi (2011) provides a sense of overview of school reform:

Today's school reform movement conflates [merges] the motivations and agenda of politicians seeking reelection, religious figures looking to spread faith, and bureaucrats trying to save a dime. Despite an often earnest desire to help our nation's children, reformers have spread some fundamental misunderstandings about public education.

Farhi (2011) also talks about charter schools, a central part of the reform movement. Contrary to many public pronouncements, he relates that a 2009 study of charter schools by Stanford University found that

Nearly half of the charter schools nationwide have results that are no different from the local public school options and over a third, 37 percent, deliver learning results that are significantly worse than their students would have realized had they remained in traditional public schools.

Sometimes school reforms not only don't help but, instead, do harm. In the *Education Week* blog on "The Futures of School Reform," Jal Mehta (2011), assistant professor at Harvard Graduate School of Education, shares that

Bureaucratic structures erected in the Progressive Era seek to address the problem [inadequate school performance] but only compound it. Policymakers distrust teachers and schools; teachers and schools distrust policymakers. Efforts to rationalize schools through NCLB [No Child Left Behind] style accountability just double down on the existing structure, and are largely impotent to create the kind of significant improvement we say we seek. *If we keep doing what we're doing, we're not going to get there.*

Joel Klein (2011), former chancellor of New York City's School System, writes in his article, "The Failure of America's Schools," that

Nearly three decades after *A Nation at Risk,* the groundbreaking report by the National Commission on Excellence in Education warned of "a rising tide of mediocrity that threatens our very future as a Nation and a people," the gains we have made in improving schools are negligible— even though we have doubled our spending (in inflation-adjusted dollars) on K–12 public education. (p. 1)

As we ponder past and future school reforms, the wise words of Linda Darling-Hammond, founding director of the National Commission on Teaching and America's Future and current director of the Stanford Center for Opportunity Policy in Education, might be helpful to us. In her article, "Restoring Our Schools" in the *Nation,* she writes,

While we have been busy setting goals and targets for public schools and punishing the schools that fail to meet them, we have not invested in a highly trained, well-supported teaching force for all communities, as other nations have; we have not scaled up successful school designs so that they are sustained and widely available; and we have not pointed our schools at the critical higher-order thinking and performance skills needed for the twenty-first century. (Darling-Hammond, 2010, p. 2)

Among the key things that our comprehensive system presented in this book, the Change Creation system endeavors to promote are strategies— through relearning, learning and relearning, collaborative relationships, and the creation of new teaching and learning approaches—to help deal with the three concerns that Linda Darling-Hammond addresses in the above quotation.

THE ROOTS OF THE CHANGE CREATION SYSTEM

The primary approach in this book, the Change Creation system, is about creating new effective learning environments and new successful learning practices; that is, creating innovative schools and meaningful *student learning* change. This system has its roots in the schoolwide change system referred to as Whole-Faculty Study Groups (WFSG) that was first introduced in 1998 in the book *Whole-Faculty Study Groups: A Powerful Way to Change Schools and Enhance Learning* by Murphy and Lick. From their related research, and that of many others in the WFSG movement, this book was followed by two further editions in 2001 and 2005, a field-book in 2007, and a book in 2008 on the schoolwide action research process embedded in the WFSG system. Over the years, these books have laid the foundation for the WFSG movement to become one of the few successful whole-school improvement processes available to schools across North America.

An example of a major school system that showed significant success with the WFSG system was the Springfield, Missouri, Public Schools. Anita Kissinger (2007), director of staff development, reported the following:

1. In the early 2000s, the Springfield Public Schools were 1 point above being "provisionally accredited."

2. During the first year of implementation of the WFSG System, the percentage of schools using the system was 60% and increased to 90% in years 2 and 3.

3. During years 2 and 3, the Springfield Public Schools were "accredited with distinction" and have continued to maintain a high level since then.

4. The Springfield Public Schools continues to use a locally enhanced WFSG system in its schools.

Kissinger (2007) also discussed Springfield Public Schools perspectives on their rationale for continuing to employ "collaborative teams" (e.g., *study groups* in WFSG and *action teams* in this book) from the WFSG system:

- They work!
- They have the greatest chance of changing the culture.
- They provide a vehicle for dealing with change, now and in the future.
- They can be accomplished with a limited budget.
- Professional development became site specific, which creates buy-in.

Research by the authors on school improvement and the WFSG system has continued during recent years. We have attempted to look not only at new approaches to various aspects of school improvement processes, but also how such processes, including the WFSG system, could be improved, for example, what needed to be added, deleted, or changed in some way; what needed to be refined, simplified, or adjusted; and what new concepts could be incorporated to make the system more effective. The result of all these efforts, the Change

Creation system, has as its basis the WFSG system, but goes well beyond it in substance and practice and, we believe, in total effectiveness.

The Change Creation system, relative to the WFSG system, has been simplified and streamlined to make it easier to use and to provide additional new materials and approaches for such things as

- Leadership and leadership development
- Creation of a culture more consistent with the goals of school innovation and student performance improvement
- A transition plan that more clearly and effectively develops an environment for accepting and creating change
- Generation of sponsorship and a broad base of support both from above and below

NO SILVER BULLET, ONE BRICK AT A TIME

School reform efforts over the past twenty years tell us that there will be no silver bullet for significantly improving our schools. If we want to improve our schools substantially, especially teaching and student learning, we'll have to do it ourselves one brick at a time, that is, one improvement after another. If major buildings can be built one brick at a time, then we, as educators, can also do it one improvement at a time, together, over time.

There is a powerful old saying that appears to be very true for education improvement in the future: "If it is to be, it is up to me." For us, as educators, this translates into, "If real, ongoing school improvement is to be, then it is up to us as educators to find ways of doing it." We know that genuine progress requires crucial change. Consequently, through our knowledge, experience, and ingenuity, we must lead the critical efforts *to create* the changes that are needed to make our schools and learning approaches more meaningful and effective.

The whole sum and substance of this book is about doing just that, giving a step-by-step process, called the Change Creation system, so that together, we can create the right school environment and culture, preparation of personnel, support, and road map to help our schools become more innovative and measurably increase student performance. This may sound reasonably easy, but it won't be; it will challenge each of us to the fullest. In particular, as an example, it will require a *culture of discipline.* As Jim Collins (2001) explains in his book *Good to Great,* it will require us developing and implementing in our schools a culture of

- Disciplined people
- Disciplined thought
- Disciplined action (p. 142)

But, haven't we been waiting for years for the freedom and appropriate circumstances to do just that?

Jim Collins (2001) gives additional depth to our understanding of this level of "freedom and circumstances" in "Level 5 Leadership: The Triumph of Humility and Fierce Resolve," *Harvard Business Review,* by sharing that

> When you have disciplined people, you don't need hierarchy. When you have disciplined thought, you don't need bureaucracy. When you have disciplined action, you don't need excessive controls. When you combine a culture of discipline with an ethic of entrepreneurship, you get the magical alchemy of great performance. (p. 5)

STANDARDS FOR PROFESSIONAL LEARNING AND PRACTICE

As part of the right framework needed for our successful effort toward accomplishing the goal outlined in the last paragraph above (i.e., our developing and implementing in our schools a culture of disciplined people, disciplined thought, and disciplined action), we must also follow the necessary professional standards. There are three especially relevant sets of professional standards relating to professional learning that this book will subscribe to closely. These are the Standards for Professional Learning by Learning Forward (formerly the National Staff Development Council), 2011 Edition; Educational Leadership Policy Standards: ISLLC 2008 by the Council of Chief State School Officers; and the National Board for Professional Teaching Standards.

The Standards for Professional Learning, adopted by Learning Forward (2011, p. 21), are the following.

Professional learning that increases educator effectiveness and results for all students

- Occurs within learning communities committed to continuous improvement, collective responsibility, and goal alignment (*Learning Communities*)
- Requires skillful leaders who develop capacity, advocate, and create support systems for professional learning (*Leadership*)
- Requires prioritizing, monitoring, and coordinating resources for educator learning (*Resources*)
- Uses a variety of sources and types of student, educator, and system data to plan, assess, and evaluate professional learning (*Data*)
- Integrates theories, research, and models of human learning to achieve its intended outcomes (*Learning Designs*)
- Applies research on change and sustains support for implementation of professional learning for long term change (*Implementation*)
- Aligns its outcomes with educator performance and student curriculum standards (*Outcomes*)

The Learning Forward standards for professional learning are especially relevant to this book because of their emphasis on learning communities as an essential condition of professional learning for all educators, which is central to our Change Creation system for schools. Throughout the book, we make connections between our Change Creation system and the Learning Forward standards.

The Educational Leadership Policy Standards (2008, p. 19) reflect the wealth of new information and lessons learned about education leadership over the past decade. These leadership standards and requisite functions specified for principals to attain these standards are particularly relevant to the actions principals take to create and sustain a school culture of "collaboration, trust, learning, and high expectations"; "develop the instructional and leadership capacity of staff"; and "ensure a system of accountability for every student's academic and social success" (pp. 14–15).

In addition to the standards for professional learning and the leadership standards for principals, standards for teachers are also important for understanding the context of schooling. The National Board for Professional Teaching Standards (NBPTS), founded in 1987, has developed standards for accomplished teaching in sixteen different subject areas with students at various developmental levels and offers twenty-five certificates for teachers who wish to become National Board Certified Teachers (NBCTs). The standards and certificates for NBCTs are based on a set of Five Core Propositions (NBPTS, 2002, pp. 3–4) that describe the NBPTS perspective on accomplished teaching. These NBPTS core propositions emphasize the importance of teachers being reflective practitioners who work collaboratively with others to continually improve their practice and student learning.

Taken together, these standards for high quality professional learning, leadership, and teaching provide a rich framework for our Change Creation system.

THE CHANGE CREATION SYSTEM

The Change Creation system is a schoolwide change and creation system. The two critical things that the Change Creation system effectively helps schools generate are

1. The right leadership, vision, culture, and relationships within the schools for innovation and creativity

2. A change process for developing new teaching and learning approaches that measurably improve student performance

Right Leadership, Vision, Culture, and Relationships

The right leadership, vision, culture, and relationships essence of the Change Creation system for school innovation and increased student performance is given in the first paragraph of this chapter. The Change Creation system will model the way and assist schools and their personnel in becoming what is imagined there—and even more. It will help the school and its people develop an overarching culture (i.e., how we do things in this school and what is appropriate and inappropriate—the assumptions we make, our values and beliefs, and our behaviors) and climate (i.e., how we feel about things), and relationships. In particular, this includes, among other things, the following characteristics:

- Being humble and having respect for one another
- Nurturing an environment of excellence, trust, risk taking, creativity, and fair and balanced reward and incentive systems
- Having an intense will to be part of a change creation process to build innovative schools and increase student performance
- Seeing the big picture for the school and its improvement, with broad and motivated support from within and from above
- Having the right values for the school and the people connected to those values
- Developing transparency across the school
- Collaborating effectively and working together in teams and across teams
- Sharing general leadership and with everyone being a leader in their area of focus
- Accepting of relearning, learning and relearning, sharing, creating, testing, reflecting, and repeating (as necessary) together

New Teaching and Learning Approaches

The second key to the Change Creation system, in addition to appropriately changing the culture, is the creation of new, more effective teaching and learning approaches. As we have seen earlier in this chapter, virtually all of the traditional school improvement reforms of the past have had minimal or no success, with some even doing damage. Consequently, isn't it time to turn school improvement—especially academic school innovation and increased student performance—more directly over to the school leaders and teachers and provide them with the environment, time, and support necessary to create the new learning approaches that will make measurable differences?

Many teaching approaches of earlier times predate much of the scientific knowledge about learning and intellectual development. Current job responsibilities for most teachers and professional school personnel provide little discretionary time for them to think, inquire, and plan, modify, and test new teaching and learning approaches. As a consequence, teachers too often must ignore research literature, including literature on such things as cognitive development, behavior analysis, learning strategies and theory, collaboration, reflection, simulation, metacognition, learner strategies, assessment, and the serious application of technology.

What this says is that "academic improvement" progress will be limited if we continue to use only the current teaching and learning approaches. That is, if we want to increase student learning performances, then we must create new teaching and learning approaches. The Change Creation system, on the other hand, has the potential to modify significantly teaching and learning approaches, giving new opportunities for generating new, more effective teaching and learning approaches for increasing student learning performance.

New approaches to teaching and learning are generated through the Change Creation process.

Change Creation Process

Schools follow a general cycle of work over the course of a school year—from new beginnings at the start of the school year when new and returning staff and students are welcomed and goals are set for the new year, to teaching and learning over most of the year, and ending with celebration and reflection on accomplishments and preparation for the next school year. Within this general cycle, a Change Creation system school follows a Change Creation process that is an annual five-step cycle guiding the school's action teams (i.e., designated groups of school personnel who work together to help accomplish the school's set goals) in improving teaching and increasing student learning. The five-step process is as follows:

The Faculty and Leaders

Step 1: Identify student learning needs and form action teams.

Each Action Team

Step 2: Create team action plans.

Step 3: Implement inquiry cycles to change practice and improve student learning.

Each Action Team and the Faculty

Step 4: Assess the impact of action teams' work on teacher practice and student learning.

Step 5: Share results and best practices across the school and apply lessons learned.

Figure 1.1 shows how these key elements relate. Having the right leadership, vision, culture, and relationships and a strong Change Creation process enables a school to create and sustain new approaches to teaching and learning.

Figure 1.1   The Change Creation System

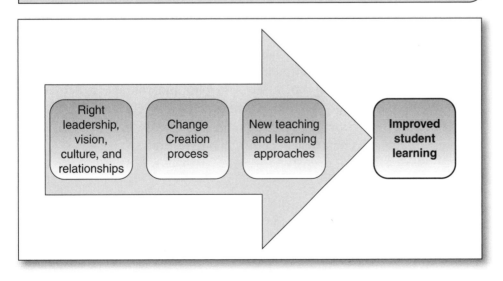

The Change Creation system, as unfolded in the remaining chapters of this book, provides the opportunity and mechanism for schools, school leaders, and teachers to regain their professional role as leaders of innovative schools and increased student learning.

SUMMARY

Most of the major, general initiatives (e.g., A Nation at Risk and No Child Left Behind) have been disappointingly ineffective. As we compared these various general school improvement initiatives, we found that they were inconsistent and often at odds with the various professional standards for school leaders and teachers and for professional learning. As a consequence, there is no "simple silver bullet" for improving our schools effectively.

Instead, for genuine effectiveness in school improvement, it will take leaders and teachers intimately and creatively involved in a broad-based, creative change system that is aligned closely with the professional standards for leaders, teachers, and professional learning. One such system that has proven over the years to be successful in schools across the country when fully applied is the WFSG system introduced in 1998 and updated in 2001, 2005, and 2008. The Change Creation system with the three components shown in Figure 1.1, the right leadership, vision, culture, and relationships, a strong change creation process, and new approaches to teaching and learning, has its roots in the WFSG system but goes well beyond it in substance and practice and, we believe, in total effectiveness.

In the next three chapters of the book, Part I, we focus on creating the right leadership, vision, culture, and relationships. We discuss a number of *critical fundamentals of effectiveness* that are *required* for schools successfully becoming professional learning communities and improving teaching and increasing student learning, including fundamentals relating to school improvement (e.g., school culture, discipline, and leadership); successful change; and creating teams, learning teams, and professional learning communities.

In Part II, Chapters 5–12, we go into detail to explain how the Change Creation process helps schools become and function as professional learning communities of action teams by (1) becoming powerful learning teams; (2) taking direction from the school vision and improvement plan and, like experimental laboratories, generating content, materials, and instructional practices that improve teaching practices and increase student learning; and (3) sharing across the school and learning from each other.

And finally, please note that a set of helpful and valuable resources for implementing the Change Creation system in schools is provided online. A list of these resources is provided after the table of contents. You will find these resources by going to www.corwin.com/schoolscanchange.

Part I

Fundamentals of Effectiveness

This part of the book addresses the critical fundamentals of effectiveness for understanding and dealing with school culture and cultural change, school vision and change, and authentic teams, learning teams, and professional learning communities. These fundamentals create the right leadership, vision, culture, and relationships that are *required* for schools to be successful in becoming professional learning communities, improving teaching, and increasing student learning. Chapter 2 explains the essentials relating to cultures of discipline, change creation, collaboration, transformational leadership, and school change. Chapter 3 discusses school vision and the power of vision, the basics of change and support of and resistance to change, and the overarching Universal Change Principle and its application. Chapter 4 covers authentic teams, learning teams, and professional learning communities, groups such as action teams becoming learning teams, and schools developing into professional learning communities. These chapters provide the foundation for the process of the Change Creation system, which is the focus of Part II of this book.

Fundamentals of Effectiveness for School Improvement 2

Can you imagine a school that is transforming its culture (mindsets and behaviors) to support successful school improvement and increased student learning performance? Where creative change is welcomed and leaders and teachers create the future that serves their students and society best? Where there is progressive discipline in leaders and teachers, in thought, and in action? Where collaboration and teamwork are fully supported and practiced across the school? Where innovation and creativity are encouraged and successful? Where school leadership is not only strong, but also transformational? Where everyone, leaders and teachers, see themselves as leaders and function as learning leaders?

The above elements are key characteristics for meeting school goals and potential outcomes of an effectively implemented school change system. In this chapter, we will discuss these major "cultural fundamentals of effectiveness for the school improvements." These cultural fundamentals include the following:

- The school culture and how to alter it
- Discipline in leadership, in thinking, and in action for school personnel
- The Change Creation process
- Relationships and collaboration in schools and among school personnel
- Transformational leadership

One might logically ask, "Why are the above items presented here and now?" and "Why are they so important?"

In school change efforts, we have learned that the closer schools get to fulfilling the above characteristics, the cultural fundamentals for effectiveness, the more likely they are to accomplish their goals and their vision for the future. That is, schools that meaningfully move to take on the characteristics discussed in this chapter are typically the ones more likely to become successful at innovation and at increasing student learning.

What we encourage you to do *now* is to seriously study the materials in this chapter, getting them in mind as much as possible for future use. And then, return to this chapter again and again to refine your understanding and increase your capacity (i.e., your willingness and your ability) to apply this knowledge readily in all of your future school change efforts.

UNDERSTANDING THE CULTURE

School culture is not always visible to outsiders and even to many within it, but it is always there and always powerful and rigid. The culture is the social and normative glue, the common bond, that holds together the educational and other aspects of a school and creates the central features, structures, and approaches that characterize it (Birmbaum, 1988, p. 72). Among the many elements in schools that determine the culture are norms and values, accepted paradigms, organizational structures, career paths, leadership and management, forms of communication, power and status, things measured and controlled, policies and procedures, institutional stories, legends, myths, rights, biases, stereotypes, rituals and symbols, design and use of physical facilities, and reward systems.

The culture is what sets one school distinctly apart from another; it is a school's self-concept, analogous to an individual's personality. The culture of a school, for example, establishes a unique set of ground rules, both stated and unstated, for how people in the school think and behave and for what they assume to be true and appropriate.

School Culture

Schools have evolved over a long period of time, and our general approaches to schooling have been in place for over a century. As a consequence, schools have well-established cultures. School cultures give schools and their programs stability and govern how issues are addressed and what can happen in schools. However, school cultures are fairly rigid and make schools far less open to change than might be desirable when trying to introduce new concepts and practices for the enhancement of student learning and school improvement.

Among the best mechanisms for bringing about meaningful cultural change are the change processes that we will be presenting later in this chapter and in the remaining chapters of this book. When these change processes are properly supported and applied, they have the potential to modify aspects of a school culture to allow for enough change so that educational practices and schools can be significantly improved.

Why is this so important to us now? Because school cultures, like many others cultures, are so difficult to change productively and qualitatively. And, in particular,

Although not all cultural changes are valuable, meaningful school change will come about only when the school's culture is changed adequately and appropriately.

The concept of school culture has generated many definitions and approaches to the subject. Because our interests in culture focus on its relationship to change (e.g., student learning enhancement and school improvement), we use a definition adapted from Conner (2006, p. 166) that has been employed extensively and successfully in organizational research and change efforts.

> School culture reflects the interrelationship of shared assumptions, beliefs, and behaviors that are acquired over time by members of a school.

Building Blocks of School Culture

As stated in the above definition, the key building blocks of the culture of a school are the assumptions, beliefs, and behaviors of the school and its personnel. To change the culture of the school for its improvement, you must change one or more of the assumptions, beliefs, and behaviors.

Assumptions in a school are the unconscious and, therefore, unquestioned perceptions concerning what is important and how people and things operate in and relating to the school—that is, the unconscious rationale for people continuing to use certain beliefs and behaviors. For example, teachers in schools often have the unconscious assumption that the lecture approach is the best way to teach something, whereas research tells us that, in fact, for certain kinds of learning, there may be more effective approaches. So, for example, changing your assumptions to what the research tells us would allow expanded thinking and the consideration of a broad array of teaching and learning practices in addition to the lecture approach.

Beliefs are the values and expectations that people hold to be true about themselves, others, their work, and the school. They provide a basis for what people in the school hold to be right or wrong, true or false, good or bad, and relevant or irrelevant about their school and its operation. Belief statements in schools, for instance, relate to such things as the vital role played by the personal interaction of the teachers and students, value of the grading system, importance of lesson plans, and the need for staff development. Our assumptions and beliefs, together, make up our *mindsets*.

Behaviors are the ways people conduct themselves on a day-to-day basis. They are perceptible actions that are based on our mindsets, our assumptions and beliefs, and are ideally aimed at carrying out the school's mission. Whereas our mindsets often reflect intentions that are more difficult to discern, behaviors are observable and can be noted objectively. Behaviors of teachers, for example, might include such things as how they teach, prepare lesson plans, advise students, and use technology, whereas behaviors for administrators might include how they assess teaching, involve faculty in decision making, encourage innovation, and relate to other administrators.

Relative to the school culture, for example, the Change Creation system, unfolded fully in subsequent chapters, has been shown to have the potential to change the assumptions of teachers and raise their level of self-esteem and professionalism. Through these system efforts, for instance, teachers may change their assumptions about their self-esteem and professionalism and see themselves differently, more like other professionals. Such changes in these assumptions can also bring about changes in teachers' beliefs. Teachers, more often, began to believe that they had professional training they could be proud of, that they were professionals, as physicians, lawyers, and other professionals, and that they could and should function fully as professionals in their activities and responsibilities. As a result, the behaviors of these teachers changed substantially, including taking more responsibility for colearning with colleagues, having greater confidence in themselves, and functioning more professionally and assertively in their experimentation and creativity. These shifts reflect important changes in the assumptions, beliefs, and behaviors of the teachers and the school and represent positive, major shifts in their culture.

Cultural Shifts

School cultures can be realigned through a process called *cultural shift.* Such a cultural transformation requires realigning and modifying assumptions, beliefs, and behaviors to make them more consistent with the new directions and new goals of the school. An especially important strength of the Change Creation system presented in this book is its capability to bring about cultural shifts. Through appropriate culture shifts, desirable changes in how teachers, leaders, and schools function are possible. The key, then, to making schools more innovative and to increasing student learning is to bring about appropriate cultural shifts.

Figure 2.1 illustrates the potential of cultural relationships, where the flow is more like a wave than a sequence.

Figure 2.1   Cultural Change–Student Learning Loop

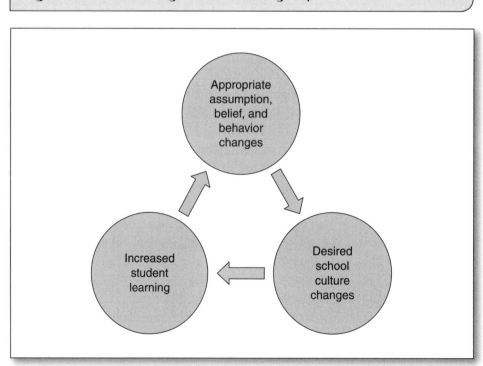

For example, by making the school culture more open to collaborative approaches to learning or to the use of technology in learning (i.e., by changing some of the assumptions, beliefs, and behaviors), we modify the school culture, giving new potential for increased student learning by using collaboration and teamwork or practices involving technology, respectively. In addition, success tends to breed a successful feedback loop; that is, increased student learning, resulting from using collaborative approaches or practices involving technology, encourages additional use of and support for the use of these changes, that is, further modification of assumptions, beliefs, and behaviors.

CULTURE OF DISCIPLINE

Business and social sector researcher, Jim Collins (2005, p. 34), tells us that a culture of discipline is essential for genuine effectiveness in an organization. Collins (2001) also says that

> A culture of discipline involves a duality. On the one hand, it requires people who adhere to a consistent system; yet, on the other hand, it gives people freedom and responsibility within the framework of that system. A culture of discipline is not just about action. It is about getting disciplined people . . . who engage in disciplined thought and . . . who take disciplined action. (p. 142)

Consequently, if schools are going to meaningfully change, for example, become more positively innovative toward increased student performance, then these three discipline elements of their cultures—discipline of leaders and teachers, discipline of thought, and discipline of action—will be fundamental to their success. This means that school personnel must approach their work, thoughts, and actions with diligence and a great sense of responsibility to themselves, their schools, and society.

Disciplined Leaders and Teachers

Disciplined leaders and teachers live in alignment with the school's vision, purpose, and goals and in accordance with their values regardless of what is happening around them. In the school setting, they are

- Clear as to who they are and where they are going
- Motivated by the vision or purpose of the school
- Committed to a consistent system or framework, within which they have freedom and responsibility, for example, leaders manage the system or framework not the people

In addition, disciplined leaders and teachers

- Help each other stay on track by reminding each other through ongoing feedback and being a role model

- Address contradictions honestly, first in themselves, and then in others, and resolve them
- Examine on a regular basis their thinking, behavior, and decisions
- Typically finish things they start (Diedrich, 2007)

Collins (2001) emphasizes that disciplined leaders and teachers "have the discipline to do the right things and, equally important, to stop doing the wrong things" (p. 141).

Disciplined Thinking

Gerry Wienholt (2010) relates that *disciplined thinking* is a method of personal leadership and explains that

It is an ongoing act of self-control that, when practiced effectively and consistently, will reap great benefits for the individual and the organization. It is a practice where the individual focuses on a predefined vision that represents a desired ideal picture of the future. Once we articulate our vision, the consistent action of disciplining our thoughts around this pre-defined vision effectively eliminates distractions and deterrents. Consistently staying focused on this positive vision will noticeably decrease doubt and skepticism and dramatically accelerate the attention needed to make the vision a reality. . . . The sobering reality is, what we think is what we create.

Those practicing disciplined thought in schools do the following:

- Keep the school's vision or purpose in the forefront of their thinking
- Confront the brutal facts and circumstances they find
- Retain resolute faith that they can and will create a path to greater effectiveness
- Persist in the search for understanding until they get to their strategic focus
- Seek continual improvement
- "Create a climate where truth is heard by leading with questions, not answers; engaging in dialog and debate, not coercion; conducting autopsies without blame; and building 'red flag' mechanisms—to turn information that is critical to competitive advantage into information that cannot be ignored" (Collins, 2001, pp. 74–80)

Disciplined Action

People can talk about doing things, plan for them, and have good intentions about getting them done, but until they actually take serious action toward their accomplishment, there won't be success! Consequently, the *discipline of action* is one of the most important elements in meaningfully changing schools and increasing student learning.

Aristotle reminds us that "We are what we repeatedly do. Excellence, then, is not an act, but a habit" (as quoted in Covey, 1990, p. 46). As regularly practiced, the discipline of action becomes a habit. And as the great educator, Horace Mann, said, "Habits are like a cable. We weave a strand of it everyday and soon it cannot be broken [it becomes strong]" (as quoted in Covey, 1990, p. 46).

One good place to begin our discussion of the discipline of action is with four of Covey's (1990) habits:

- Be proactive (i.e., we take the initiative and have the responsibility to make things happen). (pp. 71)
- Begin with the end in mind (i.e., we know where we're going so that we can better understand where we are now and so that the steps we take are always in the right direction). (pp. 98)
- Put first things first (i.e., we have an independent will, the power to do something when we may not want to do it, to be a function of our values rather than a function of our impulse or desire at any given moment). (pp. 149)
- Sharpen the Saw (i.e., we keep progressing to increasingly higher planes of effectiveness by upward action spirals requiring us "to learn, commit, and do," and then "to learn, commit, and do" again). (pp. 306)

Among other important discipline action steps we take are the following:

- Reframe the content and context of negative situations to turn them into positive and beneficial opportunities for actions.
- Stimulate progress—change, improvement, innovation, and renewal—in the operating practices, cultural norms, goals, strategies, and tactics that are consistent with the vision or purpose.
- Take each project seriously and complete it.

CULTURE OF CHANGE CREATION

Change Basics

Change has always existed. The difference is that for schools, like most of society, the intensity (i.e., speed, magnitude, and momentum) of change is potentially so much greater now. In fact, change has become a silent juggernaut, a persistent, irresistible force. It silently permeates almost everything and, frankly, is no respecter of persons, professions, or organizations, including leaders and teachers, academic environments, and schools. Perhaps change expert Daryl Conner (2006) explains this best: "Never before has so much changed so fast and with such dramatic implications for the entire world" (p. 3).

So it is natural to ask, How do schools usually respond to this dynamic, ubiquitous change? What we have found over the years is that they, consciously or by default, resist, ignore, or sidestep the realities and impact of change, all losing and self-defeating responses. They often turn to change management, especially when new things are involved, in the hope that once a change is upon them, they can manage or control the change and its effects—a reactive approach to change. Change management, being reactive, requires a quick and nimble response to understanding and managing change. This reactive approach frequently prevents one from defining useful change before being overtaken by it. In particular, change management is based on people sensing that their world, internally or externally, has changed, such as with a new policy requiring better results in some area of the school that can no longer be ignored.

To increase their potential for success, instead of schools being just reactive when something new is required, the leaders and teachers and school must become *proactive*. They must alter the school culture so that they can more effectively understand the change and its ramifications and then "join" the desired change, embrace it as a partner, and use it creatively to advance the school's and society's goals. Remember, you can't have progress without change!

We will go deeper into understanding change and how to lead it in Chapter 3.

Change Creation

With dramatic and omnipresent change being the order of the day, it becomes harder than ever to predict the future. To deal with tomorrow, management guru Peter Drucker (1985) provides a simple yet powerful answer: "Since you can't predict the future, you must *create* it" (p. 34). That is, organizations must exploit change and *create* the future that serves organizations and society best. To do this, a school and its people must shift its culture (i.e., mindsets and behaviors) sufficiently to become effective leaders and practitioners of change creation.

Change creation, introduced by Dale Lick and Roger Kaufman (2000), is the process whereby an organization and its people

1. Invite, accept and welcome change as a vital component in defining and achieving future success

2. Define the future they want to design and deliver

3. Develop and implement a change plan that capably transitions its people, processes, and circumstances, especially its culture, from the existing paradigm to the new, desired one (pp. 25–26)

Change creation is proactive. When schools enact change creation, they intentionally move from being victims of change to becoming masters of change. Change creation is especially important when organizations are faced with dramatic, or second-order, changes. Waters and Marzano (2006, p. 18), in their meta-analyses of leadership practices that significantly improve student achievement, define second-order change as change that is perceived as "a break with the past, outside of existing paradigms, conflicting with prevailing values and norms, and requiring new knowledge and skills to implement." They state, "what determines whether stakeholders perceive a change to be first-order or second-order is their own knowledge, experience, values, and flexibility."

For example, to support dramatic, second-order changes, just as the grapevine is pruned back to allow it to bear more fruit, we must organizationally "prune"—prepare for nurture and change—some of what we take for granted and/or believe and do and how we do it to allow for the development of more effective approaches and processes. Leaders and teachers must often prune processes, sometimes radically, to develop the most effective types of approaches, including modifying parts of the existing culture that inhibit effectiveness, questioning the solutions of the past toward modifying or eliminating conceptual approaches and processes that interfere with new, potentially more effective practices, and they must replace comfortable practices and processes with new ones that give potential for greater quality and productivity.

In summary, one of the most critical issues facing schools today is the urgent need for schools to design, implement, lead, and manage meaningful, intentional, planned, second-order change—change creation. Such changes will be difficult and take us out of our comfort zones, but they are essential to our future educational success.

The process of the Change Creation system is discussed in detail in Chapters 5–12 and provides a step-by-step formal mechanism for a school to change its cultures sufficiently to help it move toward becoming an effective change creation school.

CULTURE OF RELATIONSHIPS AND COLLABORATION

Collaboration is one of the most critical parts of relationships. A common dictionary definition for *to collaborate* is "To work together, especially in a joint intellectual effort." Schools, in general, have a fair amount of collaborative ventures, probably more than most other sectors of society. But even in schools, the collaboration often does not go deep enough or broad enough.

Looking at schools from a major change perspective, a deeper, more explicit definition of collaboration is given by Rick DuFour (2003):

> *Collaboration* is the systemic process in which we work together to analyze and impact professional practice in order to improve our individual and collective results.

DuFour adds that

- The first key term is systemic (i.e., of or concerning the whole body)
- Collaboration is embedded in the routine practices of the school
- Teachers are organized into teams and provided time to meet during the school day
- Teachers are provided specific guidelines and asked to engage in creative activities that help focus on student achievement

With this definition and discussion of collaboration in mind, the following research highlights the critical nature of a collaborative culture:

The single most important factor for successful school restructuring and the first order of business for those interested in increasing the capacity of their schools is building a collaborative internal environment that fosters cooperative problem solving and conflict resolution. (Eastwood & Louis, 1992, p. 215)

A precondition for doing *anything* to strengthen our practice and improve a school is the existence of a collegial culture in which professionals talk about practice, share their craft knowledge, and observe and root for the success of one another. Without these in place, no meaningful improvement—no staff or curriculum development, no teacher leadership, no student appraisal, no team teaching, no parent involvement, and no sustained change—is possible. (Barth, 2006, p. 13)

High performing schools tend to promote collaborative cultures, support professional communities and exchanges among all staff and cultivate strong ties among the school, parents, and community. . . . Teachers and staff collaborate to remove barriers to student learning. . . . Teachers communicate regularly with each other about effective teaching and learning strategies. (DuFour, DuFour, & Eaker, 2008, pp. 15–17)

[N]urturing a professional collaborative culture was one of the most significant factors in successful school improvement efforts. (Newmann & Wehlage, 1995)

And most importantly, relating to relationships,

[W]hen the relationships among teachers in a school are characterized by high trust and frequent interaction—that is, when social capital is strong—student achievement scores improve. . . . In other words, teacher social capital was a significant predictor of student achievement gains above and beyond teacher experience or ability in the classroom. (Leana, 2011, p. 19)

All of these tell us that a culture of relationships and collaboration is an essential part of school improvement and increased student learning performance.

The process of the Change Creation system explained in Chapters 5–12 will provide a step-by-step formal mechanism for a school to develop a successful culture of relationships and collaboration.

CULTURE OF TRANSFORMATIONAL LEADERSHIP

What kind of leadership in schools will to be required to successfully lead the necessary cultural shifts discussed in the above sections? Typically, leadership of the past (often called transactional leadership) won't be adequate, even with what has been thought of as traditionally good leadership. The required leadership, in addition to being what we've regarded as genuinely effective leadership, must include leadership that helps *transform* (i.e., change the condition, nature, or function of something) the school culture and the school from where they are presently to what is envisioned for the school's future. The essential leadership now called for is referred to as *transformational leadership.*

Transformational Leadership

Researcher Gary Alger (2012) tells us that

> The most significant challenge of leadership is to build and sustain an organizational culture that focuses on continual improvement of educational programs, teachers' capacities and skills, and student learning. . . . Transformational leadership is a desirable style for school leaders involved in improvement efforts because it raises the level of awareness of workers so that they come to value organizational goals and strategies to achieve those objectives. (p. 1)

Simply stated, transformational leadership acts as a catalyst for innovation in organizations and for change in individuals (*Guide to Transformational Leadership,* n.d.). A common definition for transformational leadership is as follows:

> *Transformational leadership* is defined as a leadership approach that causes change in individuals and social systems. In its ideal form, it creates valuable and positive change in the followers with the end goal of developing followers into leaders. Enacted in its authentic form, transformational leadership enhances the motivation, morale and performance of followers through a variety of mechanisms. These include connecting the follower's sense of identity and self to the mission and the collective identity of the organization; being a role model for followers that inspires them; challenging followers to take greater ownership for their work; and understanding the strengths and weaknesses of followers, so the leader can align followers with tasks that optimize their performance. (*Guide to Transformational Leadership,* n.d.)

In today's fast-changing and more demanding educational environment, schools require more effective leadership than just traditional transactional leadership can provide. As a result, the more change-oriented and powerful transformational leadership is required, as the discussions below suggest.

Su-Tuan Lulee (2011) describes the importance of transformational leadership in the conclusion of her EDUCAUSE blog:

> It is important for educational leaders to lead the organization not based on a give-and-take relationship, but on the leaders' personality, traits, intelligence, and ability to make a change through being the moral exemplars of working toward the good of the team or organization as well as constantly committing to shared visions and goals. The concept of transformational leadership is a compelling model for education leaders today. (Beaudoin, 2007, pp. 391–402, as quoted by Lulee)

Education leader Dale Lick (2007) summarizes the concept of transformational leaders and their key characteristics as follows:

Transformational leaders are distinguished by their ability to bring about meaningful innovation, successful change and transformation, and broad-based effectiveness.

Transformational leaders (Lick, 2007)

- See the big picture, create shared values and vision, and empower and inspire others in the organization
- Serve as an institutional model by being humble and respecting others ideas and skills and developing trust and integrity
- Commit to learning, sharing, and relearning by all
- Understand the essentials of change, share them broadly, and execute them effectively
- Develop sharing and relationships, team building and synergy, and learning communities across the institution
- Create an environment that nurtures excellence, risk taking, and creativity
- Provide fair and balanced reward and incentive systems

Figure 2.2 illustrates these characteristics of transformational leadership by focusing on what transformational leaders *do*—the action verbs in these characteristics.

Figure 2.2   What Transformational Leaders Do

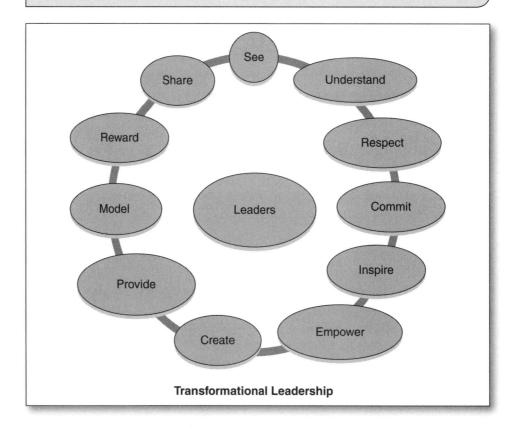

Transformational Leadership

The Principal as a Transformational Leader

Although it is desirable for many leaders and teachers in a school to be transformational leaders, the most critical one, though, is the principal. For example, the principal helps to (1) lead the development of a compelling and inspiring school vision or fails to do so; (2) make things happen or discourages them from happening; (3) create an environment that nurtures excellence, risk taking, and creativity or something less; (4) bring about a respect for others' ideas and skills and an atmosphere of trust and integrity or something less desirable; and (5) motivate sharing and relationships, team building, and learning across the school or a less collaborative school environment. What this says is that the principal being a transformational leader is the most important element for a school to innovate effectively, become a meaningful professional learning organization, and broadly increase student learning performance. Very simply, school personnel can make the right things happen, but they need the transformational leadership of the principal to do so. Each of the characteristics for a transformational leader, given in the previous section, is discussed below for the principal and builds on research by Lick (2007) and the meta-analyses of the effectiveness of school leadership practices by Waters, Marzano, and McNulty (2003, pp. 4, 9–12).

See the big picture, create shared values and vision, and empower and inspire others in the organization

One of the most important responsibilities of the principal is to "see the big picture," that is, to take a broad overview of the school and fully assess what is happening in the school, such as what is working and not working well enough, are students being effectively served, do teachers and other school personnel function in a sharing and collaborative manner, and what needs to be changed and improved? Building on these findings, the principal, then, needs to lead a shared effort with school personnel to develop a widely supported, compelling vision (see Chapter 3, p. 31) and an understanding of purpose for the school that both empowers and inspires school personnel toward the desired future for the school.

Creation of the school vision needs to be done *before* the implementation of the process for the Change Creation system, which is discussed in Chapters 5–12. An approach for developing the school vision, Vision Creation, is provided in online Resource A.

Serve as an institutional model by being humble and respecting others ideas and skills and developing trust and integrity

The most valuable asset the principal has in the school is the school personnel. The principal can say and do whatever he or she wants, but the principal must understand that it won't happen without the school personnel helping to make it happen. As a result, the principal needs to be a strong leader, but a humble one, who respects the "ideas and skills of school personnel," provides opportunities for faculty involvement in policy development, uses a leadership team in decision making, and empowers others, the building blocks for school improvement and success. To use these school building blocks most successfully, the principal, by his or her actions and decisions, needs to create a school environment that encourages people to express opinions contrary to those of authority and that provides for the most effective working conditions, one where "we are all in this together." The principal needs to create an atmosphere of respect, mutual trust, and integrity.

Commit to learning, sharing, and relearning by all

A school must be a place of learning, not only for students but also for school personnel. If the school is going to become more innovative and if students are going to perform better, then the principal must learn new things, adapt a leadership style that is open to specific situations, be able to be directive or nondirective as the situation warrants, be aware of issues that could create discord, be able to predict what might go wrong from day to day, share extensively across the school in the learning process, and relearn so as to move from things that are no longer relevant or valid to what is needed in tomorrow's schools. As the *chief leader of learning* in the school, the principal must hold strong professional beliefs and values about schools, teaching and learning, and he must work with school personnel to foster the proper climate and motivation and create appropriate professional development opportunities, especially those that directly enhance teaching and learning. The principal must continually expose the teachers to cutting edge effectiveness ideas, systematically engage teachers in discussions about current research and theory, protect teachers from issues and influences that could detract from their teaching time or focus, and provide resources, time, and incentives for helping to create a *school culture* (see earlier sections of this chapter) where learning, sharing, and relearning are the order of the day and flourish.

Understand the essentials of change, share them broadly, and execute them effectively

For a school to become more innovative and for there to be an increase in student learning performance, it will require change, *substantial* change in the school. Consequently, the principal, the leader of the school, must also become the *school change leader* and the most important *change sponsor* (i.e., the one who has the authority for and legitimatizes the change) in the school (see Chapter 3, p. 42). If the principal is to be the school change leader and be effective as such, it means that the principal must understand the essentials of change (as discussed in detail in Chapter 3), share them broadly, and execute them effectively, as well as help other school personnel understand the essentials of change and assist in their implementation. Further, the principal must be willing to consciously challenge the status quo and be comfortable with major change, lead change efforts with uncertain outcomes, systematically consider new and better ways of improving things, and be the driving force behind major change initiatives.

Develop sharing and relationships, team building and synergy, and learning communities across the institution

As all of us in education have learned over the years that bringing about genuine school innovation and increasing student learning performance is no easy task, and it doesn't get done by politicians and others who want to wave their magic wand and have it happen. Most major teaching and learning changes in schools come about by effective, proactive leadership and support by the principal and the coordinated and committed work of the teachers and other school personnel. The research in school change, such as that summarized by the Learning Forward standards (see online Resource B), tells us that the most effective schoolwide change happens through a change creation process. This happens when the school creates a supported, compelling, and inspiring vision to give powerful direction to the school change, and the teachers form into learning teams, the functional creative units, that work to develop new teaching and learning approaches and then share their findings broadly and effectively across the school, allowing it to move toward becoming a productive professional learning community (see Chapter 4, p. 69). Again, as the school leader, the principal is the one in charge of these efforts and, with the assistance of a leadership group, coordinates the various elements involved in this process for the school to move to become a professional learning community. As the Learning Forward standards, our research, and the research of many others relate, turning the school into a professional learning community requires board-based sharing and meaningful relationships across the school, consistently taking place by individuals and synergistic learning teams of school personnel with critical leadership and coordination provided by the principal.

Create an environment that nurtures excellence, risk taking, and creativity

The changes needed for a school to be more innovative and to increase student learning performance is massive. It will only happen if the process described in the previous paragraph is fully and effectively implemented. It requires leaders, teachers, and teams to truly strive for excellence, to take real risks (not wild gambles), and to be genuinely creative in their development of new teaching and learning processes. This doesn't typically happen in most schools and other organizations. However, it *must* happen if the school is going to be significantly successful with its change efforts. The principal is the single most important person in the school who can lead efforts to have this happen, that is, to "create an environment that nurtures excellence, risk taking, and creativity." For example, what creates an effective school environment is how the principal communicates and makes decisions, personally behaves and respects and treats school personnel, establishes high, concrete goals and expectations that teachers and students must meet, and nurtures discipline—in self and in others, in thinking, and in action. What creates an effective school environment is how the principal systematically acknowledges failures and celebrates accomplishments in the school, monitors the effectiveness of school practices and their impact on student learning, and gives school personnel support and freedom to be innovative with new approaches, to test those approaches, and to put successful ones in place and then to collaboratively share them with others across the school. Creating the essential ambiance for genuine school change is clearly in the hands of the principal.

Provide fair and balanced reward and incentive systems

Teachers are human with normal human traits and needs. They are generally willing to do what is needed in their professional work for the school. On the other hand, they expect reasonable things in return. For example, school personnel believe that the school should treat them and their colleagues fairly. School personnel believe and expect that if they go the extra mile (e.g., truly strive for excellence and put themselves in a potentially vulnerable position of taking major, serious personal risks in order to create new, more effective teaching and learning approaches, and work effectively and perform well), the school and its leadership will reciprocate, accordingly, and provide for them some reasonable form of a "fair and balanced reward and incentive system" rather than rely on the traditional system of rewarding seniority. The person most directly responsible for the creation and implementation of such a system is the principal. Without such a system being put in place, most creative change efforts will fail. Consequently, the principal must give time and creative thought to how he or she can devise a reasonable and effective "fair and balanced reward and incentive system" under the given constraints in the school and school system.

One of the realities of life for principals is that it is hard to be a transformational leader in one's school if the district does not expect, encourage, support, and reward the behaviors of transformational principals. Waters and Marzano (2006, pp. 3–4) found in their meta-analyses that the effective leadership practices of superintendents and district leaders do correlate with increased student achievement.

CULTURAL CHANGE

Fullan (2001) believes that transforming the culture—changing the way we do things around here—is the point in achieving successful change. The point of Change Creation system is to change the culture of schools, from one of isolation to collaboration; from individual knowledge to group knowledge; from individual work to joint work; from individual responsibility to joint and collective responsibility; from the teacher as follower to all teachers as leaders. In this book, we talk a lot about the structure of the Change Creation system. The structure gives us a set of tools for reculturing, as Fullan (2001) calls the work of change. Fullan (2001) goes on to say,

> It is a particular kind of reculturing for which we strive: one that activates and deepens moral purpose through collaborative work cultures that respect differences and constantly build and test knowledge against measurable results—a culture within which one realizes that sometimes being off balance is a learning moment. (p. 45)

The image of successful change and of reculturing that Fullan describes is a daunting mission. Such work is not for the fainthearted. Long-standing practices of isolation, traditions of territorial protection, feelings of mistrust, and histories of disillusionment are cultural fortresses. Creating new relationships forged through the Change Creation system that are built on trust, high expectations, new knowledge and skills, and more coherent instructional programs establish a culture of mutual respect.

Saphier and King (1985) identified twelve norms of school culture that should be in place and strong to create a healthy school culture (pp. 67–74). The norms were (1) collegiality; (2) experimentation; (3) high expectations; (4) trust and confidence; (5) tangible support; (6) reaching out to the knowledge base; (7) appreciation and recognition; (8) caring, celebration, and humor; (9) involvement in decision making; (10) protection of what's important; (11) traditions; and (12) honest, open communications. If these norms are in place and strong, then improvements in instruction will be significant, continuous, and widespread, according to Saphier and King. But if these norms are weak, then improvements will be infrequent, random, and slow.

Of the twelve norms, Saphier (as cited in Richardson, 1996, p. 4) points to three norms, *collegiality, experimentation,* and *reaching out to a knowledge base,* that have the highest correlation with changing the school environment and improving student achievement. Saphier (as cited in Richardson, 1996, p. 4) stated that data continue to support the 1985 Saphier and King's study. These three norms reinforce Fullan's strived-for culture above: one that activates and deepens moral purpose through collaborative work cultures that respect differences and constantly build and test knowledge against measurable results. In addition, they reinforce the elements of transformational leadership delineated in this chapter, such as being committed to learning, sharing and relearning, sharing and relationships, team building and synergy, and learning communities, and creating an environment that nurtures excellence, risk taking, and creativity.

SUMMARY

This chapter introduces several key characteristics, cultural fundamentals of effectiveness for school improvement, that can genuinely help bring about meaningful school innovation and increased student learning performance. These include the importance of school culture and why changes in it are necessary, how the culture of discipline—for leaders and teachers, for thinking, and for action—is fundamental to meaningful change, the value of shifting perspectives from change management to change creation, and the power of relationships, collaboration, and transformational leadership.

The key ideas to remember from this chapter are the following:

- *School Culture.* Transforming school cultures, that is, purposefully changing the ways we do things in schools, as well as our assumptions and beliefs, is the critical requirement for achieving successful school change for school improvement and increased student learning performance. This is creating the "Right Culture."

- *Culture of Discipline.* Disciplined leaders and teachers live in alignment with the school's vision, purpose, and goals and in accordance with their values regardless of what is happening around them. This means having the discipline to do the right things and, equally important, to stop doing the wrong things. This is creating the "Right Culture."

- *Change Creation.* Schools must become proactive. Since schools can't predict the future, they must *create* it. That is, schools must exploit change, and *create* the future that serves their students and society best. To do this, a school and its people must shift its culture (i.e., mindsets and behaviors) sufficiently to become effective leaders and practitioners of change creation. This is creating the "Right Culture."

- *Relationships and Collaboration.* When relationships among leaders and teachers in a school are characterized by high trust and frequent interaction, that is, when social capital is strong, student achievement scores improve. High performing schools tend to promote collaborative cultures, support professional communities and exchanges among all staff, and cultivate strong ties among the school, parents, and community. This is creating the "Right Relationships."

- *Transformational Leadership.* For teachers and other leaders, the principal, as a transformational leader, acts as a powerful catalyst for innovation in schools. Transformational leadership helps to lead the development of a compelling and inspiring school vision, make things happen, create an environment that nurtures excellence, risk taking, and creativity, bring about a respect for others' ideas, skills, and leadership, create an atmosphere of trust and integrity, and motivate sharing, collaboration and relationships, team building, and learning across the school. School personnel can make the right things happen, but they need transformational leadership, especially from the principal, to really make a significant difference in school improvement and student learning performance. This is creating the "Right Leadership" that enables schools to implement dramatic innovations, especially those with second-order changes, successfully.

The next chapter discusses school vision and the power of vision along with the *fundamentals of change* for successfully bringing about desired innovations in schools.

Fundamentals of Vision and Successful Change 3

Can you imagine a school with a vision "to become a national leader in school innovation and increased student learning performance"? Where creative change is welcomed and enacted to create the desired school vision? Where the basic principles of change are understood by school personnel and applied to make their school more change adaptable? Where a school will make learning better, different, and more interesting and relevant than it is today? Where leaders and teachers understand the rapidly changing nature of the society they serve and accept the necessity to introduce minor and major changes to "move their school to tomorrow"? Where a school makes a conscious decision to be at the cutting edge by taking deliberate action to make that school an important societal change agent for the future?

This chapter provides the fundamentals of successful change necessary for leaders, teachers, and their school to effectively apply the Change Creation system and move the people and the school toward what is described above. In particular, this chapter will discuss the school vision, the directional and inspirational foundation for school change; the nature and feelings of change; a process for school change; the roles of change; the sponsorship of change; and the most important principle relating to change, the Universal Change Principle.

VISION

A Vision Story

The right vision for a school or an organization can make a world of difference in its functioning and success. Consider the Walt Disney vision story from L. Mosley (1986) quoted in *The Ecology of Business* by Richard Bolstad and Margot Hamlett (n.d.).

In 1953, Walt Disney presented his proposal to the board of Walt Disney Productions. When the company turned him down, Walt decided to fund the leisure park privately.

> The vision for Disneyland was a simple but powerful one: Disneyland will be a unique world place by being a facility where people will find happiness and knowledge and parents and children will spend pleasant times in one another's company, a facility filled with the accomplishments, the joys and hopes of the world we live in, and one that reminds us and shows us how to make those wonders part of our lives. (Mosley, 1986, pp. 163)

Reading this vision, you get a sense of why "Walt had the most dedicated staff in the history of the movies—mostly because they were so proud to be working for such a visionary man" (Mosley, 1986, p. 221).

Meaning of Vision

An old Chinese Proverb tells us that "If we don't change our direction, we're likely to end up where we're headed." So, if we don't want to end up where we're now headed, we best change direction. That's what a new vision can do for you, give you a new direction toward what you hope to achieve.

Jack Welch, who was perceived to be one of the United States' most effective business leaders in the 1990s, said relative to the direction set in a new vision, "We have found that by reaching for what appears to be the impossible, we often actually do the impossible" (as cited in Rumelt, 2011).

School Vision

Definition: A *school vision* is a description of the school's desired future in the context of its society, that is, what the school wants to become.

Characteristics of a meaningful vision include the following:

- Is initiated by the leader and developed with school personnel and other stakeholders
- Provides a future orientation (say five years into the future)
- Sets an overarching direction for the future of the school
- Evokes a mental image or picture of the school's future
- Provides a standard of excellence, an ideal
- Is the basis for unique contributions to students, school personnel, community, and society
- Should be shared and supported by internal and external stakeholders
- Should be compelling and inspiring

Relative to a school vision, we encourage you to

- Think big (Overview). Think small (Important Details).
- Think tomorrow. Think creatively.
- Think student and society contribution.
- Lead and help *create* the future.

Perspectives on School Vision

According to Susan Heathfield (n.d.),

Vision is a statement about what the school wants to become. The vision should resonate with all members of your school and help them feel proud, excited, and part of something bigger than themselves. A vision should stretch the school's capacities and image of itself. It gives shape and direction to the school's future.

Hugh Burkett (2006), director of the Center for Comprehensive School Reform and Improvement, adds further to our sense of a vision with

A clear vision . . . that identifies the learning to be achieved can help keep a school and the efforts of its staff on target. A shared vision is critical to an organization's future because it provides the underlying foundation upon which all decisions are made.

In his *Forbes* magazine article, "Steve Jobs and the Power of Vision," Carmine Gallo (2011) explains that "Innovation requires a team and you cannot inspire a team of passionate evangelists without a compelling vision; a vision that is bold, simple, and consistently communicated."

In responses during the program the Role of Leadership in Sustaining School Reform: Voices From the Field, U.S. Department of Education, Nadeau and Leighton (1996) write that participants said,

Sustaining reform requires that educational leaders have a clear vision of the kind of school they want to have and operate consistently according to values and beliefs tied to that vision. These leaders seldom claim to have invented the vision or the underlying values and beliefs; instead they perceive themselves to be "keepers of the dream." They embrace it whole-heartedly and make sure that everyone else does too. And a principal commented: It has to be a collective vision; principals don't change schools by themselves. The principal is the wide-angle lens to keep the whole vision in view for the whole school.

An example of a *school vision* might be the following:

The Lincoln School will become a national leader in school innovation and increased student learning performance by fully and effectively implementing the Change Creation system.

A Vision Format

If you notice the format in this vision statement and use it to structure your own vision statement, you'll find it easier to develop your school's vision statement. This format for a vision statement is as follows:

The Lincoln School will become [What?] by {Doing What?}.

Notice in the earlier statement of the Disney vision, given again below, that the brackets contain the "What" and the braces contain the "Doing What."

Disneyland will be [a unique world place] by {being a facility where people will find happiness and knowledge and parents and children will spend pleasant times in one another's company, a facility filled with the accomplishments, the joys and hopes of the world we live in, and one that reminds us and shows us how to make those wonders part of our lives.}

And, in a similar vision format, for two school illustrations,

The Lincoln School will become [a national leader in school innovation and increased student learning performance] by {fully and effectively implementing the Change Creation system}.

The Hawaiian Avenue Elementary School will become [a professional learning community] by {ensuring that all students become high-level critical thinkers, perform at or above grade level in all subjects, and use technology competently}. (Hawaiian Avenue Elementary School, n.d.)

Take a few minutes now and try to write a version of a vision statement for your school. Later, work with others in your school to draft several school vision statements. Then, after practicing sufficiently, when the time is appropriate (See Chapter 5, p. 87), work together to create the vision statement for your school. All of this is not an easy task, but it is an absolutely critical task for effective school change for your school.

The principal and the school leadership team should lead the creation of the school vision. Creation of the school vision needs to be done *before* the implementation of the process of the Change Creation system, which is discussed in Chapters 5, pages 87–88. A process for developing the school vision, Vision Creation, is provided in online Resource A.

Power of Vision

A strong vision sets the stage for dramatic, second-order changes that lead to significant innovation. Without a strong vision, an organization is constrained to incremental, first-order changes with limited impact.

John Pellowe (2000) gives us an important sense of the power of vision when he discusses the Microsoft vision story.

Many employees at Microsoft are millionaires and yet they continue to work. Why? People volunteer to help an organization fulfill a vision that is deeply meaningful to them. . . . Effective visions help people see the "big picture," create understanding and build commitment. Ineffective vision statements are simply platitudes or statements of the obvious. . . . If you want to energize and motivate your personnel to use more of their creativity and initiative; if you want to build team spirit and commitment, then write a vision based on the desired outcomes of your [school's] success. (pp. 1–2)

The power of vision, in so many ways, is the foundation for change and is critical to transformational success, as the following discussions suggest.

Noted futurist Joel Barker (1991) in his prominent video, "Discovering the Future Series: The Power of Vision," relates that

Having a positive vision of the future is the most forceful motivator for change-for-success that companies, schools, communities, nations, and individuals possess. It inspires people in an organization to think together, dream together, and act together to make a difference.

Donella Meadows, a pioneering American environmental scientist, teacher, and lead author of the influential book *The Limits to Growth,* shares her story in the 2011 article "Donella Meadows: The Power of Vision":

My experience is, having now many times created a vision and then brought it, in some form, into being, is that I never know, at the beginning, how to get there. But as I articulate the vision and share it with people, the path reveals itself. And it would never reveal itself if I were not putting out the vision of what I really want and finding that other people really want it too.

Leadership expert Ken Blanchard (2011) says,

Vision is the vital extra ingredient for truly satisfying long-term success. Without a vision, you'll end up reacting rather than acting, and sooner or later you'll get lost. But if you have a compelling vision, you'll be clear about your purpose, so committed to it, and so sure about the ability to accomplish it that you'll be able to recognize obstacles, take them into account, and press on. (p. 19)

Additional Vision Perspectives

Vision Killers

Visions can be extraordinarily powerful, but there are things that we must guard against. Some of these are what George Barna (1992, pp. 119–129) calls "Vision Killers."

- Tradition (e.g., "but we've never done it before")
- Fear (e.g., risk raises the possibility of failure)
- Stereotypes (e.g., popular perceptions about people and conditions)
- Complacency (e.g., we fail to behave with vigor and passion)
- Fatigue (e.g., lack of commitment and energy)
- Short-term thinking (e.g., only seeking quick results and tangible benefits in the short term)

Practical Power of Vision

Timothy Clark (2011), in his *Deseret News* article "The Power of Vision Provides Organizations With Direction, Inspiration," takes us deeper:

Operationally, a vision has three functions. First is the cognitive function to educate. Second is the emotional function to motivate. Third is the organizational function to coordinate. When we hit all three, a vision becomes the ultimate economy of scale. It reduces the unit costs of performing certain types of work by answering thousands of questions, guiding employees in thousands of small decisions, and eliminating the ambiguity that might otherwise create the need for thousands of conversations. An effective vision provides for the mass production of answers and the creation of more efficient and effective coordinated action.

In addition, for success with visions, Ian Wilson (1996, p. 1) in his *On the Horizon Site* article, "The Practical Power of Vision," reminds us that

Vision is intensely practical, and that—while it should reflect our values and aspirations—it must also be built on facts. Vision is, in short, part emotional (the product of imagination, intuition, and values) and part rational (the product of analysis). Vision is a coherent and powerful statement of what a school can and should be some set number of years hence. Each element of this definition is significant—the vision:

- Must be coherent, integrating goals, strategies, and action plans into a complete and recognizable picture of the future school and its environment
- Must be powerful, to generate commitment and motivate performance
- Emphasizes what the school can be, because it should be realistic about what the future may hold and what is achievable
- Clarifies what the school should be, because it must reflect the values and aspirations of school personnel, students and other stakeholders

Shared Vision

Wilson (1996) also reminds us that

The vision must be shared. The purpose of the vision, after all, is to stimulate action and achieve results. Not to have an impressive piece of prose. If vision is to shape the future and drive action, then the leader—and other school personnel—must communicate it broadly, consistently, and continuously, until it becomes an integral part of the school's culture. (p. 1)

A Vision Reminder

A final reminder about successful visions comes from Joel Barker (1991), in his video mentioned above in the Power of Vision section: "Vision without action is but a dream. Action without vision just passes the time. Vision with action can change the world."

CHANGE

The famous scientist and science fiction writer Isaac Asimov relates about change that

> It is change, continuing change, inevitable change, that is the dominant factor in society today. No sensible decision can be made any longer without taking into account not only the world as it is, but the world as it will be. This, in turn, means that our statesmen, our businessmen, [our educators], our everyman must take on a science fictional way of thinking. (Asimov, n.d.)

Very simply, what this says to us is that the one constant in the world is change. And that change continues to accelerate at an ever-increasing pace and level of intensity, whether we like it or not. Change in society, in our schools, and in our lives will be no different. Change can be thought of as a "silent juggernaut, a persistent, irresistible force marching onward, permeating everything."

When Asimov speaks of needing to deal with change in a "science fictional way," that is, "no longer taking into account the world as it is, but the world as it will be," he means that as we plan for the future, we must develop our plan for what will be true *then* as opposed to what is true today. As an example, when Wayne Gretzky, possibly the world's greatest hockey player, retired, they asked him why he thought that he was so successful. When he answered, he said, "I skate to where the puck is going to be, not where it has been." In the same way, we have to design our change efforts for what will be needed at the time when our desired changes will take place, not what exists today.

From their research, Hord, Rutherford, Huling-Austin, and Hall (1987) concluded the following:

- Change is a process, not an event.
- Change is accomplished by individuals.
- Change is a highly personal experience.
- Change involves developmental growth.
- Change is best understood in operational terms.
- The focus on facilitation should be on individuals, change, and the context.

People's Responses to Change

In general, how do people respond to change? In response to change, we and our schools typically have chosen, consciously or by default, to resist change, ignore change, or sidestep the realities and impact of change, all losing responses.

Instead, those of us in our schools must *join* change, embrace it as a partner, and use it creatively for the advancement of our goals, schools, and society. Remember, you can't have meaningful progress without change.

A Perspective on Change

Change guru Daryl Conner (2006), gives us an overarching perspective of change and its potential as follows:

> Never before has so much changed so fast and with such dramatic implications for the entire world. . . . The magnitude of change today can prompt a doom-and-gloom vision, or it can be seen as an opportunity for a fundamental shift in how we humans define ourselves, where we are going, and how we will accomplish our goals. (pp. 3–5)

SUCCESS AND FAILURE OF CHANGE

Peter Senge, the recognized national leader in systems and learning organizations, relates in his book *Dance of Change* that "Most change initiatives fail" (Senge et al., 1999, p. 5). He goes on to report on two independent studies of hundreds of corporate programs published by Arthur D. Little and McKinsey & Company that approximately 70% failed to produce hoped-for results (pp. 5–6). And Senge further notes that Harvard's John Kotter, in a study of one hundred top management-driven "corporate transformation" efforts, concluded that

> More than half did not survive the initial phase. He found a few that were "very successful," and a few were "utter failures." The vast majority lay " . . . somewhere in between, with a distinct tilt toward the lower end of the scale." (Senge et al., 1999, p. 6)

Senge concluded his comments by saying, "There is little to suggest that schools, healthcare institutions, governmental, and nonprofit institutions fare any better" (Senge et al., 1999, p. 6).

Similarly, failure to sustain significant or transformational change in schools occurs again and again despite major school commitments to the change efforts, strong resource support, and talented and committed school personnel.

The authors of this book and others have concluded that change success requires some additional critical elements. As pointed out by Senge et al. (1999),

> Developing learning capacities (often called "learning initiatives") in the context of working groups and real goals can lead to powerful reinforcing growth processes. . . . Activating the self-energizing commitment and energy of people around changes they deeply care about has been the key to the many successes that have been achieved. (p. 9)

Consequently, these elements, "developing learning capacities," "working groups with real goals," and "self-energizing commitment and energy of people around changes they deeply care about" are part of the critical core for success in the Change Creation system presented in detail for schools in the remaining chapters of this book.

Principles for Successful Change

John Kotter (1998, pp. 27–33), in his study of why major change initiatives in the private sector usually fail, identified principles for leaders and school personnel to follow to ensure success in transforming schools. These are among the principles followed by the Change Creation system for schools, and their implementation is described in Chapters 5, 6, 10, and 12. These principles are as follows:

- *Establish a sense of urgency.* Kotter (1995) notes that over half of the organizations he has observed have never been able to create enough urgency to prompt action. He adds,

> Without motivation, people won't help and the effort goes nowhere. . . . Leaders underestimate how hard it can be to encourage people out of their comfort zones. . . . Urgency is adequate when 75% of your leadership and personnel are honestly convinced that business as usual is no longer an acceptable plan. (p. 1)

> **Kotter Principles for Successful Change**
>
> - Establish a sense of urgency.
> - Form a powerful guiding coalition.
> - Create and communicate a vision.
> - Empower others to act on the vision and eliminate obstacles to change.
> - Plan for and create short-term wins.
> - Consolidate improvements and produce more changes.
> - Institutionalize new approaches.

- *Form a powerful guiding coalition.* Change efforts may start with only a few proponents, but the number of those who believe that change is necessary should grow continually to a sizable share of believers. A guiding coalition must not only help lead the change effort, but must also bring others on board with new ideas, approaches, and commitment. Kotter (1995) tells us that "The building of this coalition—their sense of urgency, their sense of what's happening and what's needed—is crucial" (p. 1).

- *Create and communicate a vision.* Successful transformational change rests on the meaningfulness and communication of the school's vision. Kotter (1995) reminds us that

> The vision functions in many different ways: it helps spark motivation, it helps keep all of the projects and changes aligned, it provides a filter to evaluate how the school is doing, and it provides a rationale for the changes the school will have to weather. (p. 2)

- *Empower others to act on the vision and eliminate obstacles to change.* For effective change to occur, schools and leaders must allow faculty and others to make changes in their areas of responsibility, allocate funds for new initiatives, find time for personnel to do creative projects, and alter the way work is organized to allow school personnel to be where their efforts are required. Kotter (1995) points out that

Nothing is more frustrating than believing in the change but then not having the time, money, help, or support needed to effect it. You can't get rid of all the obstacles, but the biggest ones need to be dealt with. (p. 2)

- *Plan for and create short-term wins.* Progress with major change efforts typically take substantial time. This can lead to disappointment, possible loss of momentum, and a drop in urgency levels. Relative to such concerns, Kotter (1995) advises, "Commitments to produce short-term wins help keep the urgency level up and force detailed analytical thinking that can clarify and revise the vision" (p. 2).

- *Consolidate improvements and produce more changes.* Even with the best of efforts, major schoolwide change may take several years to fully accomplish. Significant school change approaches and related cultural changes take serious time and can be fragile and open to regression. To deal with such concerns, Kotter (1995) recommends that

Leaders of successful efforts use the feeling of victory as the motivation to delve more deeply into their school: to explore changes in the basic culture, to expose the systems relationships of the school which need tuning, to move people committed to the new ways into key roles. Leaders of change must go into the process believing that their efforts will take years. (p. 2)

- *Institutionalize new approaches.* We know that we have had change success when we hear "this is the way we do things around here." In this regard, Kotter (1995) cautions that

Until new behaviors are rooted in social norms and shared values, they are subject to degradations as soon as the pressure for change is removed. Two factors are particularly important for doing this. First, a conscious attempt to show people how the new approaches, behaviors, and attitudes have helped improve the school. People have to be helped to make the connections between the effort and the outcome. The second is to ensure that the next generation of school leaders believe in and embody the new ways. (pp. 2–3)

We use these principles from Kotter for leading change in Part II to frame the work of principals, school leadership teams, and central office staff to guide and support the implementation of action teams in schools.

Assimilation Capacity

Relative to successful school change, one of the major problems in schools is that they have too many change efforts going on at any one time. This is a serious problem for the personnel of the school, the various groups that are functioning in the school, and the school itself.

People and schools have only so much capacity or resources to deal with change, their *assimilation capacity.* The assimilation capacity is different for different individuals; some individuals have little capacity to deal with change, whereas others may have substantial capacity. The same is true for groups and organizations, with some having limited assimilation capacity and others having much more.

When there is so much change that an individual's assimilation capacity is surpassed, then that individual's efforts are degraded and the individual performs below his or her normal levels of productivity and quality. In such a case, we say the individual is *dysfunctional;* that is, his or her actions or feelings divert resources away from meeting the desired productivity and quality standards. Dysfunctional individuals can continue to perform, but they perform at lower levels of productivity and quality. In a similar way, groups and schools can be dysfunctional; this happens when their assimilation capacities are surpassed and they perform at lower than optimal productivity and quality levels.

Dysfunctional behavior in individuals ranges, for example, from low levels (symptoms: poorer communications, reduced risk taking, lower morale and conflicts with fellow workers) to medium levels (symptoms: lying, chronic tardiness, apathy, and interpersonal withdrawal) to high levels (symptoms: covertly undermining of the leadership, chronic depression, physical breakdown, and substance abuse). Simply put, if individuals, groups, or schools are asked to handle too much change in their total arenas of action, including work, home, family and friends, community and beyond, they will become dysfunctional and cannot perform optimally. The students, school, family, and others all lose. When this is true for all or most of the personnel in a school, then the loss is major and serious. Often, this represents reality today in our schools and other organizations in society.

Typically, schools are filled with an excess number of low-priority to middle-priority projects that have some value or would be nice to have but will have little real effect on the productivity and quality of the school. In fact, these low- to middle-priority projects actually stand in the way of accomplishing the ongoing and other potentially high-priority efforts.

In particular, most faculties have exceeded their capacities to assimilate all the changes, and many faculties, as a whole, are dysfunctional. Such discoveries bring clarity to what must be done and give a sense of hope to school leaders and teachers.

Now that we understand these assimilation and dysfunction concerns better, what can we do about them? A five-step process for dealing with such concerns follows.

1. Leaders must become aware of the concepts of limited assimilation capacities and associated dysfunctions and their serious potential negative impact on the people and effectiveness of the school and its operations.

Five Steps for Dealing With Change Overload

2. Before new projects involving major change are initiated, a thorough analysis of all existing projects should be undertaken and a list of them prepared.

3. Projects should be prioritized, ranging from low to high priority (imperatives, projects that will make a significant difference).

4. All but the highest-priority projects should be considered for termination or reduction in scope.

5. A plan should be developed and implemented to eliminate or reduce in scope as many of the lower-priority projects as is practical, timely, and cost-effective.

School leaders, as much as is possible, should use this process to clear the decks before implementing the Change Creation system.

Change Roles in Schools

As schools attempt to build commitment for change efforts that affect their people, processes, and outcomes, an understanding of the four roles of change—change sponsor, change agent, change target, and change advocate—is critical.

Change Sponsor

A *change sponsor* or *sponsor* is an individual or group who has the power to sanction and legitimize the change efforts. In schools, depending on the specific change effort, a sponsor might be the school board, the superintendent, the principal, a department chair, or a combination of these individuals, because they typically are the ones, with final authority, who can sanction and legitimize change.

The sponsor must be the champion for change. It is the sponsor's responsibility to (a) decide which initiatives and changes will be authorized; (b) communicate his or her decisions and priorities to the school and its personnel; and (c) provide the appropriate encouragement, pressure, and support for change efforts. Strong sponsors are essential to the building of commitment for change efforts and can create an environment in the school that enables the work to be effectively implemented and productive.

In school districts that seriously choose to participate in change efforts, superintendents, principals, and the board of education sponsor the implementation of the change process and legitimize it. This makes the change process both important to the schools and legitimate for principals, teachers, and others to invest time and serious commitment in. Also, in educating parents and bringing them along with the effort, they too become direct or indirect supporters of the change approach.

Change Agent

A *change agent* or *agent* is an individual or group who is responsible for implementing the desired change. Teachers, the principal, and the leadership team often play the role of change agent. Agents' success depends on their preparation as change agents, their relations with others in the school, and their ability to diagnose problems, deal with the issues, plan solutions, and implement their plan effectively. Properly prepared action teams have the potential to be especially effective change agents in their schools.

Change Target

A *change target* or *target* is an individual or group who must actually change. Targets are the people who must change if innovation is to be successful. In school improvement projects, targets typically are students, teachers, and administrators. For example, if the change calls for computer-assisted instruction, then students as well as a number of teachers and administrators would be targets and have to change by learning how to use computers in an instructional mode.

Like all of us, targets will be more responsive to our change efforts if we put things in their frame of reference and help them fully understand the desired change, why it is important, what is expected of them, and the impact that the change will have on them and the school. Fullan (1991) states that people must be able to attach their own personal meaning to the change experiences. The change agent, then, must be alert to how the meaning of change is communicated to the targets of the change.

Change Advocate

A *change advocate* or *advocate* is an individual or group who desires a change but doesn't have the authority or power to sanction it. Frequently, faculty, the principal, or nonschool persons or groups, such as parents, play the role of advocate when they want something new to happen but do not have the power to approve it.

Advocates typically recommend actions to those with the authority to approve or further recommend. For instance, a community person may advocate for a special resolution to the school board, or a department chair may ask the principal for a special budget consideration, or a principal might recommend a certain policy to the superintendent for school board consideration. However, it should be clearly noted that advocates are *not* sponsors or effective replacements for sponsors.

Playing Different Change Roles

In different circumstances, an individual or group may play different change roles. Also, various change projects might require an individual or group to serve in more than one change role. A typical example might be where a principal is a change agent to the superintendent but a sponsor to teachers. Action teams could play all four roles of change sponsor, agent, target and advocate—as a sponsor of the change they want to bring about in the school, as an agent as their team enacts one of their changes, as a target because they must change for them to bring about change, and as an advocate to another action team for an approach to learning that the original action team found successful. The important thing to remember is to determine the role you are playing in the given situation and perform it well.

EFFECTIVE SPONSORSHIP IN SCHOOLS

All four roles of change are necessary for the success of change efforts and the Change Creation system. However, the roles of those in leadership positions are especially critical. Earlier, when listing the responsibilities of the principal, the first item was "the sponsor," and for school system and district influence, the school board, superintendent, and district leaders are among the most important sponsors. For major innovations to be successfully implemented in our school, especially for innovations involving second order change, sponsors must demonstrate strong, decisive, and visible commitment to those efforts. For example, if an innovation or a change project has strong school system, district, and principal sponsorship, it has an especially positive probability for success.

Very simply, significant change will not occur without sufficient commitment and action by natural school sponsors. Sponsors must show strong commitment to ensure that agents and targets are effective in their roles. Often, the difference between success and failure in school efforts comes down to the quality of the sponsorship!

The new standards for professional learning from Learning Forward emphasize the importance of strong leadership as part of the essential conditions for effective professional learning. Their standard for leadership states, "Professional learning that increases educator effectiveness and results for all students requires skillful leaders who develop capacity, advocate, and create support systems for professional learning" and adds that

> Leaders throughout the pre-K–12 education community recognize effective professional learning as a key strategy for supporting significant school and school system improvements to increase results for all students. Whether they lead from classrooms, schools, school systems, technical assistance agencies, professional associations, universities, or public agencies, leaders develop their own and others' capacity to learn and lead professional learning, advocate for it, provide support systems, and distribute leadership and responsibility for its effectiveness and results. (Learning Forward, 2011, p. 28)

Characteristics of Strong Sponsorship

Conner (2006, pp. 116–117) outlines the characteristics of a strong sponsor. What follows is an adaptation of these sponsorship characteristics in the school setting.

- *Power:* Power in the school to legitimize the change for others
- *Pain:* A level of discomfort with some area of the school that makes change there attractive
- *Vision:* A clear understanding of what change must occur
- *Resources:* An understanding of the school resources (e.g., time, money, and people) necessary for successful implementation and the capacity (i.e., willingness and ability) to commit them

- *Long view:* An in-depth understanding of the effect the change will have on the school
- *Sensitivity:* The capacity to appreciate and empathize with the personal issues raised by the change
- *Scope:* The capacity to understand fully the impact of the change
- *Public role:* The capacity to demonstrate the public support necessary to convey strong school commitment to the change
- *Private role:* The capacity to meet privately with key individuals or groups to convey strong personal support for the change
- *Consequence management:* The capacity to promptly reward those who facilitate the change or to express displeasure with those who inhibit it
- *Monitor:* The capacity to ensure that monitoring procedures are established that will track both the progress and problems of the transition
- *Sacrifice:* The commitment to pursue the transition, knowing that a price will most often accompany the change
- *Persistence:* The capacity to demonstrate consistent support for the change and reject any short-term action that is inconsistent with the long-term change goals

The above criteria give a comprehensive set of characteristics by which to measure the sponsorship for change and the Change Creation system in a school or district. If most of these are met, there is a high probability for good sponsorship and support. However, if several of these are not satisfied, then there may be serious sponsorship problems; in such situations, leaders should work to improve sponsorship for the effort or replace the sponsors with stronger ones. In addition, if the principal is the in-school sponsor of a change effort, the sponsorship for the change is strengthened dramatically if the superintendent and district leaders also sponsor and support the change.

Action teams and their schoolwide efforts represent major change in the school. As a result, they will require the same strong and effective sponsorship as that outlined above. Learning Forward (2011) echoes the importance of strong change sponsorship in stating that leaders need to "apply understanding of organizational and human changes to design needed conditions, resources, and other supports for learning and change" (p. 29).

Dealing With Weak Sponsorship

If a major change initiative does not have a reasonably high level of sponsorship commitment or if such cannot be developed in an appropriate time frame, then the initiative has a high risk of failure.

What should be done if sponsorship is weak? When sponsors are not fully committed to the proposed change, don't fully understand it, or are unable or unwilling to provide adequate sponsorship, there are only three options (Conner, 2006, p. 115):

- Strengthen sponsorship (e.g., by applying the Universal Change Principle found later in this chapter to help the sponsor become stronger).

- Find strong alternate sponsorship (e.g., under the right conditions, the assistant or associate principal, with the full support of the principal, might become a strong sponsor).
- Prepare to fail.

Strong sponsorship is absolutely essential to the success of effective action teams and the change initiatives they hope to accomplish!

CHANGE AND RESISTANCE IN SCHOOLS

Human Nature of Change

As one considers dealing with people and change, it is important to understand the underlying human nature of people. All people have their sensitivities; these sensitivities vary greatly from person to person, but each of us has our own personal sensitivities.

Well-known author Stephen R. Covey explains this in his book *The Seven Habits of Highly Effective People* (1990):

> People are very tender, very sensitive inside. I don't believe age or experience makes much difference. . . . Inside, even within the most toughened and calloused exteriors, are the tender feelings and emotions of the heart. That's why in relationships, the little things are the big things. (pp. 192–193)

Consequently, when we work in promoting change, we must understand where people are coming from and be especially careful in how we approach them and what we say to them.

People's Feelings and Truths

People understand and accept things in two different ways, *intellectually* and *emotionally.* Relative to a change, you would like them to accept a change both intellectually and emotionally—then they are really committed. However, people often accept things intellectually, on a factual basis, and not emotionally. A powerful example of this we can see in smokers; they intellectually agree that smoking is very bad for their health and might eventually kill them, but still keep on smoking. Their emotional feelings are overriding their intellectual acceptance.

The reason for this type of inconsistency is simply that *people's feelings are their truths,* and when they are faced with a difficult decision, they go with their truths, their feelings, over their intellectual considerations. A powerful school vision, as discussed earlier in this chapter, is foundational for change and one of best sources for gaining emotional acceptance of a change effort. To gain genuine and full acceptance of a change effort, we need both people's intellectual and emotional acceptance. At the beginning of a change effort, we may not have adequate intellectual and emotional support from people. As a result, we must work with them during the transition process to more fully develop it so that we are able to gain their genuine and full acceptance of the change effort. A compelling and inspiring vision helps begin the process of gaining genuine and full acceptance of a change effort, and short term wins and meaningful feedback during the change process help toward building genuine and full acceptance of a change effort.

The Feeling of Change

To experience a *sense of the feeling of change,* do the following experiment. Put your hands together so that your fingers are alternately intermingled from each hand. Once you've done this, check and see which thumb is on the top. Now take your hands apart and put them together again with the other thumb on the top. In a word, how does that feel? Do such words as *strange, odd, uncomfortable,* or *weird* come to mind? That's the feeling of change.

This experiment was only a minor one in change, but notice the discomfort you experienced from it. As a result, this gives you some idea of what the discomfort level might be if the change were something much more significant and one that you were not familiar with. You can now more easily imagine how major, unfamiliar change causes discomfort, fear and anxiety, and resistance in people.

Resistance to Change

As humans, we take comfort in the neurological truth that doing what we have always done is a familiar route that is not easily changed due to the design of the brain and fear of the unknown. From a scientific perspective, neuroscientist Robert A. Burton (2009) explains why change is so difficult for us and why we naturally resist change.

> The concept of neural networks helps explain why established habits, beliefs, and judgments are so difficult to change. . . . The brain is only human; it relies on established ways. As interneuronal connections increase, they become more difficult to overcome. (pp. 51–52)

And in related change resistance research, organizational culture leader, Edgar Schein noted in his book, *Organizational Culture and Leadership* (2004) that "people will even retain a dysfunctional culture if it is in their comfort zone."

Conner (2006, pp. 17, 27) relates that it is actually not the change event itself that upsets us as humans; it is the *implications* that the change has for our life. The Beast of Change is the *implications of change,* the fear and anxiety within us as we encounter significant change. It is *natural* and *normal* for people to feel uncomfortable about change and for it to cause discomfort, fear, and anxiety. We explore different types of change resistance in the following sections and discuss how to deal with them.

General Change Resistance

There is one certainty with change: Someone will resist. Why? Because resistance is natural and normal for people. Nonetheless, if there were one vital point we would like to communicate, it would be this: Don't let resisters stop necessary change.

Too often, we let a small, loud percentage of coworkers rule the day. We should listen to concerns of others, try to understand, and take their concerns into consideration. Yet, at some point, we simply have to get started, include those resisting the change effort, and assume that in a small group with peers, their concerns can be worked out.

Carlene Murphy illustrates this point when she tells a story about a teacher in her school who initially was very reticent and vocal about her objection and opposition to the school improvement program. The teacher did not want to be a member of an action team; however, like all teachers at the school, she was included in an action team. From August through October, she was cool to other members and somewhat reluctant to fully participate. By January, she was demonstrating strategies to her action team colleagues and bringing student work to show how well her students were responding. By April, she was being videotaped as an example of how to effectively use the strategies and action team meetings to fine-tune a lesson. Within two years, she was a member of Murphy's staff. Suppose she had been allowed not to participate? The gulf between this teacher and those teachers in action teams would have widened, and her constructive contributions would have been lost.

Quick Fixes and Resistance

With change, one common approach is the quick fix. What often happens with the quick fix is referred to as the *attempt, attack, and abandon cycle.* Jim Knight (2006) describes this as follows:

> During this vicious pattern, a new practice or program is introduced in a school and teachers make a half-hearted attempt to implement it. Then, before it has been implemented effectively and for a sufficient length of time, various individuals in the school or district begin to attack the practice or program and, not surprisingly, many teachers implementing it begin to lose their will to stick with the program. Eventually, even though it never had a chance to be implemented properly, leaders in the district reject the program as unsuccessful and abandon it, only to propose another approach that is soon pulled into the same vicious cycle. In this manner, schools stay on an unmerry-go-round of attempt, attack, abandon, without ever seeing any meaningful, sustained change in instruction taking place.

Resisters and Innovators

Everett Rogers (2003, pp. 22, 280–285) writes that individuals play different roles in the change process. His research says the five types of roles (and their respective sizes) that are activated in change efforts are Innovators (2.5%), Early Adopters (13.5%), Early Majority (34%), Late Majority (34%), and Laggards (16%), as sketched below.

- *Innovators.* Venturesome; eager to try new ideas; able to cope with a high degree of uncertainty; willing to accept an occasional setback; play an important role in the change process; provide a gate-keeping role in the flow of new ideas; and are important to communications.

- *Early Adopters.* Respectable; opinion leaders; serve as role models; try out new ideas, but in a careful way; decrease uncertainty about a new idea by adopting it; maintain a central position in the communication structure; and change agents use them to speed up the process.

- *Early Majority.* Deliberate; adopt new ideas just before the average; interact frequently with peers; seldom hold leadership positions; adopt between very early and late adopters, making them an important link in the change process; and provide interconnectedness in the school.

- *Late Majority.* Skeptical; have a cautious air; adopt new ideas just after the average, when majority has adopted; peer pressure is necessary to motivate them to adopt; and the uncertainty of a new idea must be removed before they feel safe to adopt.

- *Laggards.* Traditional; last to adopt change; possess almost no opinion leadership; many are near being isolates in the school; their point of reference is the past; interact with mostly other traditionalists; suspicious of change and change agents; their adoption lags well behind awareness-knowledge of a new idea and slows the change-decision process; and their lateness to adopt may be more related to a system's problem than their individual problem.

The first three types will go where they need to go and do what they need to do, just at different rates. The Innovators are the first to go, not afraid to venture into the unknown; Early Adopters follow, often cutting their own paths before the roads are clear; the Early Majority wait until they have assurances that roads are clear and some bridges have been built. The Late Majority go in large groups, believing that there is safety in numbers, and as with any major movement, they will bring stability. These are the people who can be depended on once they understand and accept what is ahead of them. The Laggards don't want to move and, if possible, aren't going to let anyone else move either.

Dealing With Resisters and Innovators

The foregoing way of thinking about individuals is an important frame of reference when we are initiating and implementing major change efforts, such as with action teams. When you work with an all-inclusive system, you have all types of individuals within the circle. Knowing that in schools 16% of individuals are Innovators and Early Adopters and nearly 70% are in the Early and Late Majorities, we have a better sense of success for creating a positive and constructive environment. In particular, action teams stimulate the Early and Late Majorities and cause them to participate more than they would otherwise.

This Early and Late Majority group is the population on which we should focus. But what do we do? Too often, we see resisters, for example, Laggards, and feel their rejection and use our precious energy trying to persuade them. We must understand that it isn't just our efforts that they don't want to do.

They don't want to do anything, and they know exactly how to make enough noise so that leaders leave them alone. In Change Creation system schools, we simply include them. By including them, we have a chance to have an impact on their attitude and behaviors and to gain from their input and contributions. Also, we must remember that resisters teach children, too.

Control Resistance

We know that human beings have a strong need for control (Conner, 2006, pp. 74–75). This is especially true when it comes to change. When we have a sense of control over change and its circumstances, we typically feel comfortable. So the change we initiate, understand, and have a sense of control over is a change that we feel good about and are more comfortable with.

There are actually two types of control we all seek: direct control, where we have the direct ability to request or actually dictate outcomes that usually occur, and indirect control, where we have the ability to at least anticipate the outcomes of a change. People usually have the highest level of comfort when they have a sense of direct control. Indirect control results in less, but some, comfort with change. For example, if I am not in direct control of some change but understand it and know the implications of it, I then can anticipate what will occur. This, again, is indirect control, and I will feel less threatened by the change than if I had no sense of possible outcomes.

What all this means is that if leaders of an innovation want people to feel comfortable with a particular change, the leaders must do whatever is appropriate and necessary to give others a sense of control, either direct or indirect, for the change effort. If this can be done, leaders enhance the chances that people will be supportive of and helpful with the change.

However, if people aren't given some sense of control over the change by feeling able to directly dictate or influence its outcomes or at least anticipate its outcomes, they may feel threatened. As a result, they will do what comes naturally when people don't understand or appreciate what is going on; they will resist the change either openly and overtly or covertly. Human resistance to change is not an aberration or a reflection that something is wrong with someone. Instead, it is a natural reaction to change when one does not understand the change and its implications. Consequently, if you do not want people to do what is natural relative to change (i.e., resist it), then, very simply, you must make them feel comfortable with the change by helping them understand the change and its implications and giving them a sense of either direct or indirect control. The major change principle that describes how to do this is discussed in the next section.

Other Reasons for Resistance

In addition to the reasons for resistance to change discussed in the previous sections, there are other reasons to resist change. In Theodore Creighton's *The Principal as Technology Leader* (2003), he quotes from Kanter's book, *Evolve* (2001), additional reasons people resist change in schools, particularly in the early stages of implementation, as follows.

- *Loss of face:* Fear that dignity will be undermined
- *Loss of influence:* Anger at decisions being taken out of one's hands
- *Excess uncertainty:* Feeling uninformed about where the change will lead
- *Surprise, surprise:* Automatic defensiveness—no advance warning, no time to get ready
- *The "difference" effect:* Rejection because it doesn't fit the existing mental models and habits and routines
- *Can I do it?* Concerns about future competence and success
- *Ripple effects:* Annoyance at disruptions and interference to other tasks
- *More work:* Resistance to additional things to learn and do
- *Past resentments:* Memories of past hostilities or unresolved problems
- *Real threats:* Anger that the change will inflict pain and create losers

UNIVERSAL CHANGE PRINCIPLE FOR SCHOOLS

The Universal Change Principle is the most important principle for dealing with and helping others deal with change. This principle establishes a contextual condition that prepares people for a change. It gives an overarching approach for leading and managing change and is applicable for change virtually everywhere.

> Universal Change Principle: Learning must precede change.

For our discussion of change and the Universal Change Principle, think of *learning* as *action learning*, gaining capacity (i.e., willingness and ability) for effective action relative to the change under consideration. Effective action is to be interpreted in relation to the totality of change being considered. Ability that enhances effective action includes information, knowledge, skill, experience, and understanding about the change, as well as understanding the nuances and qualities of the culture. If people are to help bring about change, then they must be provided with the appropriate learning in advance so that they understand and appreciate the change and its implications.

Providing the appropriate learning allows people to gain a reasonable sense of control with respect to the change. As we discussed above in the section on the human nature of change, note that *appropriate learning*, as much as possible, should involve both *intellectual learning* (e.g., from facts and other related information) and *emotional learning* (e.g., from the vision, personal and professional support and information from friends and colleagues, and other emotion-related information).

Appropriate Learning

Appropriate learning does not mean that change agents have an answer for every circumstance in the initiation and implementation stages of the innovation.

In any complex change effort, such as the one in schools, there will be holes and blanks that cannot be filled in by anyone but the implementers. Appropriate learning would include knowing theoretical and practical underpinnings that support the proposition that the new process, practice, program, attitude, belief, or material would bring about the desired change in a specific school or with a particular group of students. Teachers should know what disagreements or conflicts may exist among researchers about the new practice. When the initiators or change agents confirm with teachers that there are few clear answers that fit every situation, teachers are more likely to see themselves as experts in their situation, given the latitude to find the answers for their students. Teachers with this attitude and who are part of a strong support system will be less likely to get frustrated and rebellious when the proposed change hits snags. The learning that precedes the change, then, includes a clarification of the meaning of the change and whatever information is required for the proposed implementers to agree to begin.

For example, a simple illustration of the Universal Change Principle might be that of a driver who wants to make a turn ahead. He provides learning for those behind him by lighting his turn signal a few hundred feet before the turn. As a result, other drivers learn of the first driver's desired change and then have time to make their appropriate adjustments. In this case, learning preceded change for the success and safety of all.

A school example might involve a principal who wants the mathematics teachers to use a new approach for teaching basic mathematics. If that principal just announces one day that starting next semester the mathematics teachers will teach by the new method, probably most of the teachers will be unfamiliar with the new approach, not understand its value and implementation, not feel comfortable with this new change, and as a consequence, resist rather than be helpful with what the principal desires to have happen.

However, suppose instead that the principal uses the Universal Change Principle to guide the implementation of what he or she desires to have happen. Following this approach, the principal would first ask himself or herself, "What learning must take place before this change can be successfully implemented?" In response, the principal would most likely involve the mathematics teachers in a series of discussions concerning such things as (a) what the principal is thinking about; (b) why this is important to improving student learning and to the teachers and school; (c) what the implications are for the students, teachers, and school; (d) what training and support will be provided; (e) how will people be rewarded for participating; and (f) how and when the new approach should be implemented. Doing all this doesn't guarantee that everyone will be in favor of the change and that all resistance will be averted. It does, though, ensure greater understanding of what's desired; why it's important; and what the implications are for the students, teachers and school. Furthermore, it helps teachers gain a sense of control for the project, making them feel much more comfortable with it and its implementation. As a result, teachers are far more likely to help with the change rather than resist its implementation.

Learning Leaders in Learning Forward

Principals, as schools' chief learning leaders, are embodied in the Learning Forward Leadership standard for professional learning as follows:[1]

- As advocates for professional learning, leaders make their own career-long learning visible to others. They participate in professional learning within and beyond their own work environment. Leaders consume information in multiple fields to enhance their leadership practice.
- All leaders demand effective professional learning focused on substantive results for themselves, their colleagues, and their students.
- Leaders artfully combine deep understanding of and cultural responsiveness to the community they serve with high expectations and support for results to achieve school and school system goals.
- Leaders embed professional learning into the organization's vision by communicating that it is a core function for improvement and by establishing and maintaining a public and persistent focus on educator professional learning.
- Skillful leaders establish organizational systems and structures that support effective professional learning and ongoing continuous improvement. (Learning Forward, 2011, pp. 29–30)

Application of the Universal Change Principle

The proper application of the Universal Change Principle does not guarantee that all resistance to change will be averted and that all desired changes can be accomplished. However, an appropriate application of the Universal Change Principle does significantly enhance the likelihood of these desired things happening. The proper application of the Universal Change Principle does take additional time and effort but generally pays off handsomely in terms of real accomplishment in the end. It means slowing down to speed up, that is, taking a little longer initially to do the right things and then being able to speed up the process later on as a consequence of the earlier foundation that was laid.

The Universal Change Principle also says "No surprises!" If you want to bring about a desired change, don't surprise people with it. Their likelihood of reacting favorably to the change and assisting with it will be increased greatly if you take the time to provide people with a basis of understanding from which they can make the desired transition.

If *L* represents *learning* and *C* represents *change*, a nice way to symbolize the Universal Change Principle is this:

$$L > C$$

It is read as "learning is greater than change."

---

[1]From *Standards for Professional Learning*, by Learning Forward, 2011, Oxford, OH: Author. Reprinted with permission.

Notice that this implies that if there is to be a lot of change, then there must be a lot of learning that takes place first. If the change is really major, then it may require several iterations of learning at several different times and with different groups of people, depending on the change, circumstances, and people involved. For large school changes, this is what typically must happen: In advance of the announcement of a desired change effort, leaders develop a relatively detailed plan, based on the Universal Change Principle. This means that they determine the groups that must have additional learning and then provide each of them with the appropriate and necessary learning iterations, specifically designed for their group, to precede the desired change. As Learning Forward (2011) states in its Implementation standard for professional learning, "Drawing from multiple bodies of research about change, leaders provide and align resources, including time, staff, materials, and technology, to initiate and sustain implementation" (p. 44).

SUMMARY

In previous chapters, we have focused on several crucial *fundamentals of effectiveness* that are *required* for schools successfully becoming professional learning communities and for improving teaching and increasing student learning. These include fundamentals relating to contextual conditions such as school culture, discipline in thought and action, and transformational leadership. In this chapter, we build on these earlier concepts and explore and discuss the foundational nature and importance of school vision and critical elements of successful change. Included in the latter were the human nature of change, principles of successful change, change assimilation, roles of change, the feeling of change, resistance to change, and the overarching and powerful Universal Change Principle—learning must precede change.

In addition, this chapter discusses the key ideas and concepts that the principal and other leaders will need to use to transform their schools as they prepare to implement the Change Creation system. These include the following:

- Creating a strong, compelling vision that requires new approaches to learning and teaching
- Identifying who plays which change roles—change sponsor, agent, advocate, and target.
- Assessing the capacity of the faculty to undertake a new change initiative and reduce or eliminate the "change overload"
- Understanding where staff members are with regards to their level of receptivity and resistance to the Change Creation system initiative
- Using the Universal Change Principle in planning for gaining acceptance for initiating and implementing the Change Creation system

In the next chapter, we build on our understanding of culture and change and focus on the fundamentals for creating highly effective learning teams and professional learning communities that are integral to the Change Creation system.

Fundamentals for Creating Learning Teams and Professional Learning Communities

4

Can you imagine a school where the school personnel are organized into action teams that work together to help the school accomplish its vision? Where action teams become authentic teams by developing the willingness and ability to work together in a genuinely cooperative and mutually dependent manner toward a common goal? Where action teams become learning teams that learn and recreate themselves, set and focus on challenging new goals, engage in creative inquiry, are self-directed and reflective, and take innovative and coordinated action? Where all action teams, as learning teams, improve teacher practice and enhance student learning and become part of the generative process in the school? Where schools become professional learning communities that create new approaches to teaching and learning? Where the work of action teams is an integral part of the school improvement plan, and faculty and action teams collaborate across the school and use and adopt content and best practices proven successful by other action teams?

Our research and experiences over the last twenty-five years have shown (Murphy & Lick, 2005) that the processes for school improvement and student performance enhancement are most successful when the school's *action teams* (i.e., designated groups of school personnel who work together to help the school move toward accomplishing the school vision) become *authentic teams, comentoring teams,* and *learning teams,* and the school becomes a *professional learning community.*

In this chapter, we discuss in detail and illustrate the concepts of collaboration, teams, comentoring teams, learning teams, and professional learning communities. The concepts discussed will be fundamental to meaningful school change and will be utilized throughout the remainder of this book. We encourage you to study these concepts now and then, later, return to them regularly to deepen your understanding so as to use them knowledgeably and successfully in your future work.

Action teams, when initially formed, generally don't start out as authentic, comentoring, learning teams. Instead, action teams typically begin as groups and then evolve, as indicated in Figure 4.1, to become authentic teams. Authentic teams whose members comentor one another then become comentoring teams. Finally, through a step-by-step process, comentoring teams become learning teams. That is, groups that are potential action teams grow over time into authentic, comentoring, learning teams through the intentional collaborative efforts of team members and with the support and encouragement from leaders and coaches.

Figure 4.1 The Desired Evolution of an Action Team

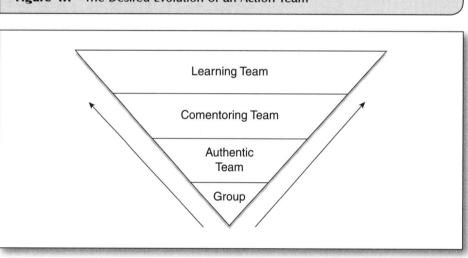

COLLABORATION AND TEAMWORK

According to the National Staff Development Council, now Learning Forward, researchers and teachers, within a reasonable school environment with adequate structure and leadership, increased teacher collaboration, and teamwork have the potential to improve schools and increase student learning performance.

National Staff Development Council

Some of the most important forms of professional learning and problem solving occur in group settings within schools and school districts. Organized groups provide the social interaction that often deepens learning and the interpersonal support and synergy [i.e., authentic teamwork] necessary for creatively solving the complex problems of teaching and learning. And because many of the recommendations contained in the standards advocated for increased teamwork among teachers and administrators in designing lessons, critiquing student work, and analyzing various types of data, among other tasks, it is imperative that professional learning be directed at improving the quality of collaborative work. (Roy & Hord, 2003, p. 41)

Researchers

An interdependent work structure strengthens professional community. When teachers work in groups that require coordination, this, by definition, requires collaboration. When groups, rather than individuals, are seen as the main units for implementing curriculum, instruction, and assessment, they facilitate development of shared purpose for student learning and collective responsibility to achieve it. (Newmann & Wehlage, 1995, pp. 37–38)

When teachers, working in teams, recognize the value of teacher leadership, engage in systematic high-level instructional talk, and have the opportunity to improve practices collaboratively and in concrete forms, they develop team loyalty, trust, and new feelings of responsibility and accountability. The collective team is responsible to each other and for all the team's students. The result is improved teaching and learning. (Troen & Boles, 2011, p. 2)

Teachers

Two-thirds of teachers who reported to the annual survey (67 percent) believe that increased collaboration among teachers and school leaders would greatly improve student achievement. [The survey polled 1,003 K–12 teachers in the fall 2009.] (Perkins-Gough, 2010, p. 67)

As the above quotations testify, increased teacher collaboration and teamwork have the potential to improve schools and increase student learning performance. Unfortunately, to do this is easier said than done, that is, there are many barriers to successful teacher collaboration and teamwork, as the following study attests:

While teacher teams may have energy and enthusiasm, team members typically lack the skills, tools, and support structures that would allow them to orchestrate significant pedagogical and curriculum changes through the collaborative work of the team. Principals generally lack the time and preparation to properly guide and supervise teacher teams. (They haven't been taught how to do it, either.) Teams are rarely, if ever, trained in the basic skills of team facilitation, such as time management, goal setting, development of team norms, and conflict resolution. (Troen & Boles, 2011, p. 1)

ACTION TEAMS AND PROFESSIONAL LEARNING COMMUNITIES

Action teams are the designated groups of school personnel who work together to help the school move toward accomplishing the school vision. They are key building blocks in the Change Creation system for school improvement and increasing student learning. Action teams not only function individually but also work with leaders, school personnel, and other teams more broadly as critical functional parts of the school becoming an effective professional learning community. As a result, the two fundamental questions about action teams and the school that should be asked at this point are as follows:

1. Do action teams in schools function as authentic teams, comentoring teams, and learning teams, and do schools function as professional learning communities?

2. How do action teams become authentic teams, comentoring teams, and learning teams, and how do schools become professional learning communities to increase school innovation and improve student learning performance?

The *typical answer* to the first question is "of course." However, too frequently, groups in schools do *not* function as authentic teams, comentoring teams, or learning teams, and schools too often function in ways that are *contrary* to the characteristics of professional learning communities. Consequently, in the balance of this chapter, we discuss in detail the fundamentals of authentic teams, comentoring teams, learning teams, and professional learning communities and explain and illustrate exactly what teachers and leaders need to understand and do in order to turn school groups (i.e., action teams) into *authentic teams* and *learning teams* and schools into *professional learning communities.*

AUTHENTIC TEAMS AND SYNERGY

An *authentic team* is a group of people with the ability to work together in a genuinely cooperative and mutually dependent manner (i.e., interdependently) toward common goals. Authentic teamwork means joint work and joint responsibility. Authentic teamwork is a vehicle that allows common people to attain uncommon results. Authentic teamwork is called *synergy.* Synergy occurs when the teamwork of a group allows it to get the maximum results from the available resources.

In a synergistic group, an *authentic team,* Conner (2006) tells us that "the members of the team function together to produce a total result that is greater than the sum of the efforts of the individual members" (p. 190). In an authentic team, members energize and inspire each other, and the diversity of ideas and openness to them provide the basis for new creative thinking and approaches (Murphy & Lick, 2005, p. 165).

Synergy Prerequisites

Change expert Conner (2006) explains that synergy is the "soul of a successful change project" (p. 188). His research found that the key requirements for a group to have synergistic capacity (i.e., be an authentic team) were *willingness*, arising from the sharing of common goals and interdependence (i.e., mutual dependence and genuine cooperation) and *ability*, growing from member and group empowerment and participative involvement (Conner, 2006, pp. 191–202). Willingness and ability are the two critical components in having capacity to accomplish desired goals.

The *four prerequisites* for *synergistic teams* (i.e., authentic teams) in schools are as follows:

1. *Common Goals.* Seek, create, and continue to focus on clear common goals for the group.

2. *Interdependence.* Operate interdependently in the group in a genuinely cooperative and mutually dependent fashion.

3. *Empowerment.* Function in the group so as to empower all members. People are empowered when they feel that they have something of value to contribute and that it may have a bearing on the final outcome.

4. *Participative Involvement.* Provide participative involvement where members are expected, encouraged, and free to openly and fully share their skills, knowledge, and ideas in a balanced approach in the group.

Synergistic relationships in schools are both powerful and productive. However, most groups don't naturally function synergistically; they either don't understand the requirements of synergy or don't choose to apply them very well.

Synergy Process

What is the process for creating the above prerequisites and synergistic teams? Conner's research (2006, pp. 203–217; also see Murphy & Lick, 2005) gives us an effective *four-step process* for *building synergy* in groups in schools, as shown in Figure 4.2. The figure illustrates that synergy increases as a group moves from interaction through appreciative understanding and integration to implementation. Each step is described below.

The elements described above in the prerequisites for synergy and synergy process are the *required norms* for a group to become a synergistic team, an authentic team. Figure 4.3 lists the norms for synergistic teams.

The thing to specifically note here is that *the more closely members follow the above norms, the more effectively their group will function as an authentic team!*

Groups can, at an initial meeting when norms are considered, discuss the concept of synergy and the illustrative synergy norms presented in Figure 4.3. After the synergy norms have been adequately discussed, the group

Figure 4.2 Building Team Synergy

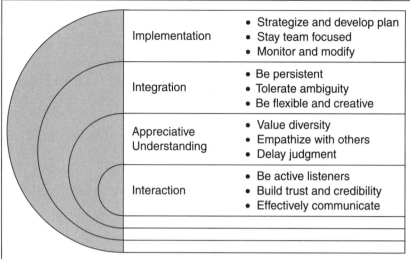

Implementation	• Strategize and develop plan • Stay team focused • Monitor and modify
Integration	• Be persistent • Tolerate ambiguity • Be flexible and creative
Appreciative Understanding	• Value diversity • Empathize with others • Delay judgment
Interaction	• Be active listeners • Build trust and credibility • Effectively communicate

Building Team Synergy

1. *Interaction.* Group members must interact with one another and reciprocate. *Required elements:* Effective communication, active listening, and creating trust and credibility.

2. *Appreciative Understanding.* Group members must understand why others see things differently than they do and work to appreciate the differences. *Required elements:* Create an open climate, delay negative judgment, empathize with others, and value diversity.

3. *Integration.* Group members must consider all input from the group, evaluate its value and usability, and collaboratively pull together appropriate ideas and perspectives to generate the best available solutions or outcomes. *Required elements:* Tolerate the ambiguity of the discussions and be persistent, flexible, creative, and selective as you work toward the best solutions or outcomes.

4. *Implementation.* Together as a unit, the group must implement the desired solution and introduce the various parts of the desired outcomes effectively in the school. *Required elements:* Strategize and develop an implementation plan; monitor, reinforce, and remain team focused during the implementation process; and update and modify the implementation as needed to reach the desired outcomes.

Figure 4.3 Norms for Synergistic/Authentic Teams

- Help create and focus on common goals.
- Operate interdependently.
- Work to empower members.
- Share fully in discussions and encourage others to do likewise.
- Communicate effectively and actively listen to others.
- Help create trust in the group and credibility for members.
- Work to create an open climate.
- Delay negative judgments.
- Empathize with others.
- Value diversity.
- Tolerate ambiguity in discussions but remain persistent and flexible.
- Be creative and selective in formulating outcomes.
- Help develop a team implementation plan and regularly monitor, adjust, and update the plan.
- Remain team focused throughout the full implementation of the plan.

should develop an agreement that the group, individually and collectively, will strive to fulfill the synergy norms and function as an authentic team. If someone violates a synergy norm, this should be diplomatically called to the individual's attention, as appropriate, either in the meeting or immediately after it.

Synergy Checklist

As groups in schools collaborate to build teams, they should stop from time to time to monitor whether the group is continuing to function synergistically or, if not, to determine which synergy norm areas require additional attention. A synergy checklist containing the synergy norms (Clauset, Lick, & Murphy, 2008, p. 45; Lick, 1999, pp. 42–43; Murphy & Lick, 2005, p. 174) is presented in Figure 4.4 and in online Resource C. The eight question sets provide a practical checklist for assessing where the synergy norms are and are not satisfied. When the norms are present, they add to the synergy of the group and its capacity for effective action, and when they are not present, the synergy and effective action of the group is lessened.

A Synergy Example: Team-Building Efforts in the Tigerville School District

Turning school groups into authentic teams is often easier said than done. Some groups find it easier than other groups, even within the same school district, as highlighted in the following example.

This case study by Koenigs (2004, 2007) took place in the Tigerville (a pseudonym) School District in a small rural community in central Kansas. The school district consisted of a primary, intermediate, middle, and high school.

Sharing was probably the most popular activity in their formed groups, according to the teachers in Tigerville. The most common activities were sharing ideas, discussing instructional practices, lesson plans, strategies and student work, personal experiences at work, aligning curriculum to state standards, creating products and projects, discussing books and educational articles, and researching best practices. For some teachers, their groups seemed almost a cathartic experience, "We did a lot of unwinding together; a lot of group building, team building," one teacher recalled.

In Tigerville, the strong cultural norms of each school faculty played a key role in collaboration and changes in teachers' practices. Elementary teachers continued to try new strategies and shared these with each other, because their culture of risk taking and collaborative sharing already existed at their level prior to the introduction of groups. Additionally, it seemed that elementary teachers felt "pressure" to try new things if they heard others in their group talk about using new strategies. This kind of team norm supported changes in practices rather than inhibit them. Middle school teachers also had a culture of working together in teams, so working collaboratively and trying new strategies was not as much of a stretch for them.

The culture of the high school, however, was not accustomed to collaboration and sharing prior to their groups. The high school culture was challenged and stretched by their groups, which reflected on members' practices and perceptions and, consequently, collaborative team building was, at times, new, uncomfortable and difficult for them.

Figure 4.4   A Synergy/Authentic Teamwork Checklist for Teams

Checklist for Team Synergy

Action Team: _____ Date: _____

Directions: As a group, rate your group using the following symbols:

* = We're there!   > = We're developing!   < = We're struggling!

Common goals

_____   Has your group discussed, agreed upon, and written a clearly and precisely stated goal or goals for its work?

Interdependence

_____   Has the interaction and sharing of your group been interdependent (i.e., mutually dependent and genuinely cooperative)?

Empowerment

_____   Does each member feel that what he or she has to offer is important and may have an effect on the outcome of decisions?

Participative Involvement

_____   Do the members of your group feel that they can and do openly and freely participate in balanced discussions and activities of the group?

Interaction

_____   Do the members of your group, individually and collectively, communicate effectively and actively listen to each other?

_____   Has a sense of trust and credibility been created in the group?

Appreciative Understanding

_____   Do the members of your group show appreciative understanding to each other and their ideas?

_____   Does your group have an open climate, value diversity, delay negative judgment, and empathize with others' ideas?

Integration

_____   Do your group members show persistence in their deliberations and tolerate ambiguity as your group works to consider input and pull it together to generate the best decision or outcome?

_____   Are members flexible, creative, and selective as they consider the issues and transition toward their final result?

Implementation

_____   Does your group create a plan for the implementation that sets its direction, manages the resources, and determines priorities?

_____   Does your group ensure that the various steps are completed, appropriate behavior and progress are monitored and sustained, the process remains team focused, and there are continual updates of the action plan?

Source: Lick, D. W. (1999). Proactive comentoring relationships: Enhancing the effectiveness through synergy. In C. A. Mullen & D. W. Lick (Eds.), *New directions in mentoring: Creating a culture of synergy.* London, UK: Falmer, pp. 42–43.

PLEASE NOTE: Now that we have talked about the critical nature of designated groups in schools becoming authentic teams, we shall, in the remainder of this book, use the term *team* to mean an *authentic team,* meeting the conditions discussed earlier in this chapter for synergistic groups.

Teams and Team Failure

Although teams are critical for the effective improvement of schools, unfortunately, research suggests that failure rates for teams and team implementations may be high, ranging from 50% to 90% (Beyerlein, 2003, p. 4). Beyerlein's research (1997a, pp. 3–4; 1997b, pp. 12–13) provides some key causes of team failures in schools:

- Team implementation in schools is imported from elsewhere and not adapted and tailored to the specific needs of the school environment.
- Teams are introduced in schools more as a fad rather than as a serious means for improved performance.
- Teams in schools are adrift as isolated islands of structural change, not linked with other teams and appropriate resources and support.
- Teams in schools are not institutionalized in a team-based system, but left to depend on a single effective champion.
- Team processes in schools are not institutionalized so as to gain the full buy-in of the organization's leadership.
- Team preparation and support in schools are inadequate.
- Teams in schools are not provided adequate time for developing teamwork and the new norms that support it.
- Organizational leadership in schools is not prepared with the new manifestations for teamwork, such as supervisors transitioning into team coaches and team members taking leadership responsibilities.
- Teams are not planned to the ebb and flow of the academic year.

In all of the above areas of failure for teams in schools, the Change Creation process and the Universal Change Principle, described in Chapter 3, were less than adequately implemented.

COMENTORING TEAMS

One important and deeper functional aspect of teamwork, in the evolution of teams (see Figure 4.1), is comentoring. *Comentoring* (Lick, 2000, pp. 43–48) means members of the team all agree to mentor each other. Peer coaching, where every member agrees to be a peer coach in the group, is one form of comentoring. In effective comentoring teams, each member acts as a sponsor, advocate, or guide. Members teach, advise, trust, critique, and support others to express, pursue, and finalize goals (Vanzant, 1980). Ideally, in a comentoring situation, "each member of a group offers support and encouragement to everyone else which expands individual and group understanding, improving the group's effectiveness and productivity" (Lick, 1999, p. 209).

A comentoring team in schools, for example, might be an action team that explores a learning area together and whose members assist one another in expanding all team members' capacity for understanding and creativity relative to some learning area. Synergy and comentoring can be meaningfully combined in groups in schools, as comentoring teams, to help generate unusually effective and productive teamwork.

LEARNING TEAMS

The concept of a *learning team* has been defined in a wide range of ways and in many types of organizations and settings. In this chapter, we define learning team (Lick, 2006, pp. 88–96) in a way that goes well beyond most definitions in the literature. This definition is based on change creation and the Universal Change Principle, discussed earlier in Chapter 3, p. 20 and p. 51, and consistent with the formal definition of *team learning* found in Senge (1990, p. 236): "A *learning team* is a team that *develops and aligns its capacity* (i.e., willingness and ability) *as a team* to create the results its members desire to achieve (Lick, 2006)."

Develop means to *expand* the team's willingness and ability toward the team's desired end. *Align* means to bring in line with other appropriate and relevant factors and characteristics in and related to the school. Alignment represents dealing with the complex system of relationships within a school so that the team can accomplish its goals.

Learning Team Capacities

Learning teams in schools, as defined above, have the potential capacities to

- Learn and recreate themselves
- Set and focus on challenging new goals
- Have a spirit and capability of inquiry
- Be self-directed and reflective
- Dialogue and think insightfully together about complex issues
- Take innovative, coordinated action
- Do things that they were never able to do before
- Invent together and experiment with their inventions
- Evaluate progress on issues and effectiveness of ideas
- Re-perceive their school, its programs, personnel and groups, and their interrelationship (e.g., as a team learns more about their situation and gains new insight about it from others, along with acquiring additional relevant information, team members and the team see things through new eyes with new perspectives)
- Extend their capacity to create and be part of a major generative process in the school's life and activities (e.g., as in the previous bullet, when that happens, the team is open to additional perceptions and options and, as a result, has increased potential for being creative and productive in new ways)

These capacities are about teams learning, thinking, and acting. Figure 4.5 illustrates the capacities above in these three areas.

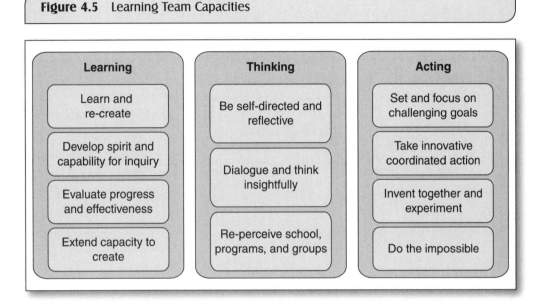

Figure 4.5 Learning Team Capacities

Learning	Thinking	Acting
Learn and re-create	Be self-directed and reflective	Set and focus on challenging goals
Develop spirit and capability for inquiry	Dialogue and think insightfully	Take innovative coordinated action
Evaluate progress and effectiveness	Re-perceive school, programs, and groups	Invent together and experiment
Extend capacity to create		Do the impossible

Learning teams are powerful and effective change agents in school improvement and student learning, as former Alabama Teacher of the Year Anne Jolly relates (as quoted in Richardson, 2001): "Learning teams are the most effective, cost-efficient way for teachers to learn what changes are needed in practice and then make changes. They also have the benefit of building rapport, trust, and support" (p. 1).

Building Learning Teams

Effective learning teams in schools are essential for genuine school change, but can be difficult to create and sustain. Consequently, actions toward the development of action teams as effective learning teams in schools have to be intentional by action teams and leaders and represent clearly defined commitments of the action teams, school leaders, and school personnel. However, when this is done properly and well, the payoffs can be significant and can move the school and its people to new levels of creativity, learning, change, and success.

Building on the earlier discussions of authentic or synergistic teams and comentoring teams, we now provide a *practical design process for creating learning teams* as an important part of generating change and new school learning. We illustrate each step with selections from efforts in Bunn Elementary School in Bunn, North Carolina.

The "building learning teams" process has three phases, the Foundational Phase, Learning and Inquiry Cycle Phase, and Recheck Phase. These three phases are illustrated in Figure 4.6 and described as follows.

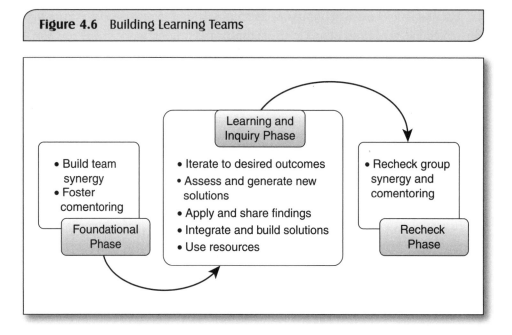

Figure 4.6 Building Learning Teams

Foundational Phase

1. *Build team synergy (i.e., an authentic team).* This was discussed earlier in the section titled Authentic Teams and Synergy (see pages 59–61 and the steps for building synergy below). Synergy represents the most important part of the process. Without synergy, the group is just *not* an authentic team and will fall short of its maximum potential. Having synergy, that is, being an authentic team, is the foundation for the team being self-directed, setting and focusing on challenging new goals, having collaboration and reflection, and dialoguing and thinking insightfully *together* about complex issues in the school. As we stated earlier, the steps for building synergy in teams are

   a. *Interaction* through effective communication, active listening, and creating trust and credibility

   b. *Appreciative Understanding* through creating an open climate, delaying negative judgment, empathizing with others, and valuing diversity

   c. *Integration* through tolerating the ambiguity of the discussions and being persistent, flexible, creative, and selective as members work toward the best solutions or outcomes

   d. *Implementation* through strategizing and developing an implementation plan, monitoring, reinforcing, and remaining team focused during the implementation process, and updating and modifying the implementation as needed to reach the desired outcomes

Building team synergy starts in the Foundational Phase and continues through the other phases as teams execute, monitor, update, and modify their implementation plans.

After individual groups had been selected, they began hour-long weekly meetings. By the end of their third week, each group had developed an action plan to guide

their work. The groups also agreed to team norms and the synergy prerequisites and process, including the use of the synergy checklist, as they implemented their work together.

2. *Foster comentoring in the team.* In comentoring teams, each member offers support and encouragement to everyone else, which expands individual and team thinking, understanding and learning, and thereby, improving the team's effectiveness and productivity. A team can foster comentoring by encouraging members to each take the lead on different relevant matters for the team and act as a sponsor, advocate, or guide for those matters, including teaching and advising other team members on such matters. Similarly, team members can also foster comentoring by supporting and critiquing team members on other relevant matters and assisting them in moving toward desired team goals.

The Radical Readers team at Bunn Elementary worked on cause and effect during the fall semester. Teachers discussed strategies used within individual classrooms. They found that using everyday examples tend to work better to explain cause and effect than using a textbook to teach. One member brought in a list of books to accompany lessons using cause and effect. Another member, whose class had the lowest average on the pre-test, brought in and explained his post-test results, which showed a vast improvement. He incorporated test-taking strategies along with the cause-and-effect strategies all members had been using. One strategy he used was to (have students) read the questions before they read the passage. The whole team decided to use his strategy within their individual classrooms and continued to incorporate the charts and various graphic organizers.

Learning and Inquiry Cycles Phase

3. *Utilize learning resources.* The team utilizes a wide variety of learning resources, including research and literature, internal and external expertise, related experiences, relevant learning models, and professional development. As the learning-team process unfolds, discovering, generating, and using appropriate learning resources provide an enhanced basis and higher plateau for increased learning and potential for new creative solutions and outcomes in the school.

After creating draft action plans, each team decided which of their specific student needs to address first, identified or developed a simple classroom assessment task to give to students to collect data on how well their students currently perform on the need, used a scoring rubric or checklist to assess student work, developed specific performance targets to achieve by the end of the semester, and updated their action plans with the baseline and target data.

Teams used teachers guides, the Internet, the school's instructional specialist, and district content specialists as resources to help them identify research and best practices related to their student learning needs and updated their action plans with the new resources they had identified.

4. *Integrate knowledge and create potential solutions.* The team pulls together all of the relevant information and knowledge available to it. These resources are then integrated synergistically and creatively into one or more potential

solutions or desired outcomes. This allows the team to take innovative and coordinated actions, through a spirit and action process of inquiry (i.e., disciplined inquiry that leads to changes in practice and performance), toward inventing together and then experimenting with its creations. Further, from this process, the team not only gains new knowledge and learning, but can recreate itself and do things that it was never able to do before.

Then teams began the "real" work—changing what they taught and how they taught to improve student learning in the specific need area each team chose to address first. During the next three-month period, teams followed cycles of "learn-plan-act-reflect," learning about the new strategies they found, planning at their team meetings what to do differently in class, acting in class to implement the lesson plans and strategies, reflecting in the next team meeting on the effectiveness of the lesson plan or strategy and planning next steps.

5. *Apply potential solutions and share findings.* As part of the spirit and action process of inquiry, the group applies the new solutions or outcomes in their classes and the school workplace and shares their findings and results with team members.

Teams reflected on the results and effectiveness of the strategies they used, decided whether to continue working as a team on the same learning need during the second semester or switch to another need, and updated their action plan with the actual results.

6. *Assess findings and generate new solutions.* The team assesses the findings and results from Step 5 above, evaluates their progress and effectiveness toward the desired outcomes, and creates new potential solutions.

Teams regularly readministered the baseline assessment tool to students and examined samples of student work to understand how the changes they were making in their classes were affecting student thinking and understanding. Later in the semester, representatives from all of the teams met for a third Instructional Council [the coordinating group] meeting to share interventions and what they were learning about improving student learning.

7. *Iterate to desired outcomes.* The team considers intermediate findings, results and solutions, and modifies them accordingly by repeating Steps 3–6, as often as necessary, until the team is satisfied with the final outcomes.

During the school year, the team at Bunn Elementary assessed the results of their work with students at the end of the fall semester and then decided whether to continue working on the same need or to shift their focus to a new need.

Recheck Phase

8. *Recheck group synergy and comentoring.* The team must also periodically recheck its levels of synergy (using the Synergy Checklist) and comentoring (see the discussion in the Comentoring section above on page 63), and make appropriate adjustments to continue to satisfy the criteria of Steps 1 and 2.

For a midyear Instructional Council meeting, the principal asked each team to complete the Synergy Checklist for Groups given earlier in Figure 4.3 and to review their results and share their findings with other teams.

PROFESSIONAL LEARNING COMMUNITIES

The ability to collaborate—on both a large and small scale—is one of the core prerequisites of modern society. . . . [W]ithout collaborative skills and relationships, it is not possible to learn and continue to learn as much as you need in order to be an agent for social improvement.

Michael Fullan (1993, pp. 17–18)

Definition of a Professional Learning Community

What Fullan has highlighted above, the "collaborative, learning and improving relationships" in a community (e.g., a school) is the essential nature of a professional learning community. The critical essence of what Fullan suggests here is strongly reinforced for school improvement efforts by the results of recent research by Carrie R. Leana (2011):

[W]hen the relationships among teachers in a school are characterized by high trust and frequent interaction—that is, when social capital is strong—student achievement scores improve. . . . In other words, teacher social capital was a significant predictor of student achievement gains above and beyond teacher experience or ability in the classroom. (p. 19)

Definition: A *professional learning community* or *learning community* is a community that can effectively collaborate, experience and learn, and then collectively share learning across the entire community and apply their new learning to improve the community and its members. DuFour and Eaker (1998) tell us in their book, *Professional Learning Communities at Work,* that in school professional learning communities, "educators create an environment that fosters mutual cooperation, emotional support, and personal growth as they work together to achieve what they cannot accomplish alone" (p. xii). They outline the key characteristics of professional learning communities as follows:

- Shared vision, mission, and values
- Collaborative teams focused on learning
- Collective inquiry
- Action orientation and experimentation
- Commitment to continuous improvement
- Results orientation (pp. 25–29)

And relating to learning communities, they state,

The school that operates as a professional learning community recognizes that its members must engage in the ongoing study and constant practice that characterize an organization committed to continuous improvement. (p. xii)

The most promising strategy for sustained school improvement is developing the ability of school personnel to function as professional learning communities. (p. xi)

The most critical question educators must confront as they consider an initiative to create a professional learning community is this one: Do we believe in our collective capacity to create a better future for our school? (p. 286)

In its new Standards for Professional Learning, Learning Forward refers to professional learning communities as learning communities and views them as part of the essential conditions for "professional learning that increases educator effectiveness and results for all students." Their standard for learning communities states, "Professional learning that increases educator effectiveness and results for all students occurs within learning communities committed to continuous improvement, collective responsibility, and goal alignment." They further elaborate as follows:

Professional learning within communities requires continuous improvement, promotes collective responsibility, and supports alignment of individual, team, school, and school system goals. Learning communities convene regularly and frequently during the workday to engage in collaborative professional learning to strengthen their practice and increase student results. Learning community members are accountable to one another to achieve the shared goals of the school and school system and learning community members work in transparent, authentic settings that support their improvement. (Learning Forward, 2011, p. 24)

Professional learning communities are powerful and effective change structures and approaches to improve schools and increase student learning, as the following research reports.

And it is not hard to be convinced by the growing body of evidence that shows when schools and districts with the necessary capacity set about by organizing themselves as professional learning communities, and when schools operate on these principles are compared with counterparts that do not, PLCs have a consistently positive impact on student achievement results. (Hord & Sommers, 2008, p. ix)

After an overview of the characteristics of professional learning communities (PLCs), this manuscript presents a review of 10 American studies and one English study of PLCs on teaching practices and student learning. . . . The collective results of these studies suggest that well-developed PLCs have positive impact on both teaching practices and student achievement. The studies reviewed . . . leave us hopeful that learning communities offer an avenue to build the momentum of a shifting paradigm in the professional development of teachers and the learning of students. (Vescio, Ross, & Adams, 2008, pp. 80, 90)

On the other hand, we have learned only too well from our many experiences over the last twenty-five years that most communities of educators are *not* professional learning communities. The fact is that genuine professional learning communities are difficult to develop. The fundamental lesson learned here is the following: *To create an effective schoolwide professional learning community, you must first develop strong action teams across your community!*

Change Creation System Schools as Professional Learning Communities

Action teams are the critical building blocks for larger professional learning communities. They are the groups in the community that "separately collaborate, experience, and learn" and then "collectively share and apply their knowledge and know-how meaningfully across the entire community to improve the community and its members."

So, if groups in a school are functioning effectively as action teams, how do you move them to the next plateau to turn your school into a learning community? The best process we have seen for doing this is the approach utilized in this book, the Change Creation system.

Change Creation System Goal and Process

The *goal* of the Change Creation system is to focus the entire school administration and faculty on creating, implementing, and integrating effective teaching and learning practices into school programs that will result in an increase in school innovation, student learning, and school improvement.

The process of the Change Creation system, as described in Chapter 1 and in detail in Chapters 5–12 in this book, is a job-embedded, self-directed, action team-driven approach to professional learning and creative inquiry designed to build communities of learners in which professionals continuously strive to increase student learning and improve their practice. The driving force in the Change Creation system process is its self-directed action teams as they function as learning teams and do collective inquiry.

At the onset, administrators and faculty members, as a collective group, commit themselves to the Change Creation system and a shared vision and general plan, requiring everyone's best efforts, for improving the school and increasing student learning in the school. Once the above commitments are made, the collective group analyzes relevant student and school data to identify the priority student needs that action teams will address. After priority needs have been established, each faculty member decides which priority-need action team he or she will join, and then each team becomes a self-directed team and develops their action plan for what its members will do when the team meets to address their specific student need.

Action teams employ the "practical learning-team design process" to become a synergistic, comentoring team and engage in effective collaborative collective inquiry, including the learn-plan-act-reflect cycles. As action teams meet and address their action plan, they post logs of their efforts publicly for everyone in the school to see, and the principal or a designee reads and responds to all logs, providing such things as general responses, advice, assessment, encouragement and offers of support.

At regular intervals, action teams or their representatives meet together with the principal and the other members of the leadership team, the school-wide coordinating body, to share collectively their efforts and findings, new knowledge and know-how, problems and successes, needs and wishes, and future actions. Leaders provide extensive communication mechanisms among action teams and with other groups, including students, parents and the parent-teacher association (PTA), district, superintendent and board officers and staff, and the general public. Leaders also arrange midyear and end-of-the-school-year celebrations and sharing events to let teachers know that they appreciate and recognize the work action teams are doing, and for special times for teams to have fun and do creative things to inspire others and raise the status of learning at the school.

DuFour, DuFour, and Eaker's six "key characteristics of professional learning communities" are comparable to the elements of the Change Creation system described above. Districts, such as the Springfield Public Schools in Missouri and DeKalb County School System in Georgia, that have studied both the professional learning community and the Whole-Faculty Study Groups designs, from which the Change Creation system evolved, have used the Whole-Faculty Study Groups design as a concrete and practical approach to implementing professional learning communities. Table 4.1 below highlights these six key principles of professional learning communities, as articulated by DuFour, DuFour, and Eaker (2008, pp. 15–17), and compares them with key principles of the Change Creation system approach.

Where properly implemented, the Change Creation system of action teams can be successful in facilitating schoolwide action inquiry, schoolwide change, and the enhancement of the school and student learning because action teams

- Work to produce a schoolwide learning community
- Plan and learn together, construct subject-matter knowledge, and engage broad principles of education that modify perspectives, policies, and practices
- Immerse everyone in sustained work with ideas, materials, and colleagues
- Cultivate collective inquirers, producing, evaluating, and applying relevant related knowledge and research
- Struggle with fundamental questions of what teachers and students must learn, know, and apply (Murphy & Lick, 2005, pp. 177–178)

In his doctoral dissertation research, Koenigs (2004) found that professional learning community models, such as a version of the Change Creation system, showed great promise to affect positively teachers' instructional practices and school culture if thought and care are taken during the implementation process.

Table 4.1   Comparing Elements of Professional Learning Communities and the Change Creation System

Professional Learning Communities	Change Creation System
Theoretical framework with guiding principles, tools, and examples	Practical, structured, job-embedded, self-directed, student-driven system to create action teams that increase student learning
Shared vision, mission, and values	Compelling and inspiring vision for improving school innovation and increasing student learning performance Guiding principles: • Students are first. • Everyone participates. • Leadership is shared. • Improvement requires learning. • Responsibility is equal. • The work is public.
The focus: Instruction, curriculum, assessment practices, and strategies for improving the effectiveness of schools	Action teams address *how* and *what* staff teach (instruction, curriculum, and assessment practices).
The question that drives change must be enhanced student achievement.	Guiding question: What are students learning and achieving as a result of what teachers are learning and doing in action teams?
Collective inquiry	All action teams engage in cycles of collective learning and inquiry to improve educator practice and student performance.
Collaborative teams focused on learning	All certificated staff work in action teams of three to five members focused on professional learning and inquiry to increase student learning. Action teams become collaborative, synergistic, comentoring learning teams as they work together to address specific student learning needs.
Time for collaboration built into the school day and year	Within the school day, action teams meet weekly or biweekly.
Highly structured meetings	Action teams plan meetings in advance, rotate leadership, prepare and post meeting logs, and use protocols for examining student work.
High levels of trust	Team norms, size limits, and shared leadership help each action team develop trust.
Action orientation and experimentation	Action teams experiment with new teaching strategies and content, act in their classrooms on their plans, and reflect on the impact.
Commitment to continuous improvement	Action teams engage in cycles of learning and inquiry during the school year to improve their expertise and practice and increase student learning.
Results orientation	Every action team sets specific, measurable targets for improved student learning in their classrooms for each cycle of learning and inquiry during the school year, measures progress toward these targets, examines student work samples and data, and modifies its work with students.
Role of the principal	The principal, the primary sponsor for action teams within a school, provides support, encouragement, and pressure for teams, and models Change Creation system principles and best practices.
Role of teachers as professionals	The Change Creation system embodies the Learning Forward standards for teacher involvement in learning communities.

A School District Example of Change Creation System Learning Communities

The example below involves the Springfield Public Schools, where almost all of the fifty-one schools are implementing a constructive version of the Change Creation system. It illustrates how the schools in that school system created professional learning communities in their schools and shared and applied their knowledge and know-how effectively to turn their schools and school system into successful professional learning communities with exceptional results.

> *The year 2000/2001 found the Springfield (Missouri) Public Schools only one point, on the Annual Performance Rating of the Missouri accreditation process, above the cut-off for "provisional accreditation." Subsequently, they implemented a major improvement process in approximately 90% of their schools with a version of the Change Creation system being a central feature.*
>
> *By the 2006/2007 school year, the district scored 100 out of 100 points on their Annual Performance Rating for their last three accreditation reports and earned the state's coveted Distinction in Performance award (Kissinger, 2007, pp. 37–39).*
>
> *The Missouri Commissioner of Education, D. Kent King, said, "This award is unique and demanding, because it requires districts to demonstrate growth and progress across the board. Districts must show improvement or high performance at every level—elementary, middle and high school" (Kissinger, 2007, pp. 37–39).*

In March 2007, Springfield Public Schools was one of five districts in the state to receive the 2007 Missouri Staff Development Council (MSDC) Commissioner's Award of Excellence for Professional Development. The award honors Missouri school districts with quality professional development that is data driven, job embedded, and results based. Springfield Public Schools demonstrated how professional learning positively impacts students and teachers and how practices are aligned with national standards for professional learning. A version of the Change Creation system is a key component of the district's professional development program.

Earlier, the Springfield Public Schools' fifty-one campuses demonstrated wide variances in performance and were seeing little districtwide improvement. To fulfill their vision of academic excellence for all students, they had to face the reality of their data and implement a change process that began with a focus on student learning, moved to process alignment at all levels, and continued with district-level support for introducing action teams and an uncompromising expectation for results. In their successful approach, they found seven key learning principles, as described below (Kissinger, 2007):

1. A clear and uncompromising focus on student performance is required.

2. Accountability created a sense of urgency.

3. Systematic and well-aligned planning models caused meaningful reflection and resulted in action appropriate for the stated goals.

4. A version of the Change Creation system was a systematic and well-aligned implementation model for school improvement plans.

5. A sense of urgency was harnessed to facilitate change.

6. District leaders had to provide organizational changes and support required for effective implementation.

7. Schools improved and student performance increased when effective, well-aligned models were combined with dedicated professional teachers, focused district leaders, and supportive board members.

Since 2007, Springfield, now the largest school district in Missouri, has strengthened the implementation of the Change Creation system of teacher collaboration and professional learning, now called the Site Professional Learning Systems, and expanded the implementation of the Continuous Classroom Improvement (CCI) process. The CCI process involved a weekly Plan-Do-Study-Act cycle that mirrors the Action Teams Learning and Inquiry Cycle (see Chapter 10, p. 153). Teachers and students set weekly learning goals and teachers guided students through learning activities and diagnostic assessments Monday through Thursday after pre-assessing their levels of proficiency and understanding. On Fridays, students completed post-assessments, discussed with the teacher what worked during the week and what didn't, and set goals for the coming week (Clauset et al., 2008, p. 199). As a result of these efforts, the district has continued to improve teacher practice and student learning, which led to another state "Distinction in Performance" award in 2010/2011. The district is now developing the SPS Learning Model that "incorporates the key capabilities necessary for student success in the 21st century and the key processes to guide both learning and work in the district" (Springfield Public Schools, 2011). This learning model will encompass both the continuous classroom improvement process and the district's Site Professional Learning Systems.

SUMMARY

In this chapter, we introduced the concepts of authentic teams and learning teams and discussed and illustrated the process for action teams actually becoming authentic and learning teams. We described the fundamentals and key characteristics of professional learning communities, showed how action teams are critical building blocks for professional learning communities, and explored how, using a major change process, such as the Change Creation system, schools could be turned into professional learning communities with the potential to become more innovative and to increase student learning performance and improve schools.

At the beginning of the chapter, we framed two guiding questions. For the first question, if action teams in schools function as authentic teams and learning teams and if the school functions as professional learning community, our answer is, "It depends."

Schools implementing schoolwide action inquiry function as professional learning communities when (1) they enable action teams to become learning teams and enable them to share and learn from each other; (2) the work of action teams is embedded in the school's improvement plan so that action teams take direction from the improvement plan goals and drive its implementation; and (3) action teams, like experimental laboratories, generate content, materials, and instructional practices that improve student learning and that other faculty use and adopt. On the other hand, if schools implement schoolwide creative inquiry *without* (1) assuring that action teams are learning teams; (2) providing opportunities for action teams for sharing and learning among action teams; and (3) connecting the work of action teams to the school vision and improvement plan, schools have little hope of becoming professional learning communities.

Our second guiding question has two parts: "How do action teams become authentic teams and learning teams to improve teacher practice and enhance student learning?" and "How do schools become professional learning communities to increase school innovation and improve student learning performance?"

The answers to these questions are a function of "how action teams operate" and "what action teams do." Action teams become authentic teams and learning teams by how they operate. Action teams that embrace the synergy norms in how they work together can become learning teams. Action teams, as authentic teams and learning teams, improve teacher practice and enhance student learning by following the collective inquiry process described briefly in this chapter and in detail in Chapters 10 and 11 and by working with content and instructional practices that are directly related to the learning needs of their current students.

Likewise, schools become professional learning communities that improve teacher practice and enhance student learning by "what action teams do" when (1) the student learning needs that action teams address are driven by the school vision; (2) the work of action teams drives the implementation of the school improvement plan; (3) each action team is improving teacher practice and student learning for the students its members serve; and (4) faculty and action teams collaborate across the school and use and adopt content and best practices proven successful by other action teams.

In Part II and subsequent chapters, we will build on the material from this chapter and earlier chapters to discuss and illustrate the steps in the process for the Change Creation system and what action teams do at each step.

Part II

The Process of the Change Creation System

The Change Creation system is a schoolwide change and creation system that has these two components:

1. The right leadership, vision, culture, and relationships within the schools for innovation and creativity

2. A change creation process for developing new teaching and learning approaches that measurably improve student performance

In Part I of this book, Chapters 2–4, we described the fundamentals of effectiveness for ensuring that schools have the right leadership, vision, culture, and relationships to support and sustain innovation, creativity, and the Change Creation process. In this part of the book, we outline and unfold the process of the Change Creation system through what we term the Decision-Making Cycle. Chapter 5 introduces the Decision-Making Cycle, and Chapters 6 and Chapters 9–12 discuss the Decision-Making Cycle process and its application in detail. Chapters 7 and 8 describe action teams in depth and what leaders need to do to guide and support action teams as they evolve into learning teams. Action teams are the primary vehicles for implementing the Change Creation system.

The steps and chapters for the Decision-Making Cycle are as follows:

The Faculty and Leaders

Step 1: Identify student learning needs and form action teams. (Chapter 6)

Each Action Team

Step 2: Create team action plans. (Chapter 9)

Step 3: Implement inquiry cycles to change practice and improve student learning. (Chapters 10 and 11)

Each Action Team and the Faculty

Step 4: Assess the impact of action teams' work on teacher practice and student learning. (Chapter 12)

Step 5: Share results and best practices across the school and apply lessons learned. (Chapter 12)

Introducing the Decision-Making Cycle 5

This chapter presents an overview of the Action Teams Decision-Making Cycle (DMC), which is the process at the heart of the Change Creation system and the *critical preparation* schools need to make *before* beginning the DMC. Chapter 6 and Chapters 9 through 12 will address in detail the steps in the cycle, while Chapters 7 and 8 examine action teams and how to guide and support them. These seven chapters also make connections to the fundamentals of effectiveness introduced in Chapters 2 and 3 and the fundamentals of teams, learning teams, and professional learning communities introduced in Chapter 4.

All schools follow cycles of work. One cycle is a multiyear improvement cycle linked to the school's vision and strategic plan or to an instructional focus, such as reading comprehension, critical thinking, or problem solving. A second cycle is the annual school-year cycle—from new beginnings at the start of the school year, when new and returning staff and students are welcomed and goals are set for the new year, to a focus on teaching and learning during the year, and ending with celebrating and reflecting on accomplishments and preparing for the next school year.

ACTION TEAMS DECISION-MAKING CYCLE

Within multiyear school improvement cycles and the annual school-year cycle, the Change Creation system provides a five-step Action Teams DMC that guides the school's action teams in improving teaching and learning.

Figure 5.1 illustrates how each year's Action Teams DMC supports the multiyear improvement plan.

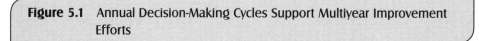

Figure 5.1   Annual Decision-Making Cycles Support Multiyear Improvement Efforts

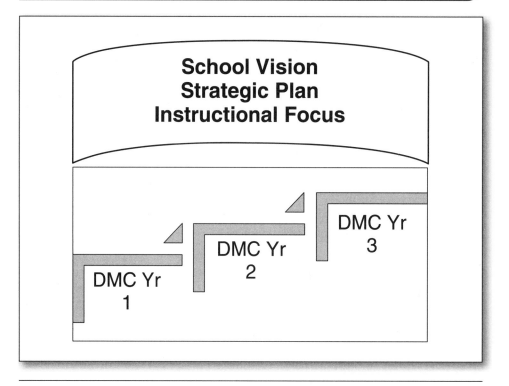

DMC = Action Teams Decision-Making Cycle

The Action Teams DMC involves the whole school. Every faculty member at a school is a member of an action team focusing on data-based student instructional needs. Action teams with no more than five members improve their practices and increase student learning by engaging in cycles of learning and inquiry that are driven by data and the application of what they know and are learning. The five steps in the DMC that guide the work of action teams are listed in Figure 5.2.

How each school implements these steps should be based on the school's uniqueness. We can describe how we recommend each step be implemented based on our experience working with schools, but the final decision rests with each school's leadership team and faculty.

The Action Teams DMC shown in Figure 5.2 and in online Resource D is a revised and streamlined version of the DMC for Whole-Faculty Study Groups (WFSG) first introduced by Carlene Murphy, the founder of WFSG, in 1992. A comparison of the original WFSG Decision-Making Cycle and the Action Teams Decision-Making Cycle can be found in online Resource E.

In Chapter 4, we described the evolution of action teams from groups when they are initially formed to authentic or synergistic teams, then comentoring teams, and finally learning teams through the intentional collaborative efforts of team members and with the support and encouragement from leaders and

Figure 5.2 Action Teams Decision-Making Cycle

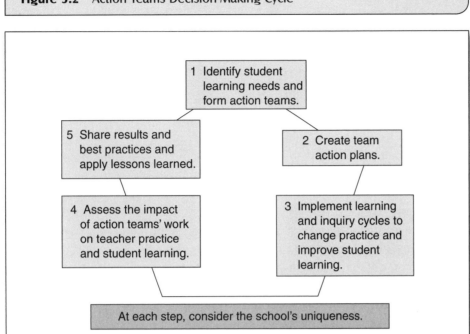

Source: Adapted from *Whole-Faculty Study Groups: Creating Professional Learning Communities That Target Student Learning,* 3rd edition (p. 111, Figure 7.1), by C. U. Murphy and D. W. Lick, 2005, Thousand Oaks, CA: Corwin. Adapted with permission.

coaches. The Action Teams DMC supports the evolution of action teams and aligns with the process for building learning teams we described in Chapter 4, page 65.

Steps 1 and 2 in the DMC are part of the Foundational Phase for the process of creating learning teams. Step 3 in the DMC, implement learning and inquiry cycles, corresponds to the Learning and Inquiry Phase in creating learning teams. Steps 3–7 in the creating learning teams process occur within the learning and inquiry cycles in Step 3 of the DMC and at the end of the school year when action teams engage in Steps 4 and 5 in the DMC to assess impact, share results, and apply lessons learned. The Recheck Phase in the creating learning teams process occurs at the end of each learning and inquiry cycle in the DMC and at the end of the year as part of Step 4 in the DMC.

Step 1: Identify Student Learning Needs and Form Action Teams

The school's faculty and administration complete the first step of the Action Teams DMC—identify student learning needs and form action teams—usually at the beginning of the school year over a period of several weeks.

Step 1 has three desired outcomes:

1. The school creates a list of student learning needs informed by its analysis of data on student learning.

2. Action teams are formed to address specific student learning needs.

3. Each action team reaches consensus on the specific student learning needs it will address.

In creating a list of schoolwide student learning needs that are informed by data, we are referring to concrete and specific student learning needs that are tied to specific content standards and the 21st-century skills that students need to be college and career ready. For example, students' need to improve their ability to solve multistep problems and explain their approach is a specific student learning need; students' need to improve math performance is not.

There are different ways to form action teams. In our work with schools, we have seen three options: form action teams based on (1) common student learning needs, (2) existing grouping patterns, and (3) new grouping patterns.

Regardless of how action teams are formed, the expectation is the same—each action team formed is committed to working collaboratively on a common set of specific data-informed student learning needs. The decision-making process that teams use to select the student learning needs they will address will affect whether the team is committed to working collaboratively, with full participation by all members, on a set of student needs. We describe Step 1 in Chapter 6.

Step 2: Create Team Action Plans

The first major task for action teams is to select the student learning needs that each team will address. Step 2, create team action plans, is the second major task for each action team after teams are formed.

Action plans are important because they help team members plan what they want to do and keep track of what they have accomplished. The action plan guides the work of the team during each cycle of learning and inquiry. Every team creates its own action plan, even if more than one team is working on the same student learning needs or using the same instructional strategy.

Teams should not spend an entire term or semester trying to create a "perfect" action plan. We have found that it is best for teams to develop an initial draft plan in two or three meetings and then revise it as they engage in their learning and inquiry cycles (Step 3). We describe Step 2 in Chapter 9.

Step 3: Implement Learning and Inquiry Cycles to Change Practice and Improve Student Learning

This is the heart of the process of the Change Creation system and the *action* in action teams. This is the step in the DMC where action teams learn about the latest research on teaching, learning, and assessment and apply that research to specific student learning needs in their classrooms.

Working independently, each action team implements learning and inquiry cycles by engaging in the following tasks:

> **The Learning and Inquiry Cycle**

- Clarify the focus, determine current student performance, and set targets.
- Identify content and best practices, develop expertise, and plan and practice interventions.
- Implement interventions, examine student work, assess impact, reflect on lessons learned, and plan next steps.
- Assess and reflect on end of the cycle results and plan for the next cycle.

Action teams are engaged in Step 3 for most of the school year. Most teams engage in two or three cycles a year. We describe Step 3 in Chapters 10 and 11.

Step 4: Assess the Impact of Action Teams' Work on Teacher Practice and Student Learning

Action teams cannot improve the quality of their work and their impact on their practice and on student learning without assessing and reflecting on the work they have done. In addition to the reflection each team does at the end of each learning and inquiry cycle, we expect teams to conduct an end-of-the-year review. In this review, teams look back on their work for the year to ask "So what have we learned and accomplished?" In addition, we expect the faculty as a whole to assess how well the system of action teams has functioned during the year and to ask and answer the "So what?" question about the collective work of all the action teams.

Although the primary focus of Step 4 is on summative evaluation at the end of the year, formative evaluation should occur throughout the time that action teams meet. Regular meetings to share the work of action teams provide an opportunity to surface issues or concerns and monitor the work of action teams.

The assessment and reflection in Step 4 of the DMC is the "so what" that leads directly to the "now what" of Step 5: share results and best practices and apply lessons learned. Individual action teams and the whole faculty complete Steps 4 and 5. We describe Step 4 in Chapter 12.

Step 5: Share Results and Best Practices and Apply Lessons Learned

This is a new step in the Action Teams DMC, but it has always been part of our design and our work with schools. The step encompasses three related tasks: (1) sharing results and best practices, (2) ensuring that teams learn from each other and that lessons learned are applied throughout the school, and (3) embedding best practices and lessons learned in next year's school improvement plan. This step is crucial for the school if it is to become a learning community. We describe this step in Chapter 12.

The Decision-Making Cycle Repeats Itself Each Year

At the end of a school year, all action teams complete Step 5 on the DMC. At the beginning of the next school year, all action teams begin the DMC again and return to Step 1. It does not matter if action teams are continuing their work from the year before or if they have reconfigured; all action teams return to the new data collected for guidance as to what action teams will do in the new school year. As Figure 5.1 illustrated, each year's DMC is part of a multiyear effort toward schoolwide improvement.

The beginning of the new school year is a time for the school leadership team to reconsider the school's vision and to reconnect the work of action teams to that vision. Before beginning the DMC anew, school leaders announce changes in the Change Creation system of action teams for the new year based on the feedback and reflection in Step 4 of the DMC and celebrate the changes to the school improvement plan based on the work of action teams the previous year.

Action Teams and the School Improvement Plan

Most schools have a school improvement plan (SIP) that the district expects them to implement. The SIP is an operational plan for achieving the school's multiyear goals that are embedded in its school vision, strategic plan, or instructional focus. In Change Creation Schools, action teams *drive* the SIP.

Action teams are the *vehicle* for the faculty to work together collaboratively to address the goals in the SIP. The specific learning needs that action teams address are aligned with these performance goals. Through sharing results and best practices from individual action teams and embedding these best practices and lessons learned into next year's SIP and the work of next year's action teams, the school as a whole builds on, and learns from, the action teams.

Since the SIP gives direction to action teams regarding performance goals and areas of focus, the interaction between action teams and the SIP is two-way. This interaction is illustrated in Figure 5.3.

PREPARING TO START THE DECISION-MAKING CYCLE

A key question is, "How do principals, school leadership teams, and district staff prepare to start the Decision-Making Cycle?"

Prepare the Foundation

Any major schoolwide initiative, such as the Change Creation system of action teams, represents a major shift from business as usual. As we described in Chapter 3, John Kotter (1998, pp. 27–33), in his study of why major initiatives in the private sector usually fail, identified three principles for leaders to follow to ensure success preparing organizations for major change initiative,

Figure 5.3   Action Teams Drive Plans for Improvement

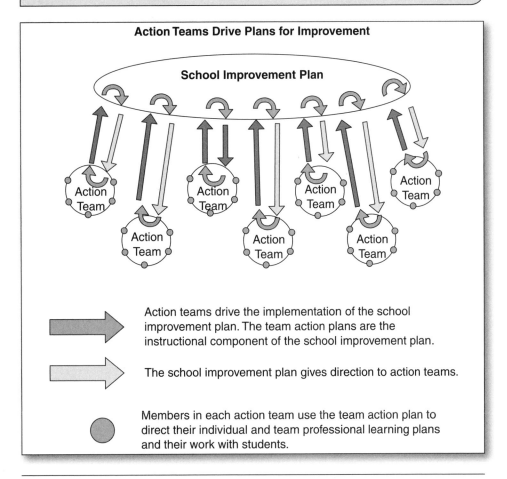

Action Teams Drive Plans for Improvement

School Improvement Plan

Action teams drive the implementation of the school improvement plan. The team action plans are the instructional component of the school improvement plan.

The school improvement plan gives direction to action teams.

Members in each action team use the team action plan to direct their individual and team professional learning plans and their work with students.

Source: Adapted from *Whole-Faculty Study Groups: Creating Professional Learning Communities That Target Student Learning,* 3rd edition (p. 135, Figure 7.4), by C. U. Murphy and D. W. Lick, 2005, Thousand Oaks, CA: Corwin. Adapted with permission.

which is what the Change Creation system for schools is all about: (1) establish a sense of urgency, (2) form a powerful guiding coalition, and (3) create and communicate a compelling vision.

Establish a Sense of Urgency

Organizations tend to operate to maintain the status quo, and schools are no different. Implementing a new initiative like action teams is a change to the status quo. Leaders *create a sense of urgency* for launching action teams based on data about student learning and effective and productive professional learning communities. By *leader* we mean the principal, assistant principal(s), instructional or curriculum specialists, and teacher leaders who together share responsibility for leading and supporting teaching and learning. In this section, we use *leader* as shorthand for all these school leaders.

Federal and state pressure to ensure that students in every subgroup are proficient in core content areas and college and career ready provides every school with ample opportunities for creating a sense of urgency for improving student learning. In addition, most schools have vision and mission statements that define learning more broadly than reaching proficiency on standardized tests and recognize that they have much still to do to reach these goals. Faculty examining a variety of data together about student learning can create a sense of urgency that supports implementation of the action team initiatives as vehicles for improving student learning.

Another element to creating a sense of urgency is the quality of collaborative work around teaching and learning. While schools have a plethora of committees, teams, and task forces, the fundamental work of creating learning opportunities that challenge and engage students and assess their impact on student learning often takes place in isolation.

But this view of teaching is changing. Learning Forward (2011, pp. 24–25) states that every teacher should be part of a learning community and that "communities of caring, analytic, reflective, and inquiring educators collaborate to learn what is necessary to increase student learning." The Learning Forward expectations for teachers are that every teacher convenes regularly and frequently in learning communities "during the workday to engage in collaborative professional learning to strengthen their practice and increase student results" and that "learning communities apply a cycle of continuous improvement to engage in learning, inquiry, action research, data analysis, planning, implementation, reflection, and evaluation." This describes what action teams do.

District office staff can help school leaders create a sense of urgency for effective collaboration, improved educator practice, and increased student learning by establishing clear district goals in these areas, publicizing progress toward these goals, and through providing feedback and support to school leaders. It is far easier for school leaders to communicate a sense of urgency to their staff when their messages are being reinforced at the district level.

Form a Powerful Guiding Coalition

Kotter (1996) emphasizes that a "smart" leader assembles a group of people within the organization, a guiding coalition, to help the leader lead the change effort—recognizing that the initiative becomes more credible if others beside the titular leader are actively engaged in planning and leading the initiative (p. 57). In the Change Creation system, the *principal* and the *school leadership team* play the role of a guiding coalition. School leadership teams focus on improving teaching and learning in the school and are usually composed of administrators, teacher leaders, both formal and informal, and instructional coaches. Teacher members of the school leadership team join teacher action teams and serve as regular, participating members. The principal is often a member of an administrative action team.

The primary responsibilities of the school leadership team for leading the Change Creation system and the school's action teams are the following:

**Role of the
School Leadership Team**

- Deepen their understanding of the Change Creation system and the action team process
- Lead the whole faculty in an orientation to define and explain the Change Creation system

- Lead the whole faculty through the launch of the DMC (Step 1) that results in establishing action teams and what they will do
- Lead and support action teams through the remaining steps of the DMC (Steps 2–5) over the rest of the school year
- Establish a variety of communication networks and strategies to share the work and results of action teams and apply lessons learned

District office staff can help principals in creating an effective school leadership team that is a strong guiding coalition by providing training for principals and school leadership teams in both the Change Creation system and action team process and in effective meeting practices, establishing clear expectations for principals about school leadership teams, and through providing feedback and support to school leadership teams. School leadership teams want and need to be successful.

Create and Communicate the School Vision

A clear vision answers the question "Why are we doing this?" Leaders can enhance the success of their action teams by creating a vision for the school that incorporates action teams as a primary strategy for achieving that vision. The Learning Forward Leadership standard reinforces the importance of vision in stating that "leaders work collaboratively with others to create a vision for academic success and set clear goals for student achievement based on educator and student learning data" and that they "clearly articulate the critical link between increased student learning and educator professional learning" (Learning Forward, 2011, p. 29).

Kotter (1996) reminds us that it is not enough to create a vision (p. 9, pp. 85–100). For the vision to be an effective staff motivator, the guiding coalition, the leadership team, needs to communicate the vision repeatedly through every vehicle possible, develop strategies for achieving the vision, and teach new behaviors through the actions of the leadership team—"walking the talk." For the principal and assistant principals, *walking the talk* means protecting time for regular and frequent action team meetings, actively and regularly giving feedback and support to action teams, participating in an administrative action team, and being an advocate for action teams to the district and community. For teacher members of the school leadership team, *walking the talk* means being productive members of their own action teams and representing action teams well in school leadership team meetings.

A corollary to defining and communicating a vision about the transformative power of action teams is being clear about the expectations for action teams and their members. That is, the expectations for whole-faculty participation in action teams and that working collaboratively to improve educator practice and student learning are the professional responsibility of every educator in the school. Just as in communicating the vision, it is important for leaders to communicate the expectations repeatedly through every vehicle possible and model behaviors that meet these expectations through the actions of the school leadership team.

Launching action teams requires consensus among the faculty to embark on the process. Prior experience in working collaboratively also increases the likelihood of a successful launch. How long the consensus building process takes depends on a number of factors that relate to the culture of the school and the faculty's prior experience with change initiatives.

Creating and communicating a clear and compelling school vision for collaboration, learning, and improved performance is far easier when there is a corresponding district vision and when district office staff provide training and support for school leaders as they design and implement their school visions. It is also easier for school leaders to set expectations and build consensus for change when faculties see that all schools in the district are expected to engage in the same changes.

Please note, as we discussed earlier in Chapter 2, pages 24–25, and Chapter 3, pages 33–34, the principal and the school leadership team should lead the creation of the school vision. The creation of the school vision needs to be done *before* the implementation of the Change Creation system and the DMC in the first year, and serious reconsideration needs to be given to the vision in subsequent years. A process for developing the school vision, Vision Creation, is provided in online Resource A.

Decide to Implement the Change Creation System

The fundamental decision to be made by the school leadership and the faculty is whether or not the Change Creation system will be put in place at the school. This decision is made after the leadership and all faculty members have had an orientation to and been given information about the Change Creation system. Typically, this is done in a general faculty meeting. In some schools, the principal or other school leaders meet with grade level or department groups. In other schools, printed materials are distributed and the principal follows up with individuals.

Regardless of the process used, it is important to let faculty know up front how the decision will be made and what the criteria for approval are. If the faculty is to vote, everyone needs to understand what percentage of approval (e.g., 70%) will require all faculty members to be members of action teams. If approval will be by consensus, everyone needs to understand how consensus will be determined. However, once the decision is made, it is expected that *all faculty members* will participate in an action.

Directly related to the decision to begin the Change Creation system is the commitment of active support (i.e., strong sponsorship; see Chapter 3, pages 44–46) by the principal for the preparation, launch, implementation, and institutionalization of the Change Creation system. Schools must have the daily, active support of the principal and assistant principals for the system to succeed. In the Change Creation system, the principal is expected to support and facilitate the orientation of staff to the system and take the faculty through the preparation and launch process (Step 1) and through the remaining steps on the DMC.

Regardless of how effective the decision-making process, how thorough the orientation, how compelling the vision, or how strong the sense of urgency, once the action team process (or any complex initiative) begins, there will still be individuals who will feel some resentment about beginning the initiative.

As we discussed in Chapter 3, pages 47–49, leaders can expect differences in how individuals respond and the level of consensus among faculty members. Even those individuals who were most willing to begin may become less so when the real work of collaboration begins. We have found the old adage "It's not real until it's real" to certainly be true. Commitment to the work and genuinely and fully accepting the change comes when teachers see the positive impact of action teams on student learning.

Find Meeting Time for Action Teams

A crucial decision that needs to be made *before* beginning the process of the Change Creation system, the steps in the DMC, is *when* action teams will meet or, at least, the options for finding time for them to meet. It is important to decide this before beginning Step 1 of the DMC, because teachers always want to know that time will be provided for action team meetings before they make choices about student needs and forming action teams. Since many teachers are skeptical of new programs and the school and district's support for implementation, deciding up front when action teams will meet demonstrates commitment to support the Change Creation system and the faculty.

Action teams should meet every week or at least every other week for 45 minutes. Action teams that meet less than this will not be as successful in changing practices and improving student performance. Since *all* certificated staff in the school *are members* of action teams, the time for action teams to meet must be built into the school schedule in a way that respects teacher's contractual obligations. Usually action teams meet during the school day, before school, or after school. In Chapter 6, page 98, there is a section that describes a number of options schools have used for action teams time. An expanded list of time-option approaches is given in online Resource F. It is not uncommon for schools to use one approach in the first year and then try a different approach in the second year.

How this decision about time is made can be just as important as the decision itself. Ideally, the exploration of options and dialogue and discussion about these options should involve the school's shared decision-making team and/or the leadership team and the entire faculty to ensure understanding and ownership of the decision.

Determine Data to Identify Student Learning Needs

Finally, school leaders decide what data will be examined to determine student needs when the faculty begins Step 1 in the DMC. Data must be collected and organized for the faculty to use in making decisions about student needs, what action teams will do, and how action teams will be organized. What student data and general information about students that the faculty and school leadership will review is one of the most important decisions made by the leaders of the Change Creation system. All future decisions will be shaped by what data the faculty and school leadership analyze. If that data won't lead to the most serious instructional needs, the whole process will be in danger of not accomplishing intended results. If, for example, the most serious student need is in the area of reading and the faculty does not have data to validate that need, the faculty may miss its opportunity to address that critical need. Guidelines for selecting and organizing data are discussed in Chapter 6.

How the decisions are made about what data to bring to the Change Creation system launch (Step 1) is important for convincing faculty and school leadership that the Change Creation system is different from traditional top-down interventions. A school's leadership team should lead the discussions about what data to bring to the faculty so that everyone knows before starting Step 1 how and why data decisions were made.

SUMMARY

This chapter introduced the five-step Action Teams DMC that Change Creation system schools follow in improving teaching and learning and the *critical preparation* that schools need to make *before* beginning the DMC. The five steps are as follows:

Step 1: Identify student learning needs and form action teams.

Step 2: Create team action plans.

Step 3: Implement learning and inquiry cycles to change practice and improve student learning.

Step 4: Assess the impact of action teams' work on teacher practice and student learning.

Step 5: Share results and best practices and apply lessons learned.

Schools implement the DMC anew each year as part of their multiyear improvement effort guided by their school vision, strategic plan, or schoolwide instructional focus. The work in each successive DMC builds on the accomplishments in the previous year's cycle.

Prior to starting the DMC, the school leaders need to prepare the foundation by establishing a sense of urgency for change, building a guiding coalition to lead the change efforts, and communicating a compelling vision. They also have three concrete tasks to accomplish: (1) lead the faculty to decide to implement the Change Creation system, (2) find time for action teams to meet, and (3) determine which data to use to identify student learning needs. As is indicated in Figure 5.2 on page 81, it is important for each school's leaders and faculty to think about how best to adapt the DMC to the school's unique context.

Chapter 6 and Chapters 9 through 12 explore the steps of the Action Teams DMC in detail. Chapter 6, "Identifying Student Learning Needs and Forming Action Teams," focuses on Step 1 in the DMC and offers strategies that the principal and the school leadership team can use to identify specific schoolwide student learning needs, form action teams, and help each action team reach agreement on the specific learning needs it will address.

Identifying Student Learning Needs and Forming Action Teams 6

This chapter focuses on Step 1 in the Action Teams Decision-Making Cycle (DMC) and offers strategies that the principal and the school leadership team can use to identify specific schoolwide student learning needs, form action teams, and help each action team reach agreement on the specific learning needs it will address. There are three desired outcomes for this step:

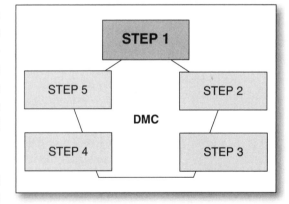

1. The school creates a list of student learning needs informed by its analysis of data on student learning.

2. Action teams are formed to address specific student learning needs.

3. Each action team reaches consensus on the specific student learning needs it will address.

Depending on the processes used, schools can achieve the first two outcomes in as little as two hours in a faculty meeting or over a period of several weeks. Action teams can achieve the third outcome in the first two team meetings.

STUDENT LEARNING NEEDS THAT ACTION TEAMS ADDRESS

By *student learning needs* we mean the most important specific concepts and skills across grade levels and content areas that students need to master to improve their performance. Each action team identifies the student learning needs it will address for the students the team members serve and works on these needs over the entire school year. We focus on instructional or academic needs rather than behavior needs, but we recognize that there is overlap between instructional and behavior needs.

We share the beliefs imbedded in the Positive Behavior Support (PBS) or Positive Behavioral Interventions and Supports (PBIS) system that "successfully addressing problem behavior requires an increased emphasis on proactive approaches in which expected and more socially acceptable behaviors are directly taught, regularly practiced in the natural environment, and followed by frequent positive reinforcement" (Sugai et al., 2010, p. 11).

Research suggests that the likelihood of disruptive behavior increases as student success with academics decreases and that students are more successful when curriculum and instruction match student ability (Epstein, Atkins, Cullinan, Kutash, & Weaver, 2008, p. 17). Action teams are a structure for educators to work together to ensure that each student experiences success in every classroom.

In addition to addressing student learning needs related to academic standards and content, teacher action teams may also address needs related to underlying skills such as the ones listed below.

Students need to

- Understand and follow multistep directions
- Improve listening skills
- Demonstrate good note-taking and study skills
- Be actively engaged in their own learning
- Solve problems/make good decisions

Nonteaching staff can be in teacher action teams or their own action teams and can work together to help students develop the skills they need to be successful in school. Some examples of student learning needs that nonteaching staff might address in action teams include the ones listed below.

Students need to

- Demonstrate socially respectful and responsible behavior (aides, administrators, and counselors)
- Apply research skills (media and technology)
- Demonstrate leadership skills (administration and counselors)
- Solve problems/make good decisions (counselors)

Examples of illustrative student learning needs at the elementary, middle, and high school levels are shown in online Resource G.

Other noninstructional student needs are important and should be addressed, but not by action teams. Needs not appropriate for teacher action teams may be assigned to an administrative team, a task force, a committee, student council, advisory councils, or any other team that oversees general student and school needs (Murphy & Lick, 2005, p. 251).

We have found that action teams are most successful when they target student learning needs that are

- Important
- Specific
- Under their direct control
- Connect to what they do with students
- Measurable—seen in what students do

A student learning need is important if the concept or skill is critical to mastering a key state standard in the content or courses for which team members have responsibility and if data show that a number of students have not mastered it. Team members will not put in the time and energy required for action teams to be successful if they do not feel the needs they are addressing are important for their students.

The more specific and measurable a learning need is, the easier it is for an action team to assess their students' current proficiency, identify and implement interventions, and see results. Specific and measurable student learning needs are the first step in creating action team targets. Those are SMART learning goals—specific, measurable, attainable (but challenging), relevant, and time-bound (Conzemius & O'Neil, 2002, p. 4). Teams that have ill-defined student needs to address may take weeks or months to achieve enough clarity to begin to take action.

As we described in Chapter 3, change initiatives engender resistance when participants do not feel a sense of control. Nothing frustrates team members more than working on needs that are not under their direct control and do not connect to what they do with students. For example, an action team of teachers should not be working on improving student behavior in the cafeteria because this need does not relate to the work they do with students in their classrooms.

Action teams work on student needs that affect what students do or produce. Teams need to be able to measure the quality of what students do or produce and determine whether their interventions with students have led to changes in what students do or produce.

HOW TO IDENTIFY STUDENT LEARNING NEEDS

Every K–12 public school in the United States examines data each year on student performance to determine areas of strength and weakness, including achievement gaps between student subteams. They use this information to prepare or revise their achievement goals for their school improvement plans.

But these goals, such as "increase the percentage of students in Grade 8 who are proficient or above on the state English language arts assessment," do not tell a school's faculty what specific concepts and skills students need to master to reach proficiency. While Learning Forward, in its new standards for professional learning, emphasizes the importance of using a wide range of data to identify learning community goals (Learning Forward, 2011, p. 36), we have found that data disaggregated by student subgroup, types of performance tasks, and specific content standards are more useful than aggregate summative data for identifying specific skills and concepts for action teams to address.

Faculty need time together to dig deeper to identify, analyze, and discuss student data, standards, assessment items, and pacing guides in order to identify the specific concepts and skills students need to master to reach proficiency. As the Learning Forward standard on using data explains, "[p]robing questions guide data analysis to understand where students are in relationship to the expected curriculum standards and to identify the focus for educator professional learning" (Learning Forward, 2011, p. 36). Some of this digging work can be done before forming action teams by looking at schoolwide data. A second round of digging occurs when action teams select specific student learning needs and analyze the data for their students that relate to the selected need.

The transition to the Common Core standards in the United States provides a rich opportunity for schools to identify student learning needs that their faculty must address in their work in action teams. States are analyzing their current content standards in English language arts and mathematics to revise and align them with the Common Core standards. In addition, the Common Core literacy anchor standards for history/social studies, science and technical subjects (NGA Center and CCSSO, 2012), which focus on reading comprehension, critical thinking, and narrative, argumentative, and explanatory/informational writing, provide clear expectations for reading and writing across content areas. Part of the data that a school leadership team presents to faculty in this step of the DMC can be a gap analysis between current district and state grade level standards and the new Common Core standards.

If a faculty is unfamiliar with a school's data or lacks skills in interpreting data, a workshop should be held for the purpose of teaching the faculty how to interpret the school's data. It is a mistake to try to develop data analysis skills at the same time the faculty is using data for identifying student learning needs and organizing action teams.

Two approaches to developing a set of schoolwide specific student learning needs, the whole-faculty process and grade level or content area process, are described in the following sections.

Whole-Faculty Process

One process for creating a list of student learning needs for action teams to address is to use the whole-faculty process we developed for the Whole-Faculty Study Group design (Murphy & Lick, 2005, pp. 117–123):

1. The school leadership team of administrators and teacher leaders assembles the data for faculty to review and prepares data folders with five or six separate sets of data in a user-friendly format. "Where possible, data

should be disaggregated for specific skills, concepts, and understandings within each subject area; types of performance tasks; and different student group characteristics" (p. 117).

2. The faculty, seated at tables in mixed groups of five or six, all have data folders with the same five or six data sets. Each person reviews one of the data sets and shares with others at the table what they see in the data as patterns and trends, gaps or anomalies, and areas of strength and weakness.

3. After sharing observations about the data, each table group brainstorms a list of student learning needs that they see in the data. Lists from each table are combined to create a master list of student learning needs.

4. Then, the faculty sort the needs on the master list into different categories, recognizing that some needs may belong to multiple categories.

Examples of illustrative lists of schoolwide student learning needs created by this process at the elementary, middle, and high school levels are shown in online Resource G. A number of the needs listed in these examples directly relate to the Common Core standards.

Bunn Elementary School and Western Harnett High School, both in North Carolina but in different districts, used the whole-faculty approach to identify student learning needs and created cross-grade and cross-content area teams.

Grade Level or Content Area Process

Another process is to invite faculty to work in grade level or content area teams to analyze their data and develop separate lists of student learning needs that can then be combined into a schoolwide list of student learning needs. Grade level or content area groups

1. Collect student data, assessment instruments, and standards for their grade level or content area

2. Analyze the data for patterns and trends, gaps or anomalies, and areas of strength and weakness

3. Brainstorm a list of student learning needs that they see in the data and create categories of needs

4. Send their lists to the school leadership team to compile a master list and share with faculty

Granby High School in Norfolk, Virginia, used the content area process to identify student learning needs and created teams within each of its four academies.

A challenge to using content area groups to identify student learning needs is that some content areas may have more student learning data, such as English language arts and mathematics, than other areas.

The desired outcome from either process is a list of concrete, specific student learning needs that action teams can use to select student needs to address.

FORM ACTION TEAMS AND SELECT STUDENT NEEDS TO ADDRESS

The desired outcome is forming a set of action teams, each with three to five members, that involve the whole faculty and with each action team committed to working collaboratively on specific data-informed student learning needs that they have selected from the list of schoolwide student learning needs. This expectation meets the Learning Forward Learning Communities standard that "Professional learning that increases educator effectiveness and results for all students occurs within learning communities committed to continuous improvement, collective responsibility, and goal alignment" (Learning Forward, 2011, p. 24).

> **Selecting Student Learning Needs—Five Key Questions**

What is most important is that each action team formed is committed to working collaboratively on a common set of specific data-informed student learning needs. Action teams achieve this outcome when every member of the team can answer yes to the following five questions:

1. Are the student needs we are addressing concrete and specific?

2. Are the student needs we are addressing important for the students with whom I work?

3. Are these student needs ones that I can address through the content of my teaching or my work with students?

4. Are these student needs ones about which I need to learn more?

5. Do we have genuine consensus that we all will commit time and energy to working on these needs in our team meetings and in our work with students?

How action teams are formed depends on two interrelated contextual issues: the desired grouping configuration and the current grouping structures within a school and when action teams can meet within the contract day or week.

How to Form Action Teams?

We have seen three grouping options for forming action teams—by (1) common student learning needs, (2) existing grouping patterns, or (3) new grouping patterns.

By Common Student Learning Needs

This option forms action teams based on common student learning needs, regardless of other current grouping patterns. It works best when schools have dedicated time for all action teams to meet, such as time on common late start or early release days. The whole faculty meets together and each person identifies from the master list of student learning needs the category of needs and the specific needs he or she would like to address. Then faculty members are grouped by selected category. If more than five people choose a category, the group is subdivided into teams of three to five, based on specific needs they want to address.

The advantage to this approach is that teams are formed based on their common interest in a category of student learning needs that they feel are important for their students and that they can address through the work they do with students. For schools in the United States, this approach may be used to support the transition to the Common Core standards. Action teams would be formed around categories of needs that relate to the Common Core standards, such as close reading, argumentative writing, mathematical reasoning, and mathematical applications.

A disadvantage is that the team members may not have worked closely together before and will need time to create a team identity.

In schools that do not have dedicated time to meet, teams meet during common planning times. Faculty with the same common planning period meet together and subdivide into teams of three to five based on common categories of student learning needs. The advantage is the common planning time is already in the schedule. A disadvantage is that reaching consensus on a set of common student learning needs may be hard if the number of people is small and they teach different grades or subjects.

By Existing Grouping Patterns

Some schools may want action teams to be created from existing grouping patterns, such as cross-subject grade-level teams, content area teams, or cross-subject multigrade teams. They reason that transforming existing teams into action teams will increase their impact on teaching and learning. One advantage is that time already exists within the school schedule for these teams to meet. If grade-level teams meet daily for 45 minutes, one day per week can be designated for action team time. Another advantage is that faculty members may be more comfortable working in these groupings. But this can also be a disadvantage. The teams may have developed habits, such as overrelying on the appointed leader of the team or ineffective meeting practices, which might undermine their effectiveness as action teams.

By New Grouping Patterns

Some schools may want action teams to be composed of people who do not normally work together to stimulate new ideas and new interactions. They might reason that they already have effective content or grade level teams but they want to encourage new opportunities for collaboration. For example, middle schools and high schools might want to form cross-grade and cross-content teams with English language arts, science, technical subjects, and history/social studies teachers to work on the Common Core literacy standards for writing across these content areas. One advantage is that there are no ingrained habits around group dynamics to unlearn. Everyone is a new team member. A disadvantage is that it takes new action teams time to develop their new team identity. Another disadvantage is that the school leadership team may have greater difficulty finding time within the contract day or week for action teams to meet.

Team Size and Meetings

Team Size

Keep the size of the action teams between three and five members. The research on small group productivity is clear (Hackman, 2002, pp. 116–122). Productivity declines as group size increases beyond five members. As group size increases, it becomes increasingly difficult for teams to adhere to the key principles of the action team system—everyone participates, leadership is shared, and the responsibility is equal. In teams larger than five, individuals can "hide" and not assume their share of the work (Murphy & Lick, 2005, p. 89).

The size of teams affects how comfortable individuals feel about serving different roles—leader, recorder, timekeeper, process observer—to help the team operate effectively. With small teams, rotating leadership roles is comfortable.

If time is not provided within the school day for teams to meet, the larger the team, the more difficult it is to find a common time when all members can be present (Murphy & Lick, 2005).

When to Meet

The decision about how to form teams may be complicated by the decision about when to meet. When action teams will meet is a major decision that is ideally made in the year before action teams are launched. This is the third guideline: Develop and keep a regular action team meeting schedule, with teams meeting weekly or at least twice a month for at least 45 minutes per meeting.

In more than twenty years of working with schools, we have seen several options for holding team meetings within the contract day or week:

1. All teams meet at the same time on the same day, which might be a late start or early release day.

2. All teams meet at the same time but on different days.

3. Teams meet at different times during the school day and/or week during common planning time.

4. Teams meet once a month on a late start or early release day and other times during common planning time or other common time which members choose.

We describe in online Resource F eighteen different strategies schools have used to find time for action team meetings. The important thing to remember is that there are "pots" of time throughout the work day, week, month, and year that can be combined and used for action team time—before and after school time, after school meeting time, planning periods, and staff-development days. As Murphy and Lick (2005) said with conviction, "There is time in the school day for teachers to collaborate, if the administration and faculty are willing to change other things!" (p. 56).

Decisions about when action teams meet and how teams are formed are fixed for the year but can change from year to year. For example, a school might have to form action teams in year 1 around teachers with the same common planning period because it is too late to change the student schedule, but in year 2, the school plans ahead to change the student schedule to allow all staff to meet for action teams at the same time (Clauset, Lick, & Murphy, 2008, p. 153).

SELECTING STUDENT NEEDS TO ADDRESS

Regardless of how action teams are formed, the expectation is the same—each action team that is formed is committed to working collaboratively on a common set of specific data-informed student learning needs.

The decision-making process that teams use to select the student learning needs that they will address will affect whether the team is committed to working collaboratively, with full participation by all members, on a set of student needs. We emphatically urge action teams to make important decisions, such as selecting needs to address, by consensus.

We emphasize making decisions in action teams by consensus for several reasons. Based on our principles for action teams, we expect everyone to participate and for members to share responsibility both in the meetings and for implementing decisions made by the team. Making decisions by majority rule undermines trust, sharing, equal participation, and follow-through.

An illustrative process for action teams making decisions about student learning needs by consensus is shown in online Resource H.

SUPPORT FOR IDENTIFYING STUDENT NEEDS AND FORMING ACTION TEAMS

A key question is, "How do principals, school leadership teams, and district staff support faculty in Step 1, identifying student learning needs and forming action teams?"

As we described in Chapters 3 and 5, John Kotter (1998, pp. 27–33) identified principles for leaders to follow to ensure success in transforming organizations, which is what the Change Creation system is about. These include establish a sense of urgency, form a powerful guiding coalition, create and communicate a vision, and empower others to act on the vision and eliminate obstacles to change.

In Chapter 5, we discussed the first three principles in the context of "preparing the foundation" to start the DMC. Starting to implement the DMC is "leading the launch" and focuses on Kotter's fourth principle, empower others to act on the vision and eliminate obstacles to change.

Empowering Others to Act

As their staff begins to work in action teams, many school leaders find that faculty members do not believe that they control the work they do in action teams. They keep expecting the leaders to tell them what needs to address, or what to put in their action plan, or which strategy to use in their classrooms. This is especially true in schools that have a tradition of "top-down" decision making and leadership.

Action teams really do have choices and flexibility to decide what to do. The action team process empowers others to act and fosters teacher leadership by requiring members to rotate responsibilities for conducting effective meetings and for sharing their work and results. It breaks from the traditional view that teams and committees have designated leaders; all members share the leadership.

Leaders can empower action teams by encouraging and expecting risk-taking and nontraditional ideas and strategies in the interventions that action team members try out in their classrooms to improve student learning. Similarly, district office staff can empower school leaders by encouraging and expecting risk-taking and nontraditional ideas and strategies in the interventions that school leaders try out with their action teams to improve educator practice and increase student learning.

Removing Obstacles to Change

Removing obstacles to change is part of successfully implementing any change initiative and is connected to viewing change as a process rather than as an event, as described in Chapter 4, page 37. Learning Forward's implementation standard for professional learning says "professional learning is a process of continuous improvement focused on achieving clearly defined student and educator learning goals" and "when educators work to resolve challenges related to integration of professional learning, they support and sustain implementation" (Learning Forward, 2011, p. 46).

One of the biggest obstacles to the successful implementation of the Change Creation system is finding time for action teams to meet frequently and regularly and finding time for cross-action team sharing and problem solving. Faculty always have questions about time. The school leadership team should either decide on a plan to present to staff or decide on options to present to the staff for discussion and reaching a consensus decision.

We recommend that action teams meet weekly or at least twice a month for at least 45 minutes per meeting. Action teams that meet less than biweekly accomplish little because they have no sense of urgency for improving student learning and lose valuable meeting time trying to remember what they were doing at their last meeting. The reason we insist that action teams meet within the contract day or week is that action team work to increase student learning should be a school priority. As such, working in action teams is part of members' professional responsibilities and should be done "on company time," not on personal time.

Leaders also need to plan for regular meetings to promote sharing and learning across action teams. These meetings should occur at regular intervals, such as after action teams develop their action plans (Step 2) so they can get feedback on their plans, at the midpoint of each inquiry and learning cycle to share strategies they are using and to get suggestions for addressing challenges, after each inquiry and learning cycle to share results, best practices, and lessons learned, and at the end of the year to share results, best practices, and lessons learned.

We recommend developing an action team calendar for the year that lists action team meetings, sharing meetings, professional learning opportunities for action teams, and the year-end reflection, celebration, and sharing.

Other obstacles to launching action teams involve data and decision making. In Step 1 of the DMC, faculty members have to use different sets of data about students to identify important student learning needs and, once they have joined an action team, reach genuine consensus on two or three student learning needs that members all agree to work on during the school year. But faculty members have different levels of access to data and different levels of expertise in analyzing data and identifying student learning needs informed by data. They also have different levels of experience with making decisions in teams by consensus.

As we stated in Chapter 3, page 51, the Universal Change Principle is that "learning must precede change." So leaders should provide the scaffolding and learning that faculty members need to accomplish the tasks in Step 1. These include the following:

Actions to Support Step 1

- Locate, select, and prepare data in user-friendly formats or develop instructions for faculty members to use to access electronic data.
- Decide what processes to use for identifying student learning needs—whole faculty or by grade level/content area—and design meetings, procedures, and materials to support the process.
- Teach and model how to go from sharing and analyzing data to creating a list of schoolwide specific student learning needs.
- Decide how action teams are to be formed—by common needs, by existing groupings, by new groupings—and design meetings, procedures, and materials to support the process.
- Teach and model consensus decision making by action teams as they decide at the end of Step 1 which two or three student learning needs members all agree to work on during the school year.
- Publicize all of the action teams, their members, and their selected student learning needs.

In most schools that plan to launch action teams at the beginning of the school year, leaders begin these preparations in the second half of the preceding school year. Leaders should not launch action teams later than midyear to ensure that all teams complete at least one inquiry and learning cycle before the end of the school year.

Sometimes the obstacles to launching change initiatives in schools come from the central office. Just as school leaders work together to remove obstacles to launching action teams, district office staff can help to remove obstacles. They can create district calendars and schedules that provide time for action teams to meet. They can help school leadership teams access and customize data for faculty members to analyze. They can design training programs and materials that school leadership teams can use to build faculty expertise in analyzing data, identifying student learning needs, and making decisions by consensus. And they can align policies, procedures, and expectations to explicitly support active principal leadership for action teams, participation by staff in action teams as part of the job, and the role of school leadership teams in leading change.

SUMMARY

Step 1 in the DMC, identify student learning needs and form action teams, has three outcomes:

1. The school creates a list of student learning needs informed by its analysis of data on student learning.

2. Action teams are formed to address specific student learning needs.

3. Each action team has reached consensus on the specific student learning needs it will address.

There are different processes that schools may use to achieve these three outcomes. Regardless of the processes used, it is important for principals and school leadership teams to remember that they are also building commitment to the work of action teams at the same time that they are forming the teams. Transparency and frequent open, two-way communication at both the district and school level are essential for building faculty trust in the processes used and confidence in the legitimacy of the outcomes.

Leaders lead and support the start of the DMC in Step 1 by empowering faculty to analyze data to identify student learning needs and make choices in forming action teams. They remove obstacles to change by providing user-friendly data, time within the contract for teams to meet and a calendar of meeting dates, and targeted learning opportunities to build faculty expertise.

After action teams have reached a consensus decision on the student learning needs they will address together, the teams move to Step 2 in the Action Teams DMC, create a team action plan, the focus of Chapter 9. Chapter 7 describes action teams in detail and Chapter 8 describes how school and district leaders guide and support action teams.

Introducing Action Teams 7

The overarching question that educators who want to bring about meaningful school change need to constantly keep in mind is, "What are students learning and achieving as a result of what educators are learning and doing in their action teams?"

The reason we have adults in schools is to help students learn. Improving student learning and achievement is the primary purpose of faculty and staff collaboration in action teams. It is "Job #1" and what schools, leaders, and faculty are held accountable to do. We purposefully used the term *educators* instead of *teachers* because other educators besides teachers are, and should be, members of action teams.

This chapter describes what action teams are, their purposes and the work they do, the principles and process guidelines that direct them, and guidelines for effective action team meetings.

Key Action Team Concepts

- Description
- The Work
- Purposes
- Principles
- Process Guidelines
- Effective Meetings
- A Bundle of Changes

ACTION TEAMS IN THE CHANGE CREATION SYSTEM

Action teams are designated teams of school personnel who work together to help the school move toward accomplishing the school vision.

The Change Creation system includes a job-embedded, self-directed, student-driven professional learning structure of action teams. Such action teams improve their practice and increase student learning by engaging in cycles of learning and inquiry that are driven by data and the application of what they know and are learning.

Teams with no more than five members

- Take collective responsibility for the students they teach
- Clarify the focus, determine current student performance, and set targets for improved student learning

- Identify content and best practices, acquire appropriate learning, develop expertise, and plan and practice interventions to use with students
- Implement interventions, examine student work, assess impact, reflect on lessons learned, and plan next steps
- Assess and reflect on end of the cycle results and plan for the next cycle

Every faculty member at a school is a member of an action team focusing on data-based student instructional needs. The collective teamwork and results of all the action teams advance the effectiveness of the whole school toward its vision.

In this definition of action teams, we have put greater emphasis on faculty learning and the application of that learning to changing practice and student performance than we had in the definition of Whole-Faculty Study Groups (WFSG). This is the same shift that Learning Forward has made in changing its standards for staff development to standards for professional learning—to emphasize the active role of educators in their own learning and assuring that "learning for educators leads to learning for students" (Learning Forward, 2011, p. 13).

The Change Creation system has at its heart the entire faculty working together collaboratively in small teams to increase student learning. These teams are a part of a larger system for professional learning and action and are job embedded (part of the job that faculty are expected to do), self-directed (teams take responsibility for their work and their outcomes), and student driven (the focus of their work is on student learning needs). The work, to take collective responsibility for the students they teach or with whom they work and to engage in cycles of learning and inquiry to address student learning needs, is consistent with the Learning Forward standard for learning communities. The standard states "learning communities share collective responsibility for the learning of all students within the school" and engage in cycles of continuous improvement (Learning Forward, 2011, p. 25).

In the third paragraph at the beginning of this section, "Every faculty member . . . ," we continue to envision action teams as the vehicle for implementing the school's improvement plan and improving teaching and learning. This is what we mean by "advancing the effectiveness of the whole school." Learning Forward (2011) agrees when it states "the more one educator's learning is shared and supported by others (in learning communities), the more quickly the culture of continuous improvement, collective responsibility, and high expectations for students and educators grows" (p. 25).

THE WORK OF ACTION TEAMS

What do students need for teachers to do in their action teams so that teachers will

1. Collaborate with team members to become a more authentic team?

2. Gain a deeper understanding of what they teach?

3. Become more effective in how they teach?

4. Enable students to become more college and career ready?

5. Share work broadly with other teams and across the school?

This stem, "What do students need for teachers to do . . . ," distinguishes the action teams design because the primary purpose for faculty and staff collaboration in action teams remains the same as for WFSG—improving student learning and achievement. This is consistent with the most important principle of the design, "Students are first." Often the focus in grade level or content area team meetings is on the adults, what do we want to do, rather than on what students need.

Collaborate with team members to become a more authentic team.

This expectation has been part of our thinking and writing about purposeful, effective collaboration since the beginnings of the WFSG design. Students need for teachers to work together effectively when they meet so that they have productive meetings that lead to teachers improving what they teach and how they teach to address student learning needs. Teams that are more effective working together are becoming more authentic and are more productive. In an authentic team, the members of the team work together to produce a total result that is greater than the sum of the efforts of the individual members. People energize and inspire each other, and the diversity of ideas and openness to them provide the basis for new creative ideas and approaches (Murphy & Lick, 2005, p. 165; Clauset, Lick, & Murphy, 2008, p. 42).

We make this expectation explicit in the Change Creation system because teams do not automatically become more authentic over time. It requires time, reflection, and action both by team members and by school leaders.

Gain a deeper understanding of what they teach.

This expectation and the next one have always been part of our design because they represent the heart of teaching, the content and pedagogy that teachers use to help students learn. We say "gain a deeper understanding" to emphasize that professional learning is part of what action teams do as they work together to address student learning needs. By focusing on one student learning need at a time, teachers have the time to delve into the content and research about the need. The team members become the school's experts for this learning problem.

Become more effective in how they teach.

The third expectation, "become more effective," is focused on results because being effective with specific learning strategies or approaches includes both being technically skillful with teaching a strategy and using it in ways that do improve student learning. It also means becoming more proficient at assessing changes in student work that relates to the strategy.

Enable students to become more college and career ready.

This fourth expectation is important because we have found that it is easy for action teams to get focused on very discrete learning needs, such as writing a five-paragraph essay, and lose sight of why writing essays is important. The transition to the Common Core standards will require that students from kindergarten through high school learn more challenging content and read, think, and write at higher levels of performance. Improving students' reading, thinking, and writing performance against the Common Core standards and assessments will require teachers to change substantively both what they teach and how they teach. For example, teachers will not only have to teach students how to do a detailed analysis of a variety of nonfiction texts without teacher prompts, but they will also have to enable students to engage in this analysis independently and proficiently.

Share work broadly with other teams and across the school.

This fifth expectation is new as an explicit expectation, but it has always been part of our thinking and writing about the importance of communication and sharing the work of action teams in the WFSG design. Too often, faculty members have worked in isolation in schools with few opportunities for meaningful sharing that advances schoolwide improvement of teaching and learning. Schools cannot become a professional learning community without teams sharing and learning from each other. We reinforce the importance of communication and sharing by making this one of our process guidelines (described later in this chapter) for the Change Creation system, including it as an explicit step in the Action Teams Decision-Making Cycle (Step 5—share results and best practices and apply lessons learned), and by emphasizing this responsibility for leaders.

PURPOSES OF ACTION TEAMS

The *primary purpose* of Change Creation system action teams is to improve teacher practice and student learning. But action teams also may have other purposes that relate to their primary purpose. These include the following:

- Implement districtwide initiatives in curriculum, instruction, assessment, and technology.
- Monitor the impact or effects of instructional initiatives on students.
- Integrate, give coherence to, and improve the school's instructional programs and practices.
- Target specific schoolwide instructional needs.

When action teams engage in these other purposes, it is subordinate to their primary purpose—to improve their practice and to increase student learning in the specific student learning needs they chose to address. Just as teachers design lessons and units are vehicles to address more than one content standard, action teams are vehicles for school improvement that serve different purposes.[1]

---

[1]The text describing each purpose is adapted from Murphy and Lick (2005, pp. 16–20).

Implement districtwide initiatives in curriculum, instruction, assessment, and technology.

The implementation of new learning is affected by the fact that our individual abilities to understand and use new ideas in curriculum, instruction, assessment, and technology frequently encountered in courses and workshops vary considerably, as do our personal assumptions, values and beliefs, and experiences. By providing teachers of differing attitudes, understandings, knowledge, and skills with the opportunity for support of each other, new learning will more likely be used in the workplace. Action teams create such opportunities, increasing the implementation of new practices learned in courses and workshops, and the effectiveness of new curricula, strategies, and educational materials.

Some examples of district initiatives that impact classroom practice include aligning curricula and teaching strategies with the Common Core State Standards, creating common formative assessments, implementing new content area instructional materials, integrating new technologies, introducing new instructional strategies, and revising the teacher evaluation system.

For instance, teachers engage in professional learning to use new instructional strategies that are backed by a strong research base and apply to a wide variety of curriculum areas. Such strategies or models may include Danielson's *Framework for Teaching* (2007) and classroom instructional strategies identified by Marzano, Pickering, and Pollock (2001) or Lemov (2010), Thompson's *Learning-Focused Strategies* (2003), or Joyce and Weil's *Models of Teaching* (2008).

Schools and districts embarking on these initiatives expect all the teachers in a school to reach high levels of appropriate use of these strategies in their classrooms. This is not likely to happen if the workplace is not designed to prepare teachers to support each other in the immediate and sustained use of the new practices. If the school has a schoolwide design for professional learning and the application of that learning that encourages sharing successes and failures, there will be a high degree of comfort in practicing lessons together and doing joint work in preparing lessons. As a teacher's comfort level increases, so does the level of use with students and the assurance that new strategies and new materials will have a positive impact on the students in the school.

Monitor the impact or effects of instructional initiatives on students.

Action teams can monitor and evaluate the impact of a new content program or textbook series on student engagement and learning as they work to address specific student learning needs through cycles of inquiry. For example, if an action team is targeting mathematics needs, the resources will be the mathematics curriculum, pacing guide, textbooks, and instructional materials the teachers use. Many of the strategies and materials identified for classroom use will be from the textbook and supplementary materials. As the action team engages in cycles of learning and inquiry for specific student learning needs in mathematics, it assesses students' strengths and weaknesses regarding specific mathematics concepts, identifies strategies and materials to use in the classrooms, plans lessons together using the new materials, teaches the lessons, reflects on student responses, and examines student work from the lessons.

The collection and analysis of information over a period of time will indicate to teachers in the action team whether the interventions are making a difference in student learning. In this way, the impact of a new mathematics program or textbook series can be monitored and evaluated.

Integrate, give coherence to, and improve the school's instructional programs and practices.

An action team, in deciding what strategies, resources, and materials to use in interventions to address data-based student needs, can integrate and give coherence to the school's instructional programs and practices. For example, an action team may target a specific need in the category of critical thinking skills, such as synthesizing. Most likely, there are a number of instructional programs with an array of accompanying materials, textbook series in all the content areas, and learning strategies that all target critical thinking skills. Frequently, it is left to the individual teacher to try to figure out relationships and common attributes among these different strategies and resources. An action team of teachers that regularly meet over a period of time can determine what materials and training programs are available, synthesize the new information and innovations, and together develop lessons that incorporate multiple strategies to increase the critical thinking skills that the action team is targeting. This analysis minimizes the traditional layering of initiatives and brings coherence to disjointed efforts.

Target specific schoolwide instructional needs.

Many schools, as they analyze student learning data across grade levels, content areas, and student subgroups, decide to focus all of their energy for a year or more on a single area, such as reading comprehension, writing, problem solving, or critical thinking. All of the school's action teams form around, or select, specific instructional needs within that area.

For example, if the school has identified reading comprehension as the focus for their school improvement plan, then each action team would work on one or two specific learning needs within reading comprehension that their students have. Some teams might decide their students need to "increase vocabulary" to improve reading comprehension, while others might choose "infer, interpret, and draw conclusions" or "support arguments with evidence" or "resolve conflicting views from multiple sources" to improve their students' reading comprehension. Regardless of the choices made by individual action teams, they are all working to improve reading comprehension.

Even if a school's improvement plan has identified different areas of student learning needs to address, action teams may still choose to work on the same need but from different perspectives. One action team may address the need through "mathematics," another may target the need through "writing," and another may work on the same need through "study skills." The difference will be in how they approach the need or personalize the need in terms of the grade level, students, or content area they teach. In this way, across the school, there will be an increase in vocabulary development because multiple action teams are addressing the need.

School faculty and leaders often review the purposes and the work of action teams and say "we can't possible do everything expected of us and also have action teams." They think about action teams as "just another program" to be added on top of everything else they are doing. This is the problem of *assimilation capacity* we discussed in Chapter 3, page 40. Our response is that schools have found that action teams are the plate that provides coherence and holds things together. Action teams provide a place where the most important work of the school, improving teaching and learning, takes place. Figure 7.1 illustrates this idea.

Figure 7.1 Action Teams Hold Everything Together

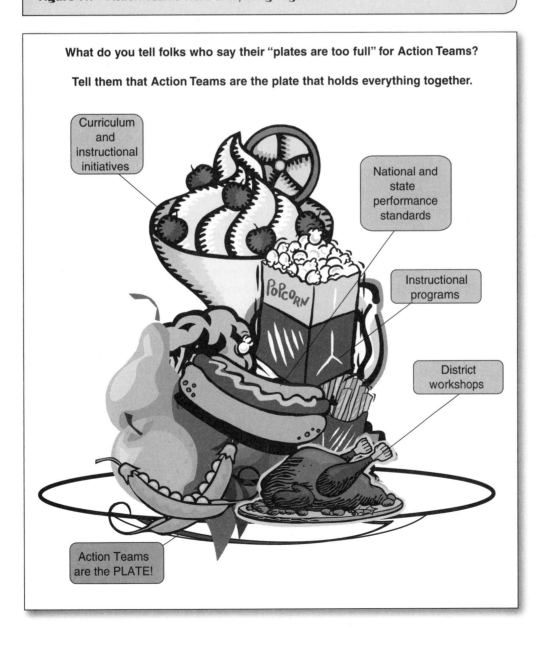

ACTION TEAM PRINCIPLES

How we act and what we do are most often based on our principles. A principle is defined as a fundamental truth, a rule of conduct, integrity (Murphy & Lick, 2005, p. 13). Guiding principles for the Change Creation system are the following:

- Students are first
- Everyone participates
- Leadership is shared
- Responsibility is equal
- Improvement requires learning
- The work is public

Our guiding principles are the same as they were for the WFSG design twenty years ago plus one, namely, "improvement requires learning." Even though school faculties are much more familiar with working together now and the technology that supports teaching, learning, and working in teams has improved, we still believe in the power of these guiding principles for shaping what action teams do and how members work together.

The First Principle: Students Are First[2]

The Change Creation system of action teams is an approach to professional learning that explicitly puts the needs of students first. The theme "what do students need for us to do" runs throughout the book and throughout the process. Members routinely examine student work collaboratively, listen to students, observe students in each other's classrooms, and pay attention to a wide variety of student data. The student voice is heard and is the factor that makes what members do in action teams authentic.

The Second Principle: Everyone Participates

Every certificated person is a member of an action team having from three to five members. Teacher members of an action team may teach at the same grade level or at different grade levels, teach in the same department or in different departments, and may be special area teachers and regular classroom teachers. If teaching assistants have instructional responsibilities, they may also be members of action teams with the teachers, or they may form action teams that have only teaching assistants as members. In some schools, nonteaching personnel, such as counselors, social workers, and media specialists, form action teams to investigate ways they can support the instructional programs or join teacher action teams. Principals, assistant principals, and instructional coaches most often are members of their own action teams and resources to the teacher and staff action teams.

---

[2]The material in this section on the guiding principles is adapted from *Whole-Faculty Study Groups: Creating Professional Learning Communities That Target Student Learning*, 3rd edition (p. 15), by C. U. Murphy and D. W. Lick, 2005, Thousand Oaks, CA: Corwin. Adapted with permission.

The Third Principle: Leadership Is Shared

The Change Creation system empowers every teacher to be a leader. Every member of the action team serves as leader on a rotating basis. Members also rotate responsibility for other roles that help teams be effective—recorder, time-keeper, and process observer—and for sharing their work with other action teams and with the whole faculty.

The Fourth Principle: Responsibility Is Equal

No one person in an action team is more responsible for the work than any other person. Everyone is equally responsible for every aspect of the team's work. Team norms are established at the first meeting, and every member holds themselves and every other member responsible for respecting and adhering to the norms. Contributions from each member are encouraged, expected, and respected. Action team members work collaboratively to increase their expertise, plan interventions, reflect on student work and results, and improve their effectiveness as a team.

The Fifth Principle: Improvement Requires Learning

Working collaboratively in action teams to engage in cycles of learning and inquiry is still a significant change for many educators. To be effective in an action team, they need to learn how to collaborate effectively and how to engage in inquiry. For teaching and student learning to change, action team members must also be continually learning new skills, new content, and new approaches for their work with students, and sharing these with other teams and across the school. As the saying goes, insanity is expecting different results in schools if educators are doing the same things over and over again.

The Sixth Principle: The Work Is Public

All the work that action teams do and their impact on teacher practice and student learning are public. For example, action plans and logs are regularly shared publicly. Any faculty member can ask someone in another action team about the work of that team. There are whole-faculty sharing times and printed summaries of what every team is doing. Sharing action teams' work, their successes, failures, and new approaches, is on the agendas of faculty meetings, grade-level meetings, and department meetings.

ACTION TEAM PROCESS GUIDELINES

Learning Forward (2011), in its new standards for professional learning, describes standards for data, learning designs, and implementation as the "attributes of educator learning processes that define quality and effectiveness of professional learning" (p. 19). These three Learning Forward process standards for professional learning that increase educator effectiveness and results for all students are

- *Data*: Uses a variety of sources and types of student, educator, and system data to plan, assess, and evaluate professional learning
- *Learning Designs*: Integrates theories, research, and models of human learning to achieve its intended outcomes
- *Implementation*: Applies research on change and sustains support for implementation of professional learning for long-term change

Process guidelines were part of the learning design for WFSGs and continue in the learning design for action teams in the Change Creation system. These process guidelines are the result of the work of Murphy, Clauset, Jenkins, Baber, Weiskopf, and many others since 1987 with hundreds of schools and thousands of study groups in those schools—in high schools, middle schools, elementary schools, and charter schools and in schools in large urban cities, suburban communities, and rural communities.

There are seven (7) procedural or process guidelines that characterize the Change Creation system of action teams. The first four guidelines focus on the system of action teams established in a school. The last three apply to the work of each individual action team.

For All Action Teams

1. Form action teams that are committed to work collaboratively on specific data-informed student learning needs.

2. Keep the size of the action teams between three and five members.

3. Develop and keep a regular action team meeting schedule, with groups meeting weekly or at least twice a month for 45 minutes or more per meeting.

4. Establish a variety of communication networks and strategies to share the work and results of action teams.

For Each Action Team

5. Create a preliminary action plan by the end of the third meeting and update it at least after each inquiry cycle.

6. Use effective meeting processes, including norms, rotating roles, equality of members, agendas, and logs.

7. Implement inquiry cycles during the school year by engaging in the following:
   - Clarify the focus, determine current student performance, and set targets.
   - Identify content and best practices, develop expertise, and plan and practice interventions.

- Implement interventions, examine student work, assess impact, reflect on lessons learned, and plan next steps.
- Assess and reflect on end-of-the-cycle results and plan for the next cycle.

We have integrated the explanation of these seven process guidelines into Chapters 6 through 12 and included a brief summary of the guidelines in online Resource I that may be used as a handout for faculty.

The action team guidelines weave in and out of each other to provide a structure through which teams work. Think of a basket, a basket with great utility. The guidelines are the wooden strips of equal strength and width in the basket. All the guidelines woven together form a basket or process strong enough to hold substantive content. Figure 7.2 is a "process" basket. Each slat

Figure 7.2 Action Teams—Why They Work: Strong Process Holds Strong Content

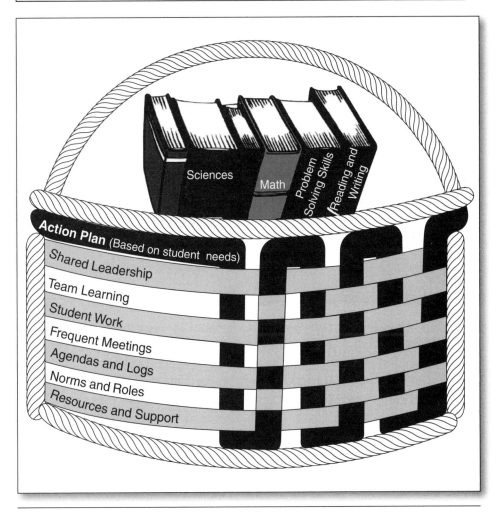

Source: Adapted from *Whole-Faculty Study Groups: Creating Professional Learning Communities That Target Student Learning*, 3rd edition (p. 86, Figure 6.1), by C. U. Murphy and D. W. Lick, 2005, Thousand Oaks, CA: Corwin. Adapted with permission.

in the basket represents one of the guidelines discussed in this chapter. The strong basket represents a strong process that can carry the weight of strong, substantive content (Murphy & Lick, 2005, p. 84).

EFFECTIVE ACTION TEAM MEETINGS

Action teams are not going to achieve results if they do not work together effectively. Effective meeting processes support genuine collaboration. In a recent review of the literature, Leach, Rogelberg, Warr, and Burnfield (2009) found five key design characteristics for effective workplace meetings: using an agenda, keeping minutes, punctuality (starting and ending on time), having appropriate meeting facilities, and having a chairperson or leader (p. 66).

The action team's design incorporates and elaborates on these five characteristics.

Using an Agenda

Leach et al. (2009) report that their survey research showed that having a written agenda in advance significantly increased participant perceptions of meeting effectiveness (p. 75). We expect action teams to create agendas for each meeting at the previous meeting and to put the agenda at the bottom of the team's meeting log. Just as Leach et al. (2009) report, we expect this because it avoids confusion and wasted time. We expect the team's recorder to share the meeting log and agenda for the next meeting with each member. Our work with teams in schools supports another finding in the survey research by Leach et al. (2009)—that an incomplete agenda reduced perceived meeting effectiveness. Often teams put too many items on the agenda and then get frustrated at not completing all the items. We recommend that teams select a single focus for a 45-minute meeting and also allow time to check in on the impact work in classrooms since the last meeting and planning their next meeting. We expect teams to improve over the school year in their ability to develop and follow agendas.

Keeping Minutes or Logs

Leach et al. (2009, p. 66) found that keeping meeting minutes or logs was important for "clarifying decisions, plans, and assignments, and recording a collective account of the meeting's viewpoint or separate comments by different people." They also report that minutes may "increase the likelihood that attendees will honor agreements made during the meeting."

We expect each action team to complete an electronic meeting log at each meeting or within 24 hours of the meeting. Consistent with the recommendations from Leach et al. (2009), an action team log is a brief, written summary of what happened at a specific meeting, and collectively the logs give a team history. Our action team log template is shown in Chapter 9 in Figure 9.3. The text that accompanies the figure describes each section of the template in more detail.

Punctuality (Starting and Ending on Time)

Leach et al. (2009) found that starting and ending meetings on time increased participant perceptions of meeting effectiveness. As they state, "waiting for latecomers serves to encourage future lateness behavior" (p. 66).

This is a perfect example of what we have advocated for years—teams need to have explicit written norms that guide their behavior, including starting and ending on time. We encourage teams to have norms in three main areas—the work, making decisions, and how members interact with each other. Each action team should develop its own set of three to five norms, but two norms are critical for all action team—starting/ending on time and making decisions by consensus. Time is precious in schools and every minute of the time allocated for action teams needs to be used effectively to improve teaching and learning. We emphasize making decisions in action teams by consensus for several reasons. Based on our principles for action teams, we encourage everyone to participate and for members to share responsibility both in the meetings and for implementing decisions made by the team. Making decisions by majority rule, rather than by consensus, undermines trust, sharing, equal participation, and follow-through.

We return to a fuller discussion of norms later in Chapter 8 when we describe the steps an action team takes in creating a team action plan.

Having Appropriate Meeting Facilities

In discussing their survey research, Leach et al. (2009) state,

Another robust finding across both studies was the importance of appropriate meeting facilities. . . . A meeting setting that, for instance, lacks the appropriate table arrangement, is noisy, is poorly lit, and is uncomfortable can impede appropriate meeting processes and thus undermine effectiveness. (p. 75)

We concur and encourage teams to hold their meetings in each other's rooms or other spaces that are convenient and comfortable and where every member of the team can see and hear each other. Many teams rotate the location of their meetings in addition to leadership roles. It is important for teams to be able to access during their meetings instructional materials, samples of student work, student data, and Internet resources. Many teams also like to have refreshments during their meetings.

Having a Chairperson or Leader

Leach et al. (2009) indicate that having a chairperson or leader at the meeting can enhance perceived meeting effectiveness and "facilitate the attainment of meeting objectives by directing the pace of the meeting and keeping the discussion on target" (p. 66). We expect action teams to rotate the role of meeting leader or facilitator and expect that the leader of an action team's meeting will

**Leader's Role
in Action Teams**

- Confirm with other team members prior to a meeting when and where the team will meet and what members need to bring or prepare
- Start and end the meeting on time
- Follow the agenda set for the meeting
- Call on team members or start a round-robin process
- Keep discussions on target without dominating the conversation
- Help search for and suggests consensus solutions
- Help resolve conflict between team members
- Revisit the action plan to keep the team focused on its intended results
- Share any comments from the principal or other support persons that may have been made on the log from the last meeting
- Ensure that all members are clear about the team's decisions and next steps

In online Resource J, we have listed the roles in the Change Creation system for the principal, the school leadership team, the action team leader and recorder, action team members, and district office staff.

Shared leadership is one of the key principles of the action team design and is based on the belief that all teachers are leaders. Members share leadership of an action team by rotating the role of leader, recorder, timekeeper, and process observer. Roles should be rotated so that all team members can become more skillful in each area and to avoid having one member become more responsible than other members for the success of the team. The leadership rotation may occur weekly, biweekly, or monthly.

All members are equally responsible for obtaining resources and keeping the team moving toward its intended results and desired ends. Individual members should look to themselves and each other for direction, not to a single person. This sense of joint responsibility for the work of the team builds interdependence and synergy within the team. When every team member feels equally responsible for the success of the team, there is a higher level of commitment, and no one leader is to blame for the failure of the team to accomplish its goals. The most positive feature arising from the use of the rotation approach is the important belief that all teams members are equals and that anyone from the action team can represent the team at any point in time, expanding the effective capacity for leadership at the school.

ACTION TEAMS AS A BUNDLE OF CHANGES

In Chapter 2, page 28, we said that the image of successful change and of reculturing that Fullan (2001) describes is a daunting mission. Successfully implementing the Change Creation system of action teams is also a daunting mission because of its complexity. The complexity of the system is that its action teams have a bundle of changes to deal with. Confronting only one, such as new materials, can be daunting. With the Change Creation system, however, the confrontation is with a collection of new things, such as picking up a bundle of clothes instead of reaching for one shirt. The Change Creation system bundle has in it all of the following changes that are expected of the school's faculty as they work in action teams.

> **The Action Teams Bundle of Changes**

- Having the whole faculty participate
- Adhering to the procedural guidelines
- Learning new content and instructional strategies
- Implementing new strategies in the classroom
- Reflecting on teaching practices with colleagues
- Monitoring student effects
- Looking at student work in a group setting
- Adjusting to new time requirements or different uses of time
- Understanding and accepting cultural shifts
- Being part of synergistic, learning teams

What makes the Change Creation system so complex (and powerful!) is that each innovation has major elements or components. For example, implementing new strategies in the classroom is preceded by (a) identifying one strategy, (b) developing lessons or using that strategy, (c) demonstrating the strategy to each other in the action team, (d) using the strategy in the classroom, and (e) reflecting on the outcomes of using the strategy. Each of the components that precede and follow implementing the strategy may be new to one or more members of an action team.

When leaders and faculties consider adopting the Change Creation system, they usually only consider the structure, meaning the guidelines. What is hidden from view is the bundle of changes. It is not long into the implementation phase that the bundle begins to unfold, and leaders need to be supported in their efforts to support individuals and action teams.

To explicate fully the complex work of action teams, we have developed the Action Teams Rubric, which can be found in online Resource V. The Action Teams Rubric measures the fidelity of action team members to the desired behaviors across a set of indicators that examine the work of individual action teams and the school's system of action teams. For each indicator, there are descriptions of behavior at four levels of implementation: "Not Yet," "Beginning Implementation," "Developing Implementation," and "Advanced Implementation." The primary purpose of the Action Teams Rubric is for action teams to use it to determine the degree to which the action team is meeting expectations. The rubric tells everyone what the system looks like in action, when fully implemented.

SUMMARY

This chapter introduces action teams in detail because action teams are at the core of the Change Creation system and are the essential structure for significantly improving teaching and learning in schools. The work of action teams is complex. They are engaged in developing mastery in new content, materials, and strategies as they work with students to address student learning needs, in becoming reflective practitioners skilled in implementing cycles of learning and inquiry, and in transforming their groups into synergistic learning teams with members using their time together effectively and productively. We describe what action teams are, their purposes and the work they do, the principles and process guidelines that guide them, and guidelines for effective action team meetings. This material is designed to give the school's faculty and leaders a deeper understanding of action teams and to emphasize that action teams are not just another name for grade-level teams or departmental/content area teams.

The next chapter, Chapter 8, "Support for Action Teams," is a companion to Chapter 7. It describes what school and district leaders need to do to guide and support action teams. Just as the work of action teams is complex, so is the work of guiding and supporting action teams.

Support for Action Teams 8

A key question is, "How do principals, school leadership teams, and district staff support action teams?"

Throughout each step in the Action Teams Decision-Making Cycle (DMC), there are eight ways that leaders can communicate the vision, empower action teams, remove obstacles, and create short-term wins. They are (1) keep the focus on student learning, (2) protect time for action team meetings, (3) establish routines, (4) provide regular frequent and constructive feedback to action teams, (5) recognize the developmental stages of action teams, (6) help struggling teams move forward, (7) establish a variety of communication networks and strategies to share the work and results of action teams, and (8) establish administrative action teams. In Chapter 6 and Chapters 9 through 12, we describe how leaders specifically support action teams as they move through the five steps of the DMC.

> ### Key Support Concepts
>
> - Learning Focus
> - Time
> - Routines
> - Feedback
> - Stages of Growth
> - Struggling Teams
> - Communication
> - Administrator Teams

KEEP THE FOCUS ON STUDENT LEARNING

Relentless communication about the vision for action teams is critical. In the absence of clear expectations and continual reminders, action team members can lose sight of their primary goal—to improve student learning this year in each of their classes or in their other work with students. Without appropriate pressure and support, action team meetings devolve into conversations about curriculum and changes that the action team members or others need to make "next year."

The three main strategies leaders use to maintain the focus on student learning are to (1) link explicitly and publicly the work of action teams to the academic improvement goals in the school's annual improvement plan; (2) encourage ongoing work on improving learning through feedback on action team action plans and logs and walkthroughs of classrooms looking for evidence of changes in practice; and (3) use cross-team meetings, faculty meetings, the school website, and staff and parent newsletters to share effective best practices and the impact on student learning.

PROTECT TIME FOR ACTION TEAM MEETINGS

After action teams are formed, a major concern of many faculty members is that action team meeting time and cross-team sharing meeting time will be usurped for other activities. For example, school leaders schedule meetings during action team time that pull members away from their meetings. Administrators ask teachers to cover another teacher's class during the period when the teacher's action team meets. The principal has to go to the district office and cancels a cross-team meeting.

When these events happen, the message faculty members perceive is that an action team meeting or a sharing meeting is not as important as the activity replacing it. When it happens often, action teams lose momentum and do not achieve their intended results, improving teacher practice and student learning.

We recommend that school leaders develop a semester or annual calendar that specifies, in advance, action team and cross-team meeting times, professional learning related to action team work, and celebration and sharing events. Then they share the calendar with staff, parents, and the district office. Once the calendar is in place, it should be followed. The hardest task for school leaders is saying no to possible disruptions.

Just as school leaders have challenges in protecting action team meeting time, so do action team members. Action team members also need to protect the action team meeting time and not schedule meetings, doctor's appointments, and other activities that will prevent them from attending their action team meetings. If a member is absent, the other members still meet. The work goes on.

ESTABLISH ROUTINES

Action team meetings are a different ways of functioning for teachers used to committee meetings and grade-level or department meetings. To begin focusing on the impact of their work on their practice and on student learning, action teams need to develop habits of working collaboratively and following team norms, rotating leader, recorder, and responsibilities for sharing the team's work, completing and submitting their action plan and logs in a timely fashion, using protocols to examine student work, planning agendas in advance, and moving through the parts of the learning and inquiry cycle.

Principals and their leadership teams can increase the likelihood that teams establish productive routines before, during, and after launching action teams. During orientation and before starting the DMC, leadership teams review the action team process guidelines (at the beginning of this chapter), provide examples of action team action plans and logs, and describe the kind of feedback principals give action teams. They also share with faculty that the work of action teams is public and that action plans and logs will be shared and displayed.

When the faculty completes Step 1 of the DMC and forms action teams, many principals send out a follow-up memo to summarize guidelines and expectations for action team work and provide a calendar for upcoming action team and cross-team sharing meetings, as well as for professional learning opportunities that will support the work of action teams.

Action team logs are the best evidence of whether a team has established routines around meeting regularly and effectively, rotating roles, using protocols, and engaging in action research. Principals can quickly get a sense of whether a team is developing routines by reviewing its log after a meeting and comparing this week's log to the previous log and to the team's action plan.

A key part of establishing routines is the process for teams submitting action team action plans and logs so that they can get feedback from the principal or other designated readers before their next meeting. The process has two special features—when to submit and how to submit.

Many schools address the "when to submit" issue by using a 24-hour rule—action team logs and action plan updates are submitted within 24 hours of the action team meeting.

"How to submit" has changed since the Whole-Faculty Study Groups (WFSG) System began in 1987. In the early 1990s, this meant managing paper. Now most schools and districts use electronic media. Some schools have an action teams folder on the school computer-network server that all staff can access. Each action team has its own folder within this folder. Action teams post their logs and action plan updates to their team folder, and the readers post their feedback to the same folder. Some districts have established districtwide systems for action teams, supported by Moodle or Blackboard Academic Suite that allows anyone in the system to access any action team's folder.

PROVIDE REGULAR, FREQUENT, AND CONSTRUCTIVE FEEDBACK TO ACTION TEAMS

While the "official" responsibility for reviewing action team action plans and logs and providing feedback rests with the principal, principals can share or delegate this responsibility if they clearly communicate to the faculty who will be responsible. The principal is usually solely responsible for providing feedback in smaller schools where the principal is the only administrator. In schools with a principal and an assistant principal or instructional support specialist, they might meet together to review action plan and logs and provide feedback. In larger schools with many action teams, the administrative team may serve as readers to action teams.

Principals and other readers need to establish their own routines to ensure that all action teams are getting regular and timely feedback. Regular feedback means action teams can count on receiving feedback on every log and action plan update. Timely feedback means that action teams can count on receiving feedback on a log or action plan update before their next meeting. This prevents action teams from feeling that they are backtracking when they receive feedback on work they did several meetings before.

The other component of the feedback routine that is important to establish right from the beginning is that the feedback is *substantive and constructive,* not superficial. Action teams expect their responders to read their logs and action plans carefully and to reply thoughtfully. We encourage readers to frame feedback in terms of "wows" and "wonders," wows for work that exemplifies quality work and indicates the team is following the action team guidelines and wonders for questions or comments that push the team's thinking or suggest resources the team might explore. Feedback can also include offers of assistance and reminders about upcoming events, such as a cross-team sharing meeting, a professional learning opportunity for action teams, or an end-of-cycle review meeting. We present additional guidance for leaders on giving feedback to action teams on their action plans and meeting logs in Chapter 9, page 151.

UNDERSTAND THE DEVELOPMENTAL STAGES OF ACTION TEAMS[1]

Action teams go through developmental stages just like all other types of teams. Teams will experience each stage to some degree, and some teams will remain in one stage longer than other teams. This section is useful information to share with action teams as they are getting started.

We have given names to four growth stages that seem to fit the various action team stages. This approach originated from the book *The One-Minute Manager Builds High Performing Teams* (Blanchard, Carew, & Parisi-Carew, 2000). The four stages, which reflect how we have seen them function, are Forming, Grumbling, Willingness, and Consequence. Others have referred to the four stages as forming, storming, norming, and performing. Figure 8.1 illustrates these four stages.

Stage 1: Forming

The forming stage begins when the faculty is first given information about the action team process, and it continues beyond the forming of the action teams. During this stage, action team members may experience the following: high expectations, anxiety, need for more information, dependence on authority, fear of differences, wonder about expectations, or concern for being a leader.

In the forming stage, individuals need much information. They must be able to express themselves and ask many clarifying questions. The principal and the leadership team should be good listeners, nonjudgmental, and accessible and open to dissenting voices. Individuals may require one-on-one attention.

---

[1]This section is adapted from *Whole-Faculty Study Groups: Creating Professional Learning Communities That Target Student Learning,* 3rd edition (pp. 101–106), by C. U. Murphy and D. W. Lick, 2005, Thousand Oaks, CA: Corwin. Adapted with permission.

Figure 8.1   Developmental Stages for Action Teams

Stage 1	Forming	
Stage 2	Grumbling	
Stage 3	Willingness	
Stage 4	Consequence	

Members' concerns focus on getting more information and details about expectations of and implications for themselves. Team members will want to know what is required of them, if the principal and district leaders are going to support action teams over time and if teachers will have adequate resources for their teams. Participants want to understand how the process will affect them, how they will be part of the decision-making process, and what the potential conflicts may be with existing structures.

It is extremely important that school leaders communicate and model the vision for action teams as well as present clear and reasonable options for teachers during the early stage of forming action teams. It is also important to give action teams clear and concise instructions as to what to do during their first several action team meetings. During these first meetings, teams establish norms and leadership rotation schedules, decide which student learning needs to address, and begin developing the action plan. These expectations keep the team members focused on tasks and not on themselves and each other.

Stage 2: Grumbling

It is usually during the grumbling stage that there is a dip in morale and commitment as the team comes to realize its tasks are more difficult than it initially expected. The saying "It isn't real until it's real" is true. Fullan (2001) refers to this dip as the "implementation dip" (p. 41). For action teams, this dip usually occurs when the initial energy wanes and the team is faced with the logistical aspects of the process, such as creating norms, developing a rotation schedule, and developing an action plan. Tasks seem disjointed and superficial.

In this stage, members realize that no one outside their team is going to tell them what to do, and this reality becomes something to grumble about. A fly on the wall might hear, "Why don't they just tell us what to do?" It is interesting that individuals can become quite comfortable grumbling. As long as they can grumble, usually about forces outside of their team, they can easily become complacent. These individuals need to feel some discomfort to move beyond this stage.

Concerns during this stage are about the processes of team membership. Members struggle with the best use of time, information, and resources. It is during this stage that members focus on the short-term value of action teams and take little time for reflection. They tend to concentrate more on themselves and the mechanics of the process than on their students. The work of the team often seems poorly coordinated and superficial. One might hear a teacher say, "I could get more done in my room by myself."

The grumbling stage is not an unproductive stage. It is a growing stage that teams go through on their way to being productive. This is usually when the seeds are sown for creativity and the valuing of differences. But action teams require much external support and encouragement in this phase to move to the next stage.

The principal and other support persons at the school and district level should respond to each team's action plan and logs. The log that each action team keeps should be carefully responded to for at least the first three or four meetings. When the logs are read, the principal will see a dominance of passive verbs, such as *discussing* and *reviewing.* At this point, the principal should ask, "And what action in the classroom will that lead you to?" This is the point at which the principal will have the greatest influence on the outcome of the action team's work. The quicker the principal acknowledges what a team is doing, the faster it will move into a more productive stage. What principals show by their actions to be important, teachers will generally take as important.

Action teams experience both support and pressure from having permission to meet in action teams, from having a content specialist meet with the team once a month, and from the principal's attentiveness to action plans and action team logs. In this context, support and pressure are positive dynamics. Without high expectations, a form of pressure, resources are wasted. Without support, individuals become alienated from the process and from school leaders. Principals need the will and skill to guide and facilitate the movement of action teams into the final two stages.

Stage 3: Willingness

It is during the willingness stage that team members become open to each other and willing to work cooperatively so the team can function successfully. Competition fades; collaboration increases. In this stage, there is a sense of expanding energy as the team pulls itself together to focus more clearly and effectively on intended results of the team's action plans. In the desired evolution of teams that we discussed in Chapter 4, page 58, action teams move through the willingness stage of development and become authentic, synergistic teams.

In the *willingness stage*, team members begin to develop new and refined instructional strategies and materials, share interdependently with each other, and introduce new practices that have a positive impact on their students. The concerns expressed are on the impact of the action team's work and the communication between and among teams. Members are refining the action team process so that it has more personal meaning to what they do in their classrooms and are integrating the work of action teams into other school structures.

When reviewing action team logs, the principal will see a shift from passive to active activities. Descriptions of team activities will most likely use active verbs. Teachers are collaborating and are taking joint responsibility for efforts in their classrooms and for their students' work. In particular, the "classroom application" section of their log is full, and student work is routinely brought to action team meetings.

When action teams are in the willingness stage, there are high levels of synergy in teams and energy throughout the school. A cultural change is evidenced in both formal and informal conversations between principals and teachers, teachers and teachers, students and teachers, students and students, and parents and teachers. Action team members are focused more on the impact their work is having on students than they were in the forming and grumbling stages.

Stage 4: Consequence

In the *consequence stage*, action team members have a high awareness of the consequences of the team's actions. Their concerns focus on the impact of their work and their professional learning on students. Teachers are continually refining the learning and inquiry process to meet the specific needs of their students. It is in the consequence stage that action teams evolve from authentic, synergistic teams to comentoring, learning teams that we described in Chapter 4, page 65.

In the consequence stage, teachers actualize the concept that students are at the center of professional learning. Teachers in action teams focus on the impact that the work of the action team is having on students. They use words such as *our students* instead *my students.* At this stage, team members require many opportunities to share what their action team is learning and doing that is changing what their students are learning and achieving. Results of increased student learning must be shared! Teachers should see the data and celebrate their successes. They need to see evidence that the collective power of their action team is making a real difference with students. At the beginning of a new school year, it is also this knowledge and its acknowledgment that will change the question "Will we have action teams this year?" to "What student needs are we going to address this year?"

More Circular Than Linear

When team conditions change, the developmental stages are repeated to some degree, and the stages become more circular than linear. Conditions change, for example, when a teacher takes a leave of absence in midyear, when a new teacher joins the team, when the team decides to rewrite the action plan and select a new student need, and when new expectations are imposed on the team. Teams that have formed and are working in the willingness stage will find themselves having to reform, if only for a meeting or two. The second time around, grumbling will be at a minimum and will have less impact on the functioning of the team. Members will quickly recommit to each other with a renewed sense of willingness to move ahead and accomplish the goals of the team.

Time in Each Stage

Typically, if action teams begin meeting weekly by the middle of the first or second month of school, it will be a month or two later before most of the teams have cleared the grumbling stage. Many teams should reach the consequence stage by the end of the first year if they are meeting weekly or biweekly. In schools in which action teams meet only once a month, the teams will most likely remain in the forming and grumbling stages the entire school year because by the end of the year, teams will have met only seven or eight times.

When the second year begins, teams will return to the forming stage, even those action teams that do not change membership. If an action team does remain intact, the reforming stage will only last a meeting or two. If people are in different action teams than they were the year before, the forming stage may continue into the fourth meeting. The grumbling stage is usually shorter during the second year because individuals have had a year of experience and they see that the action team initiative did not "go away." Most action teams will reach the consequence stage during the second year because all the teachers will be encouraged and motivated by action teams that reached the consequence stage during the first year.

When the third year begins, more teams, even those teams in which membership changed, will move more quickly though the first two stages. During the third year of implementation, most teams will reach the willingness stage by the fourth meeting.

From year to year, the factors that have the most influence on the start-up and continuation of action teams are contextual. For example, the number of new initiatives that the school has adopted, changes in leadership and faculty, and the level of ongoing district support all have the potential to inhibit or stop the process.

HELP STRUGGLING
TEAMS MOVE FORWARD[2]

Action teams, like other workplace teams, go through stages of development at different rates. We discussed earlier in this chapter the developmental stages that action teams go through and the types of pressure and support teams need at each stage. What we are focused on here are teams that from their logs, classroom visits, and anecdotal conversations appear to have lost momentum and are not making progress through a part of the learning and inquiry cycle, regardless of their developmental stage.

When an action team loses momentum, we often refer to the action team as being stuck. Just as Rosenholtz (1989) described "moving," "moderately stuck," and "stuck" groups in her work on organizational groups, we also have moving, moderately stuck, and stuck action teams. Action team members recognize when they are not being productive. Individuals feel frustrated and confused. Members are saying to each other and colleagues not in the team that action team meetings are a waste of time and nothing is being accomplished. Action team members may even be using the word "stuck." If this is not being said directly to the principal, it will surely get to him or her secondhand. In most situations, at least one team member will ask for help from someone. What we do not want to happen is for a team to remain in a nonproductive stage for as long as two or three meetings. An intervention should occur as soon as there are indicators that help is required.

An action team that seems to have lost its momentum, regardless of the stage of development, requires some type of facilitation or assistance. The assistance may be as simple as asking action team members clarifying questions, such as "How do you plan to test the instructional strategies you are identifying as effective?" or asking the simple question, "What is your problem?" or the assistance may be more complex. People available to provide such assistance are the principal, an assistant principal, a district-level support person, an instructional coach, an external consultant, and anyone within or outside the school who is familiar with the process and content of action teams.

When action teams get stuck or seem to be at an impasse, it may be due to context, process, or content issues, or a combination of factors. We have developed a set of diagnostic questions and an eight-step technical assistance plan to help leaders identify why teams are stuck and to get teams back to being productive and moving forward. Figure 8.2 summarizes the eight steps, and we outline the eight steps in the paragraphs that follow. The set of diagnostic questions and the full technical assistance plan are described in detail in online Resource K.

While the eight steps in the plan are presented in a logical sequence from collegial assistance to more direct interventions, the plan is presented with the understanding that the technical assistance provider may pick and choose what is relevant in different situations. We cannot imagine a situation in which

---

[2]This section is adapted from *Whole-Faculty Study Groups: Creating Professional Learning Communities That Target Student Learning*, 3rd edition (pp. 189–199), by C. U. Murphy and D. W. Lick, 2005, Thousand Oaks, CA: Corwin. Adapted with permission.

> **Figure 8.2**   Eight-Step Plan to Help Struggling Action Teams
>
> | Step 1: Feedback and support from other action teams |
> | --- |
> | Step 2: Reassurance |
> | Step 3: Suggestions from the reader |
> | Step 4: Direct support |
> | Step 5: Second opinion |
> | Step 6: Observe a team meeting |
> | Step 7: Share observations with the action team |
> | Step 8: Follow-up with the team |

a technical assistance provider would go through every step and every question. Most likely, it will take only one question or suggestion within a step to give the support person the direction needed.

Step 1: Feedback and Support From Other Action Teams

To reduce chances that action teams will get stuck early in the process, we recommend convening a cross-team meeting after the second or third action team meeting to share draft team action plans. This is after teams have drafted their team action plan and before they start their first learning and inquiry cycle. Depending on the number of action teams, these could be meetings with whole teams, clusters of teams, or representatives from each team. If you convene a meeting with action team representatives, each representative is expected to thoroughly share with his or her colleagues what he or she learned at his or her next action team meeting.

All teams will feel a little shaky at this first meeting, so just seeing that this is a normal state of affairs for this stage of the process will build confidence. When teams share about their action plans and their work, some might find that the team is struggling with how to keep its focus, others will say they, too, are having similar problems. Also, they will begin to give each other advice. A person will often see someone else's problem more clearly than his or her own. As a result, as people give suggestions to others, they will see the need for their teams to do something similar.

Step 2: Reassurance

When action teams are just getting started and are experiencing the DMC and learning and inquiry cycles for the first time, the number 1 question is "Are we doing this right?" If teams are in the forming stage, all they may need is more information, clearer explanations, or examples for what to do next. In the grumbling stage, an action team will express levels of dissatisfaction.

Often, to move on to the next stage, members require only additional assurance of support and confirmation that the team is on the right track.

The following steps are suggestions for action teams that require more direction; it will not be necessary to do all of them.

Step 3: Suggestions From the Reader

Sometimes, all it takes to get a team moving is for the principal or another designated person, who is reading a team's action plan and meeting logs, interacting with the team informally, and perhaps visiting classrooms to see what has not been done or what appears to be done incorrectly and to make the team aware of the oversight—"I noticed . . ."

Step 4: Direct Support

Administrative Support

The principal or assistant principal needs to provide support to action teams if they have not done what they should be doing to support teams or if suggestions to teams on logs and action plans do not yield results. Administrators can drop the ball in supporting action teams when they have not given the action team timely feedback on the team's action plan or log, responded to team requests for resources or questions and concerns, convened cross-team sharing meetings, or communicated concerns about the quality of a team's work to the team. The intervention—Just do it. Administrators also may need to give support to a team if a member is not following team norms and the other members can't correct the behavior after a Step 3 suggestion.

Content Area, Instructional or District Support

The principal or the designated reader invites a content/instructional specialist or a district-level support person to help a team if the concern relates to areas that may be beyond the administrator's expertise. Some examples might be concerns about the content and pedagogy related to a student learning need, the scope and sequence of a part of the curriculum, new materials that team members have not mastered, access to available resources, learning about or visiting teachers in other schools that are using strategies and materials with success in areas that the action team is investigating, or an action team requires specialized training.

Step 5: Second Opinion

The principal or designated reader is concerned about an action team being unproductive and is not sure about whether his or her perceptions are reasonable and what to do to help the team. He or she might ask for a second opinion from another member of the administrative team, a district support person, or an external consultant. The external person hears the concerns, conducts a thorough document review of the team's action plans and logs, and shares his or her observations.

Step 6: Observe a Team Meeting

The designated reader or another person observes a team meeting sitting at the same table with the team. The team knows about the visit in advance and the reason for the observation. At the meeting, the observer does not engage in dialogue and notes interactions among members and the substance of the work. The observer reminds the team that it should continue its work as planned and do exactly what it would do if he or she were not there. At the end of the meeting, the observer asks each member to respond in writing to a reflective question and collects the responses.

Step 7: Share Observations With the Action Team

At the second meeting, the observer shares with team members what was observed. The observer describes what he or she saw in the observation, action plan, and logs, stating what "I saw" or "I did not see." The observer reads responses to the reflective questions that he or she raised at the first meeting. The observer invites members to respond to the observations. Integrating responses from members, the observer makes recommendations to the team.

Step 8: Follow-Up With the Team

If the observer was not the principal, he or she should share the outcome of the meeting with the reader. If the recommendations require contacting a person to be used as a resource, it should be decided who will make the contact. If recommendations require obtaining a book or other material for the action team, decide who will do that. The action team should know what is expected to happen next. Whatever should be done, confirm who will do what, and communicate the results of actions with the team.

As previously mentioned, it will be a rare occurrence for all eight of the steps to be carried out. These steps are offered to provide principals and support people with a technical assistance plan from which they can choose appropriate actions. It is the principal's judgment as to the appropriateness of each step and subset of a step. Appropriateness is contextual and circumstantial.

DEVELOP COMMUNICATION NETWORKS AND STRATEGIES TO SHARE ACTION TEAMS' WORK AND RESULTS

Communication among action teams and with other groups in the school, including staff, students, and parents, is even more important today than it was when we first developed the WFSG design. It is more important now because of the increased urgency for improving student learning for all students, closing achievement gaps, and preparing students to be college and career ready. Schools cannot become learning communities if faculty members are not learning from each other throughout the school year. Boards of education and district leaders will not provide the time for action teams to meet if they do not see evidence that the work of action teams leads to more effective practice and improved student learning.

Effective sharing of the work and results of action teams is important because it reinforces the action teams principle, the work is public, and it promotes cross-team learning, an essential ingredient if the school is to become a professional learning community as we describe in Chapter 4. Effective sharing requires a variety of communication strategies. We describe these strategies in Chapter 12 rather than here because the focus of the chapter is sharing the results of action teams' work and applying lessons learned, both during the school year as teams implement cycles of learning and inquiry and at the end of the year as faculty reflect on the year's accomplishments and plan for the next school year.

FORM ADMINISTRATOR ACTION TEAMS

Just as action teams support teachers in strengthening their practice and improving student learning, principals and assistant principals need learning communities to support their work as instructional leaders. In the new Learning Forward standards for professional learning, one of the desired outcomes for principals is to participate regularly in one or more learning communities (Learning Forward, 2011, p. 24).

Administrator action teams may have foci for their work. Some, such as the administrator team in Osborne, Kansas, may choose to focus their work on supporting the teacher action teams and helping them become high-performing teams. Others, such as the team at Western Harnett High School in North Carolina, focused on how to help teacher teams use student-centered instructional more pervasively to address student learning needs.

In Change Creation system schools and districts, principals, assistant principals, and central office staff form administrative action teams that follow the same guidelines as teacher action teams. They meet weekly or biweekly in groups of three to five members, identify a set of student or teacher needs to address, create an action plan, engage in cycles of learning and inquiry, and share publicly their action plan and logs. Administrators also use their action team meetings to share and examine the feedback they are giving to action teams and problem-solve around how to help struggling action teams. When faculty see their administrators working together as an action team, they recognize that their leaders are walking the talk of action teams.

In the Franklin County Schools in North Carolina, where all fourteen schools have been implementing the WFSG system on professional learning communities since 2005, the principals and central office staff formed six cross-building and cross-level administrative action teams. The focus that guides all of the countywide teams is to strengthen and support the work of teacher teams and to improve student learning districtwide. The action plans and logs from the countywide teams are posted on the same Moodle website as the faculty study-group action plans and logs. Principals also share their action team's work at their school's cross-team meetings.

SUMMARY

Action teams do not become synergistic learning teams that transform their work with students, their implementation of cycles of learning and inquiry, and their work together as a team without the continual and ongoing guidance and support of school and district leaders. Growing action teams to engage in the complex work described in Chapter 7 is like growing a garden with a wide variety of plants and flowers—it is dedicated work that requires time and effort.

In this chapter, we have described eight concrete actions that leaders can take to "grow" action teams—keep a focus on learning, protect action team meeting time, establish routines, provide regular constructive feedback, use understanding about the stages of teams to foster growth, help struggling teams, relentlessly communicate about action teams and their work, and walk the talk by forming administrator action teams. All of these actions are important. Neglecting any one of these actions can undermine action team growth and productivity. But we do not expect principals to be superheroes who do it all. Rather, we expect principals to practice shared, transformational leadership that widens the leadership circle to encompass the school's leadership team, teacher leaders, and district staff.

The next chapter, Chapter 9, "Creating Team Action Plans," explains the tasks involved in Step 2 of the Action Teams DMC (create team action plans) and how teams use their action plan after they create it, as well as the companion to the team action plan—the team meeting log. It also describes how school and district leaders guide and support teams as they create and begin to use their action plans.

Creating Team Action Plans 9

This chapter describes the action plan template that we have created for action teams to use and explains the task in Step 2 of the Action Teams Decision-Making Cycle (DMC)—create team action plans. In addition, it explains how teams use their action plan and the companion to the team action plan, the team meeting log, and it illustrates how school and district leaders guide and support action teams as they create and begin to use their team action plans.

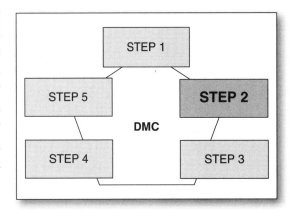

TEAM ACTION PLAN

The Whys of Team Action Plans

Action plans are important because they help team members plan what they want to do and keep track of what they have accomplished. The action plan guides the work of the team during each cycle of learning and inquiry. Every team creates its own action plan, even if more than one team is working on the same student learning needs or using the same instructional strategy.

Action plans play a role in accountability, professional learning, and recertification. The board of education, parents, and district leaders want to know how the time for action teams is being used. A team's action plan is one document that describes what the team is doing and its impact on teaching and learning. The meeting logs for each action team also document what a team is doing.

Many states and districts require educators to develop personal learning plans and to accumulate professional learning hours for recertification. Educators use their team's action plan to document their professional learning goals since the action plan addresses the question, "What do educators need to learn and do together in their action team to improve student performance for the student learning needs they have selected?" The team's action plan is, in large part, an individual team member's professional learning plan. The proposed work of an action team includes what each member must do to help accomplish district expectations. In the Springfield, Missouri, public schools, for instance, where action teams are districtwide, the team action plan is the individual teacher's professional learning plan. Figure 5.3 in Chapter 5 illustrates how the action teams, the school improvement plan, and individual plans for professional development all work together.

We emphasize that teams should develop a draft action plan within the first two or three team meetings so that teams do not spend an entire term or semester trying to create a "perfect" action plan. Schools have found that it is best for teams to develop an initial draft plan and then revise and update it as they engage in their learning and inquiry cycles.

Team Action Plan Template

A template for a team action plan is shown in Figure 9.1 and in online Resource L. An example of a completed action plan is shown in Figure 9.2. The action plan template has two pages, and each item on each page is there for a purpose. The first page focuses on the student learning needs the team has decided to address, the students each member will target, the team's essential question, the instructional strategies the team uses in the learning and inquiry cycles, Step 3 in the DMC, to address each need, and the resources the team uses in its learning and inquiry cycles. The second page focuses on data about student learning related to each student learning need the team addresses as it engages in cycles of learning and inquiry.

The example of a completed action plan using the template is adapted from work by the Radical Readers team at Bunn Elementary School in Franklin County, North Carolina. Their original action plan used a similar format. The action plan example in Figure 9.2 is an updated action plan prepared at the end of their first learning and inquiry cycle.

First Page of the Action Plan

The reason that (1) the student learning needs the team has decided to address, (2) the students each member will target, (3) the team's essential question, and (4) the instructional strategies the team uses in the learning and inquiry cycles are on the first page of the template is that they describe the work that the action team will do.

Learning Needs and Standards. The action plan and the work of the action team is driven by the *student learning needs* the team has decided to address in Step 1. These student learning needs are listed on the first page, along with the relevant state and/or district learning standards. Listing the *relevant standards* reminds action teams that the purpose of their work is to increase student learning on district and state standards as they learn and improve their practice. *The Radical Readers, a cross-grade team with teachers with Grades 3, 4, and 5 classes, selected two student learning needs in reading that were in the North Carolina*

Figure 9.1 Team Action Plan Template

Action Plan for Team # or Name: _____

Date Created: _____ Date Last Update: _____ Team Members: _____

The school's instructional focus (if applicable):

State the *specific skills or needs* (within the instructional focus, if applicable) the team will target.

List the evidenced-based teaching practices/strategies in which the team has developed expertise and used in teaching to address each student learning need addressed and, if applicable, to support the school's instructional focus.

Students need to	*Standard(s)*

Beside each student need, indicate the code or the number of the *district/state standard(s)* that will be addressed.

Member	Class or group to target

Essential question that will guide the team's work:

How can we help our students to _____

_____

_____

Our resources are (update each learning and inquiry cycle)

Our norms are

(Continued)

Figure 9.1 (Continued)

Action Plan for Team # or Name: _____

Date: _____   Team Members: _____

State *specific* student need that is being targeted: *Students need to*	Data sources: What type of pre-/post-assessments will members give to document changes in student performance? What are the criteria for GREEN, YELLOW, RED?	Current: For each team member, what number/percentage of students are GREEN, YELLOW, RED at the beginning of the learning and inquiry cycle? _____ (DATE)			Target: For each team member, what number/ percentage of students will be GREEN, YELLOW, RED after interventions at the end of the learning and inquiry cycle? _____ (DATE)			Actual: For each team member, what number/percentage of students are GREEN, YELLOW, RED after interventions at the end of the learning and inquiry cycle? _____ (DATE)		
			#	%		#	%		#	%
		Member 1			Member 1			Member 1		
		GREEN			GREEN			GREEN		
		YELLOW			YELLOW			YELLOW		
		RED			RED			RED		
		Member 2			Member 2			Member 2		
		GREEN			GREEN			GREEN		
		YELLOW			YELLOW			YELLOW		
		RED			RED			RED		
		Member 3			Member 3			Member 3		
		GREEN			GREEN			GREEN		
		YELLOW			YELLOW			YELLOW		
		RED			RED			RED		
	GREEN =	Member 4			Member 4			Member 4		
		GREEN			GREEN			GREEN		
	YELLOW =	YELLOW			YELLOW			YELLOW		
		RED			RED			RED		
	RED =	Member 5			Member 5			Member 5		
		GREEN			GREEN			GREEN		
		YELLOW			YELLOW			YELLOW		
		RED			RED			RED		

Complete a chart every six to nine weeks to track impact on students of the action team's work. Add more charts as needed for other time periods or student learning needs. Column 1: List the first student need from page 1 being addressed by the learning team. Under the need, list any subcomponents or subskills students need to master. Column 2: Indicate the common classroom assessment tasks or schoolwide assessments that will be used by members to determine the current status of each component of the student need. The data may be derived from assessment tasks designed by teachers, textbook publishers, and/or testing agencies. Columns 3, 4, and 5: Give the number and percentage of students in each members' targeted class or group that are GREEN (proficient and above), YELLOW (almost proficient), RED (far below proficient). The team members define common criteria for each performance level and use the same rubric or other rating/scoring system.

Source: Adapted from Schoolwide Action Research for Professional Learning Communities *(pp. 17–18), by K. H. Clauset, D. W. Lick, and C. U. Murphy, 2008, Thousand Oaks, CA: Corwin. Adapted with permission.*

Figure 9.2 Team Action Plan Example

Action Plan for Team # or Name: <u>Radical Readers</u>	
Date Created: <u>Sept 20</u> Date Last Update: <u>Nov 15</u> Team Members: <u>Beddingfield, Gr. 4; Joyner, Gr. 3; Kagarise, Gr. 5; Murray, Gr. 5; Watts, Gr. 4</u>	
The school's instructional focus (if applicable): Teams selected needs from categories – Reading, Writing, Math, Science, Phonics, Test Taking	

Students need to	Standard(s)		List the evidenced-based teaching practices/strategies in which the team has developed expertise and used in teaching to address each student learning need addressed and, if applicable, to support the school's instructional focus.
Demonstrate the ability to read and comprehend cause and effect within any given passage.	Gr. 3: 2.04 Gr. 4: 2.05 Gr. 5: 2.05		• Using graphic organizers • Reading the questions before reading the passage • Modeling questioning • Using real life examples before reading passages
Increase ability to draw conclusions and make inferences with given passage.	Gr. 3: 3.01 Gr. 4: 3.01 Gr. 5: 2.09		This will be our focus in our second cycle

Beside each student need, indicate the code or the number of the *district/state standard(s)* that will be addressed.	Member	Class or group to target
Beddingfield	Beddingfield	Grade 4 Class
Essential question that will guide the team's work:	Joyner	Grade 3 Class
How can we help each of our students to improve her or his reading skills and/or abilities?	Kagarise	Grade 5 Class—mostly SPED students
	Murray	Grade 5 Class
	Watts	Grade 4 Class

Our resources are (update each inquiry cycle)	Our norms are
CARS I, STARS, CARS II, Study Island, AR Extensions in Reading, Be a Better Reader, Guided Reading observations, websites, Curriculum Resource Teacher from BES & other schools, Book Room, Leveled Books—websites for cause and effect: www.longman.com/ae/marketing/sfesl/tests/grade4 and www.hartcourtschool.com/activity/trophies/rsr/build/RR_e_5_28.htm and www.quia.com (go to cause and effect).	1. Arrive/end on time 2. Listen and respect others' opinions 3. Stay on topic 4. Give constructive advice 5. Share workload

(Continued)

Figure 9.2 (Continued)

138

Action Plan for Team # or Name: Radical Readers

Date Created: Sept 20   Date Last Update: Nov 15   Team Members: Beddingfield, Gr 3; Joyner, Gr 4; Kagarise, Gr 5; Murray, Gr 5; Watts, Gr 4

State *specific* student need that is being targeted: *Students need to*	Data sources: What type of pre-/post-assessments will members give to document changes in student performance? What are the criteria for GREEN, YELLOW, RED?	Current: For each team member, what number/ percentage of students are GREEN, YELLOW, RED at the beginning of the learning and inquiry cycle? Sept 20 (DATE)		Target: For each team member, what number/percentage of students will be GREEN, YELLOW, RED after interventions at the end of the learning and inquiry cycle? Nov 15 (DATE)		Actual: For each team member, what number/ percentage of students are GREEN, YELLOW, RED after interventions at the end of the learning and inquiry cycle? Nov 15 (DATE)	
		#	%	#	%	#	%
Increase ability to recognize cause and effect within a given passage	Using CARS (Comprehensive Assessment of Reading Strategies) grade level pretests, benchmarks, and post-tests, we will have data to represent each student's basic understanding of cause and effect. GREEN = 80–100% correct YELLOW = 60–80% correct RED = 0–60% correct	**Beddingfield**		**Beddingfield**		**Beddingfield**	
		GREEN		GREEN		GREEN	
		7	29%	7	29%	7	29%
		YELLOW		YELLOW		YELLOW	
		9	38%	9	38%	9	38%
		RED		RED		RED	
		8	33%	8	33%	8	33%
		Joyner		**Joyner**		**Joyner**	
		GREEN		GREEN		GREEN	
		14	52%	14	52%	14	52%
		YELLOW		YELLOW		YELLOW	
		10	37%	10	37%	10	37%
		RED		RED		RED	
		3	11%	3	11%	3	11%
		Kagarise		**Kagarise**		**Kagarise**	
		GREEN		GREEN		GREEN	
		0	0%	0	0%	0	0%
		YELLOW		YELLOW		YELLOW	
		2	10%	2	10%	2	10%
		RED		RED		RED	
		19	90%	19	90%	19	90%
		Murray		**Murray**		**Murray**	
		GREEN		GREEN		GREEN	
		10	33%	10	33%	10	33%
		YELLOW		YELLOW		YELLOW	
		9	30%	9	30%	9	30%
		RED		RED		RED	
		11	37%	11	37%	11	37%
		Watts		**Watts**		**Watts**	
		GREEN		GREEN		GREEN	
		6	23%	6	23%	6	23%
		YELLOW		YELLOW		YELLOW	
		8	31%	8	31%	8	31%
		RED		RED		RED	
		12	46%	12	46%	12	46%

Complete a chart every six to nine weeks to track impact on students of the action team's work. Add more charts as needed for other time periods or student learning needs. Column 1: List the first student need from page 1 being addressed by the learning team. Under the need, list any subcomponents or subskills students need to master. Column 2: Indicate the common classroom assessment tasks or schoolwide assessments that will be used by members to determine the current status of each component of the student need. The data may be derived from assessment tasks designed by teachers, textbook publishers, and/or testing agencies. Columns 3, 4, and 5: Give the number and percentage of students in each members' targeted class or group that are GREEN (proficient and above), YELLOW (almost proficient), RED (far below proficient). The team members define common criteria for each performance level and use the same rubric or other rating/scoring system.

Source: Jewel Eason, Bunn Elementary School. Reprinted with permission.

standards and important for their students. They engaged in two learning and inquiry cycles over the school year, the first on "recognizing cause and effect" and the second on "drawing conclusions and making inferences."

Essential Question. The *essential question* forces teams to define in one sentence their team's focus—"How can we help our students improve their ability to . . ." When someone asks a team member what he or she does in his or her action team, that member responds by sharing the team's essential question. *The Radical Readers' essential question, "How can we help each of our students to improve her or his reading skills and/or abilities?" encompasses both of their selected student learning needs.*

Instructional Strategies. Since the action plan is a public document that summarizes the team's work over a school year, the section on *instructional strategies* allows the team to record the strategies they used with each learning need they addressed. This instructional strategies section is filled in during Step 3 when the team has begun working on their student learning needs through cycles of learning and inquiry. *The strategies listed in the Radical Readers' action plan where the strategies they listed in their meeting logs as ones they used with students and found successful—using graphic organizers, reading the questions before reading the passage, modeling questioning, and using real life examples before reading passages.*

Target Students. Specifying *target students* that each member of the action team will deal with in their classrooms or in their work setting as they address each learning need is important for the team and for others to know. Including this on the action plan enables each team member to ask, "Which students of mine need me to help them improve on a specific learning need?" We recommend that educators who work with more than one class or group of students choose for their target students one group or class or even a subgroup across several classes. For example, a high school teacher might select his third period chemistry class as a target group, or his low-achieving students in his third period chemistry class, or his English-language learners in all his classes.

For an educator working with only one class or group, she might target an entire class or choose to target a subgroup of students, such as her special needs students or her struggling readers. When teams decide to move from one student need to another, members may decide to change their target students. *The Radical Readers, all elementary teachers with self-contained classes, decided to target all the students in each of their classrooms.*

Resource Section. The *resource* section is part of the action plan because we expect action teams to be professional learning teams that regularly find and use resources in their cycles of learning and inquiry to build their expertise, design interventions to use with students, and assess changes in student learning. Resources can be books, articles, teachers' guides, Internet materials, colleagues near and far, and school, district, and state professional learning opportunities. Teams usually look for resources that help them better understand (1) the content embedded in the student learning need, such as the literature on different problem–solving strategies; (2) how to teach the content, such as different ways to teach each problem solving strategy; and (3) how to assess changes in student performance, such as assessment strategies that require students to use higher order thinking skills in problem solving. *The Radical Readers, in their September 20 initial action plan, listed the following resources: CARS I, STARS, CARS II, Study Island, AR Extensions in Reading, Be a Better Reader, Guided Reading observations, websites, Curriculum Resource Teacher from BES and other schools, Book Room, and Leveled Books. As they worked on cause and effect from September to November, they added useful websites that they found.*

> *CARS = Comprehensive Assessment of Reading Strategies (pre-tests, benchmark tests, post-tests)*
>
> *Study Island = Computer-based test prep in reading*
>
> *STARS = Strategies to Achieve Reading Success (structured modules on different reading comprehension skills)*
>
> *AR = Accelerated Reader*
>
> *CRT = Curriculum Resource Teacher*
>
> *BES = Bunn Elementary School*

Contextual Information. The first page also has space at the top of the plan for contextual information such as team name, team members, the school's instructional focus, and the date the action plan was created and last updated. We encourage teams to personalize their teams by choosing a name for their team instead of using just a number, content area, or grade level. We ask the team to list the names of team members and to indicate when the plan was initially created and last updated. In many schools, the faculty has identified through data analysis and reflection a single schoolwide instructional focus, such as critical thinking, reading comprehension, problem solving or writing, that guides the school's improvement plan and work of all action teams. We included space for the schoolwide instructional focus on the action plan template to remind each team that their work is connected to the schoolwide focus.

When Whole-Faculty Study Groups first began in the late 1980s and early 1990s, everyone created handwritten action plans, and updating action plans was a tedious process. Now we insist that teams create electronic action plans that can be easily updated.

Norms. The final section on the first page of the action plan is a space for the team to list its norms. As we stated earlier in this chapter in the section on effective meeting practices, creating norms is one important task for teams to do, especially if the action team is formed from an existing team. Teams need to have explicit written norms that guide their behavior, including starting and ending on time.

We encourage teams to have norms in three main areas—the work, making decisions, and how members interact with each other. Norms about the work include norms about time, staying focused and on-task, being prepared, rotating leadership roles, and implementing decisions. Norms about decision-making focus on how teams make decisions and deal with disagreements. Norms about how members interact include norms about respect and no fault/blame, active listening, participation, interruptions, meeting environment (such as bringing drinks and/or food), dealing with absences, and reviewing their effectiveness as teams.

Each action team should develop its own set of three to five norms, but two norms are critical for all action teams—starting/ending on time and making decisions by consensus. Time is precious in schools, and every minute of the time allocated for action teams needs to be used effectively to improve teaching and learning. We emphasize making decisions in action teams by consensus for several reasons. Based on our principles for action teams, we encourage everyone to participate and for members to share responsibility both in the meetings and for implementing decisions made by the team. Making decisions by majority rule, rather than by consensus, undermines trust, sharing, equal participation, and follow-through. *The Radical Readers' norms address punctuality, staying focused, sharing responsibilities, and how they want to interact with each other.*

Once norms are established and agreed on, members should follow them. We encourage teams to

Using Team Norms

- Post them in their meeting room or on their meeting agendas
- Review them often
- Diplomatically confront behaviors that violate them
- Revise them as needed
- Give new members opportunities for input
- Use them to evaluate team performance

Confronting behaviors that violate norms is hard for educators who often feel that being "nice" is paramount. We encourage every member to feel comfortable gently reminding each other when a norm is not being respected. We also recommend that teams create and rotate process observer role to pay particular attention to how well the team is following its norms.

Second Page of Action Plan

The second page of the team action plan template focuses on data about student learning related to each student learning need the team addresses as it engages in cycles of learning and inquiry. The data section is designed to display data for one need for the time frame the group has decided to allocate to work on the need. Teams may add additional data sections if they work on more than one need or work on the same need for several blocks of time. The data sections are completed during Step 3, but we will explain here the purpose of each column.

First Column: Specific Student Needs. (*Completed at the beginning of each learning and inquiry cycle.*) Teams write in the first column the student need from the upper left box on page 1 of the team action plan that they want to address in the learning and inquiry cycle. If the need is complex with several subcomponents, such as "demonstrate the ability to gather and synthesize information," the team lists the subcomponents in the space under the need, such as "locate information, document source, take notes, summarize, and synthesize." *The Radical Readers listed the student learning need for their first learning and inquiry cycle as "increase ability to recognize cause and effect within a given passage."*

Second Column: Data Sources and Performance Levels. *(Completed near the beginning of the learning and inquiry cycle.)* In this column the team describes the type of pre-/post-assessments members will give students to document changes in student performance on the need being addressed and they specify what their criteria are for different levels of performance. Assessments are ones that members can use in daily work with students to collect data (rather than a once-a-year state or district test). The assessment tasks may be designed by the team or adapted from materials from textbook publishers and/or testing agencies. *The Radical Readers decided to use assessment materials on cause and effect from the STARS and CARS reading materials from Curriculum Associates.*

We suggest using three performance levels—GREEN = proficient or better, YELLOW = almost proficient, and RED = below proficient. The completed action plan in Figure 9.2 shows an example of a pre-/post-assessment and performance levels. Many schools decide to use the same performance levels their state uses in its assessments.

Third Column: Current Performance. *(Data entered usually within the third to fifth action team meeting of the learning and inquiry cycle.)* Current performance data are data about the target students' level of proficiency in the selected student learning need at the beginning of the learning and inquiry cycle and before the team members have started to introduce strategies to improve students' proficiency. Team members use the same rubric or other rating/scoring system to score their students' work and calculate the number and percentage of students in each members' targeted class or group that are GREEN (proficient and above), YELLOW (almost proficient), and RED (far below proficient). We recommend that teams disaggregate student performance data by student subgroup to determine if there are achievement gaps among subgroups. The current performance date is the date the current assessment is given to students. *The Radical Readers planned their pre-test on cause and effect at their second team meeting, administered the pre-test in the following week, and then shared and recorded their results on their action plan at their third meeting on September 20.*

Fourth Column: Target Performance. *(Calculated during the same meeting as the current data for the need is entered, or at the next meeting.)* We recommend that all action teams set short-term targets, not year-long targets, for improving student performance on specific learning needs. It is too hard to stay focused on a year-long target. Many teams set their target dates to coincide with the midpoint or end of a grading period. The target performance date is the date at the midpoint or end of the learning and inquiry cycle when the same assessment will be given to students to measure changes in student learning on the selected need.

Targets are specific and quantifiable and are described in the same way as the current performance data—number and percentage of students in each members' targeted class or group that are GREEN (proficient and above), YELLOW (almost proficient), and RED (far below proficient). We recommend that teams disaggregate student performance targets by student subgroup if there are achievement gaps among subgroups. These targets are SMART goals—specific, measurable, attainable but challenging, relevant, and time-bound—and should not be achieved just with "business as usual." *The Radical Readers set their end-of-cycle targets at the same meeting when they discussed their pre-test results. Initially, they thought they would be able to complete the cycle on cause and effect by mid-October. But as they started working with students, they realized they needed to do more with students and they extended the cycle until mid-November.*

Fifth Column: Actual Performance. *(Data entered around the date indicated as the Target Performance date.)* Actual performance data are data about the target students' level of proficiency in the selected student learning need at the midpoint or end of the learning and inquiry cycle and after the team members have introduced strategies to improve students' proficiency. Team members use the same assessments and the same rubric or other rating/scoring system that they used when they collected current performance data at the beginning of the learning and inquiry cycle. They calculate the number and percentage of students in each members' targeted class or group that are GREEN (proficient and above), YELLOW (almost proficient), and RED (far below proficient). If teams disaggregated student performance data by student subgroup in the current and target performance data, members should also disaggregate the actual performance data by subgroup. The actual performance date is the date the assessment is given to students. *The Radical Readers gave their post-test to students in mid-November. For two members, Joyner and Kagarise, their students exceeded their target goals. The other three classes almost reached their targets. Kagarise's students made the most growth, moving from a pre-test average of 47% to a posttest average of 87%. The team decided to switch to their second student learning need, drawing conclusions and making inferences, for their second cycle. They added a second data section to their action plan to track progress on their second student need.*

CREATING TEAM ACTION PLANS

The first major responsibility for teams is the selection of student learning needs the team will address. This step in the DMC, create a team action plan, is the second major task of each action team after teams are formed. The section describes a process for teams to follow to create their action plans, how action plans are used after this step in the DMC, and the other tool that action teams use to document their work—the team meeting log.

Here are the suggested steps for creating a draft team action plan using the template shown in Figure 9.1. We recommend giving these instructions in writing to teams before their first meeting and that the school leadership team

Steps for Creating a Team Action Plan in the DMC Step 2

model the steps below in a faculty meeting. A copy of these instructions is included in online Resource M. When the team meets to begin creating its action plan, the team recorder uses a laptop to record team decisions on a blank template as the team works.

1. Choose a name for your team, if you haven't already, to personalize your team and put this name at the top of your action plan. List team members.

2. If there is a schoolwide instructional focus, such as critical thinking or reading comprehension, write it in the space provided.

3. Reach consensus on three to five *norms* for your team that all members in the team will observe to increase your team's productivity and effectiveness and write these norms in the box on page 1 of the template. Use these norms in this meeting and in future meetings.

   Most teams have three types of norms:

   a. Norms about the work, such as stay focused; be prepared; bring necessary materials; do what we agree to do; start and end on time; and do what our students need us to do.

   b. Norms about making decisions, such as make decisions by consensus and explore questions and concerns before making decisions.

   c. Norms about working together, such as be active listeners; be positive; and bring food.

   While stating norms isn't the same as living the norms, if teams don't have norms in all three areas, they are more likely to slip into unproductive behaviors during meetings.

4. List the two or three *student learning needs* your team selected by consensus and list the number or code for the relevant state or district standards for each need.

5. Decide which student need will be the first need the team will address and put a star beside it.

6. Write in the space in the middle of the action plan an *essential question* that captures what you want to investigate. This could be considered the problem to be solved. An essential question guides the work of an action team and should encompass the specific student needs listed on the plan. Examples of essential questions are as follows:

   - *Reading:* How can we help our students improve their comprehension of what they read?
   - *Measurement:* How can we help our students develop and use measurement skills in all content areas?
   - *Problem Solving:* How can we help our students improve their ability to use problem-solving skills and strategies effectively?

- *Writing:* How can we help our students produce writing that is well organized and thoroughly developed and reflects use of effective language? (Murphy & Lick, 2005, p. 126)

7. If team members already have some knowledge about appropriate *instructional strategies or teaching practices* to use with the student learning needs the team selected, list these strategies in the box to the right of each student need. Once the team begins a learning and inquiry cycle, you will want to update this section with the strategies the team actually uses.

8. For each team member, list the *students you want to target* for the first student need the team has selected to address. You may choose an entire class or focus on a particular subgroup within the class. If you teach or work with different classes or large groups of students, choose one class or a manageable subgroup across several classes as a focus for your work with your action team.

9. List the *resources* that are available for the group to use. Think about resources that relate to what to teach, how to teach, and how to assess the student needs you have chosen. Consider material resources associated with the textbook and instructional/curriculum programs as well as materials received in workshops and courses or Internet resources. People are also important resources, including other teachers, instructional coaches, and district support personnel.

10. Congratulations! This completes the work of action teams to create a draft action plan.

11. Send electronic copies of the draft action plan to team members and to the principal or her or his designee for feedback. Post a copy of the action plan in the network folder for other action teams.

Teams Use of Their Action Plan After Step 2

As teams move to Step 3 of the DMC, implement learning and inquiry cycles to change practice and improve student learning, they will complete the sections of the action plan on teaching practices/instructional strategies used (page 1), student needs addressed, assessment tools and data on student performance (page 2), and will update the section on resources used (page 1).

Action plans should be updated at least after each learning and inquiry cycle. We have found that many teams forget to update their action plans during the year when they find new resources, identify new strategies, and collect data on student learning. While teams might choose to update their action plans more frequently, we recommend updating the plans as part of the team's end of cycle reflection.

In online Resource N, we provide a checklist for team action plans that action teams may use as they create and update their action plans and that the principal or designated readers for the action teams may use to guide their feedback to teams about their plans.

Team Meeting Log—Companion to the Team Action Plan

In Chapter 7, we discussed effective meeting practices for action teams. One of the practices described is keeping meeting minutes or a log. This section provides more information about the action team log.

We recommend that teams record in their logs the information they think an absent member would want to know:

- When did the team meet and who was present
- What they worked on during the meeting and key insights, decisions, and proposed next steps related to that work
- What members reported about classroom interventions members did since the last meeting and the impact on student learning and engagement
- What members decided to do in their classrooms between this meeting and the next one
- What questions or concerns members had
- What the details are for the next meeting—date, time, location, roles, agenda, and what to bring or prepare

In our work with schools over the past ten years, we have taken the meeting log template through several refinements to make it easier and simpler for team members to complete a meeting log during a meeting on a computer. Our latest version is shown in Figure 9.3 and in online Resource O. You will note that the sections of the log correspond to the bullets listed above.

There are two ways for a team to describe its work during a team meeting. The first is in the box at the upper left of the template, where teams can check the part of the learning and inquiry cycle that they addressed during the meeting. The second is the text box at the upper right of the template, where the recorder summarizes important points about their work. In online Resource P, we provide a checklist for team logs that action teams may use as they start preparing logs and that the principal or designated readers for the action teams may use to guide their feedback to teams about their logs.

We have found that there is no one perfect template for logs. We encourage schools to use our template for a full year before experimenting with alternative formats. In thinking about revisions, remember that each part of the log should be there for a purpose.

The team should rotate responsibility for being the recorder. The recorder

Role of the Team Recorder

- Writes down ideas as they are expressed
- Frames comments so they can be understood by all
- Checks accuracy of perceptions
- Helps give a sense of direction and completion
- Helps people feel their concerns have been heard

After meetings, the recorder e-mails members a copy of the completed log, sends a copy of the log to the principal or his or her designee, and posts a copy in the school's shared network folder for other action teams.

Figure 9.3   Action Team Meeting Log Template

Log for Team # /Name

School _____ Log # _____ Date _____ **Leader** _____

Members Present: _____

What specific student learning need did the team work on today? _____

Check the step on the inquiry cycle that best describes what the team did today.

	Describe what the team did today, including key findings (from research, data analysis, and examining student work), decisions, and insights.
____ Determine current student performance and set targets.	
____ Identify content and instructional strategies, develop expertise, and plan and practice interventions.	
____ Implement interventions, examine student work, assess impact, and plan next steps.	
____ Assess and reflect on end of the cycle/year results and plan for the next cycle/year.	
____ Update action plan.	
____ Other	

Did the team examine student work today? _____ If yes, who brought? _____

What resources/materials did members use during the meeting today? _____

Since the last meeting, describe the specific instructional strategies members used in their classrooms that were the focus of last meeting.

MEMBER	STRATEGY	STUDENT RESULTS

What have members agreed to do in their classrooms prior to the next meeting? _____

Is the team ready to share a proven strategy with the whole faculty? _____

Questions, concerns, and comments: _____

NEXT MEETING: Date _____ Time _____ Location _____ Leader _____ Recorder _____

Materials needed: _____

Focus: _____

Source: Adapted from *Schoolwide Action Research for Professional Learning Communities: Improving Student Learning Through The Whole-Faculty Study Groups Approach* (pp. 166–167), by K. H. Clauset, D. W. Lick, and C. U. Murphy. 2008, Thousand Oaks, CA: Corwin. Adapted with permission.

Each member keeps a hard copy or electronic notebook of his or her action team's work, including the action plan, the logs, and artifacts from meetings. Using the logs, a team can refer to past meetings and confirm why they decided to take a particular action. Members can see their progress in their relations with one another, their thinking, and their actions.

It is expected that the principal or his or her designee will review team logs and give regular, constructive feedback on the team's work. The log is not used in evaluations but as a tool for determining what outside support may be helpful or promptly addressing concerns of the team.

For action teams to be successful, they need ongoing feedback and support. There must be one or more people in the school, such as the principal, assistant principals, or instructional coaches, who are specifically designated to help action teams as they begin and go about their work. Teams need someone to answer a wide variety of questions and give suggestions on where to go for additional assistance.

Giving regular, timely, constructive feedback and responding to action teams' questions and concerns is a crucial part of leading the Change Creation system of action teams. In Chapters 10, 11, and 12, we expand on the responsibilities for leading action teams through Steps 3, 4, and 5 of the DMC.

SUPPORT FOR ACTION TEAMS ON THEIR TEAM ACTION PLANS AND LOGS

A key question is, "How do principals, school leadership teams, and district staff support action teams as they create and use their team action plans and logs?"

Feedback and Support on Team Action Plans

The team action plan is the single most important document that action teams produce. The action plan identifies the student needs a team will target and indicates what the team will do when it meets. If the plan is off target, the team will be off target. Action teams need to know immediately if their readers have questions or concerns about their action plans. Clearly written procedures for submitting the action plans to the principal or readers should be distributed to all staff when action teams are formed.

Guidelines for Action Plans

We recommend the following guidelines for team action plans:

- The first page of the team action plan is completed by the end of the third action team meeting and given to the principal (refer to the action plan template in Figure 9.1).
- The first page of the team action plan is reviewed by the principal or a designee, and written feedback is given to the team *before* the team meets again; the written feedback is given to the leader of the next meeting or to the entire team.

- The first page of the team action plan is revised at the fourth action team meeting, copied and given to each member of the team, and put in a public place or posted electronically.
- Team action plans are reviewed at the first cross-team sharing meeting. Each action team, or representative, is given a set of all action plans. At the next action team meeting, the representatives will share feedback on their action plan and what the other action teams are doing.
- After action teams create their initial team action plans, they update their plans at least at the end of every learning and inquiry cycle to add baseline data, targets, and actual results for each need they address, add new resources, modify or add data sources, review and modify their norms, if necessary, and instructional strategies used. Using electronic templates, action teams have the option to add revisions to the original action plan rather than rewriting it completely.
- Each time an action team revises its action plan, the principal or reader reviews the revisions against the earlier version and gives the team feedback, along with feedback on the log for the meeting when the revisions were made.
- Feedback may be written directly on the action plan, on a sticky note and stuck on the plan, in a memo on separate paper, in an e-mail message, or in a dialogue box on an electronic action plan form.

Since the draft action plan is a guide for team action, it is important that every team get constructive feedback on its plan before it starts a learning and inquiry cycle. Typical feedback includes positive reinforcement, suggestions regarding norms and resources, and questions or suggestions about the specific student needs the team plans to address and the instructional strategies and assessments it plans to use. This is a key responsibility of the principal and assistant principals, or a designated instructional coach.

Feedback by principals and other readers on action plans and logs is constructive, not evaluative. Its purpose is to help action teams be productive and successful and is not linked with the district's formal teacher evaluation system.

Strong action plans help ensure team success. The most important part is the student needs the team selects at the end of Step 1. The selected student learning needs should be those that are concrete and specific, important for the students the team serves, can be addressed through the content each member teaches or the work members do with students, require learning by team members, and all members agree to devote time and energy to address. If the selected student learning needs do not meet these criteria, teams run into problems in the cycles of learning and inquiry in Step 3. Table 9.1 below and the online Resource Q describe typical problems with each criterion, the impact on team effectiveness, and some solution strategies.

A second part of the action plan that helps create strong action plans are the norms the team creates. As noted above, teams should have norms about the work, making decisions, and working together.

In addition to receiving feedback from administrators, many schools organize a meeting for teams to share their action plans with other teams and

Table 9.1   "Strong" Student Learning Needs—Typical Problems and Solution Options

Criteria for "Strong" Student Learning Needs	Typical Problems	Solution Options
Concrete and specific	Big undefined needs, such as reading comprehension, writing, and student engagement are complex with many components, are hard to measure, and require more time to address than teams typically have.	Help teams to realize that they have selected big, undefined needs and encourage them to spend time to define the need, specify the specific skills, concepts, or behaviors that students should master, and select a specific component to address, such as one thinking skill, one reading comprehension strategy, one element of the writing process, or one element of student engagement. Every need selected should be measurable through assessment tasks or observation protocols that the members of the action team use in their classrooms or work settings with students.
Important for their students	If the selected need is not linked to important standards or if students already are proficient for the need, then team members will feel that spending team meeting time on this need is a waste of their time.	Help teams realize that the need they selected isn't important and invite them to select a different student learning need that is linked to important standards and in which the team's students lack proficiency.
Can be addressed through content/ work	If team members cannot envision how they can address the need through what they teach or their work with students, they will not contribute fully to the work of the team and will feel that the meetings are a waste of time.	(1) Help team members reframe how they think about their content or work with students to be able to address the need, such as how to work on vocabulary development, or problem solving in physical education classes; (2) invite the team to select a different student learning need that all members can address; or (3) consider moving a team member to another team that is addressing a more compatible need.
Requires learning	Team members select an "easy" need to address and "coast" in team meetings by sharing and using what they already know. They don't push themselves to find, learn, and master new content, instructional strategies, or assessment tasks to use with students, and their impact on student learning is negligible.	Encourage teams to select needs that are challenging for members and connect to their personal professional learning goals.
All committed to devote time and energy	Often members will say they agree to a student need just to be nice and have no intention of doing real work on the need. They are unproductive in team meetings and hamper the work.	Help team members to determine why they aren't fully committed to the need and address root causes. This may require helping the member reframe how they think about a need, the team selecting a different need, or moving the member to a different team.

receive feedback from peers. Online Resource R has a protocol for action teams to use to give each other feedback about their action plans. It is a modified version of the Tuning Protocol (Blythe, Allen, & Powell, 2008).

Feedback and Support on Action Team Meeting Logs

As action teams work to create their team action plans, they also start completing team meeting logs. The action team logs (see Figure 9.3) describe what a team does at an action team meeting, and the log should be consistent or aligned with the team's action plan. The log should be electronic. Principals use logs to give support, guidance, encouragement, and suggestions to action teams and communicate expectations. Clearly written procedures for submitting action team logs to the principal should be distributed to all staff when action teams are formed.

We recommend the following guidelines for action team logs:

> **Guidelines for Team Logs**

- Logs are completed during every action team meeting and copies made for all action team members to put in their team binders. The electronic log is posted or e-mailed to the principal and to others, as appropriate.
- Logs are sent to the principal or reader within 24 hours after an action team meets.
- Logs are reviewed and responded to by the principal or reader before the next action team meeting or on a rotating schedule.
- In reviewing logs, the reader compares the current log with the previous one to check for leader rotation, whether the team is meeting as scheduled, and whether the team is doing what they planned to do at the previous meeting. The reader also reviews the action plan to check to see if the team is working on needs listed in it and if it has been revised or updated.
- Logs have boxes at the bottom for readiness for sharing and questions or concerns from the action team that *must* be promptly responded to if the log is to have any credibility.
- Action teams attach artifacts, such as rubrics, assessment tools, data, strategies, samples of student work, and resources, to logs that document the work of the action team during the meeting.
- Feedback may be handwritten directly on the log, on a sticky note and stuck on the plan, in a memo on separate paper, in an e-mail message, as a different color text directly in the electronic document, or in a dialogue box on an electronic log form.

The challenge for leaders in giving feedback on team meeting logs is helping action teams move from discussion to action. Typically, when teams start to meet, their logs contain verbs such as discuss, share, and research. These verbs are safe, require no action, require no change, and they have little or no classroom impact on students.

So what do we want to see in logs? Action verbs, such as *design*, *build*, *compose*, *create*, *model*, *develop*, and *demonstrate*, that lead to the production of artifacts to which all members contribute, all members can utilize, and all members *do* utilize.

SUMMARY

Imagine action teams as teams of medical practitioners working to keep the children they serve healthy and free of disease. Action teams work to keep the students they serve learning and growing so that they will be college and career ready and responsible adults. Now imagine how you would feel as a patient if your medical team had no plan to keep you healthy and kept no records of the tests and the treatments they give you.

This is why action plans and team meeting logs are critical components of the process of the Change Creation system. Expecting teams to draft action plans as they begin their work together requires faculty to think about what they want to accomplish in their team meetings before they start the work of changing what they teach and how they teach to improve student learning. Throughout the school year, action plans serve as both a guide to future work and a record of accomplishments. Expecting teams to complete a log during each meeting holds teams accountable to their students. The collection of team logs over the year documents the work of the team and the decisions members have made. In subsequent years, logs are a resource to the team that created them if they continue to work on the same student learning needs and a resource to other teams working on similar needs.

This chapter focuses on the tasks involved in creating team action plans, explains how teams use their action plan after they create them, and introduces the companion to the team action plan, the team meeting log. It also describes how school and district leaders provide feedback and support for action teams as they create and use their action plan and meeting logs.

The next two chapters, Chapters 10 and 11 describe the work that action teams do to implement their action plans through cycles of learning and inquiry in Step 3 of the Action Teams DMC and how school and district leaders guide and support teams. Chapter 10 focuses on the first two parts of the learning and inquiry cycle, and Chapter 11 focuses on the last two parts.

Implementing Learning and Inquiry Cycles for Innovation and Improving Student Learning

10

Parts 1 and 2

This chapter addresses Step 3 in the Action Teams Decision-Making Cycle, implement learning and inquiry cycles to change practices and improve student learning, and examines in detail Parts 1 and 2 of the learning and inquiry cycle. It focuses on what teams need to do for each part of the cycle and how the principal and the school leadership team can ensure that the work of action teams in their learning and inquiry cycles leads to learning and innovation.

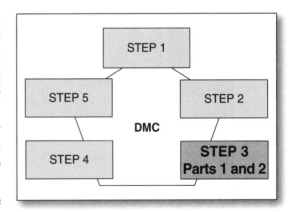

Step 3, as outlined below and in Figure 10.1, is the cycle of learn-plan-act-reflect and the heart of the learning and inquiry cycle that action teams follow. It is the *action* in action teams. This step also corresponds to the Learning and Inquiry Cycles Phase for building learning teams in Chapter 4. It is in this step that action teams move toward becoming the authentic (synergistic), comentoring, learning teams we described in Chapter 3 and reach the more advanced stages of team development, willingness and consequence, that were presented in Chapter 8.

IMPLEMENTING LEARNING AND INQUIRY CYCLES

Working independently, each action team implements learning and inquiry cycles by engaging in the following tasks, organized in four parts:

Part 1: Clarify the focus, determine current student performance, and set targets.

Part 2: Identify content and best practices, develop expertise, and plan and practice interventions.

Part 3: Implement interventions, examine student work, assess impact, reflect on lessons learned, and plan next steps.

Part 4: Assess and reflect on end-of-the-cycle results and plan for the next cycle.

Typically, if action teams form and create their action plans within the first two months of the school year, they can complete at least two learning and inquiry cycles within the school year. If action teams launch in the middle of the school year, they can usually only complete one cycle before the end of the school year.

Engaging in cycles of continuous improvement to increase educator effectiveness and results for all students is an essential element of the Learning Forward standard for learning communities (Learning Forward, 2011, p. 24). In the standard, Learning Forward describes the characteristics of each application of a continuous improvement cycle:

- The use of data to determine student and educator learning needs
- Identification of shared goals for student and educator learning
- Professional learning to extend educators' knowledge of content, content-specific pedagogy, how students learn, and management of classroom environments
- Selection and implementation of appropriate evidence-based strategies to achieve student and educator learning goals
- Application of the learning with local support at the work site
- Use of evidence to monitor and refine implementation
- Evaluation of results

Each of these characteristics is incorporated into the four parts of the learning and inquiry cycle that action teams implement. Action teams engaged in multiple cycles of learning and inquiry sustain the implementation of job-embedded professional learning when they

meet to learn or refine instructional strategies; plan lessons that integrate the new strategies; share experiences about implementing those lessons; analyze student work together to reflect on the results of use of the strategies; and assess their progress toward their defined goals. (Learning Forward, 2011, p. 45)

Figure 10.1 and online Resource S illustrate how teams move through the four parts of the learning and inquiry cycle.

Figure 10.1   The Learning and Inquiry Cycle for Action Teams

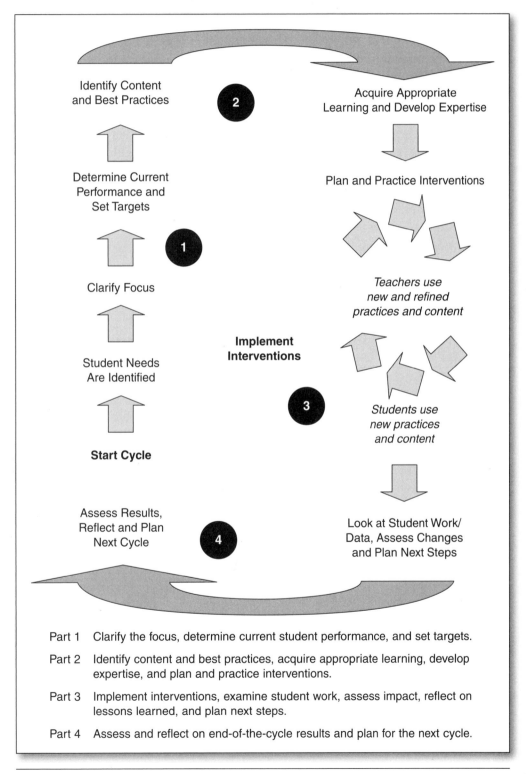

Part 1   Clarify the focus, determine current student performance, and set targets.

Part 2   Identify content and best practices, acquire appropriate learning, develop expertise, and plan and practice interventions.

Part 3   Implement interventions, examine student work, assess impact, reflect on lessons learned, and plan next steps.

Part 4   Assess and reflect on end-of-the-cycle results and plan for the next cycle.

Source: Adapted from *Schoolwide Action Research for Professional Learning Communities* (p. 57), by K. H. Clauset, D. W. Lick, and C. U. Murphy, 2008, Thousand Oaks, CA: Corwin. Adapted with permission.

This figure illustrates the learning and inquiry cycle that each action team follows. We shall provide an overview of the learning and inquiry cycle here and then give a detailed explanation for the first two parts in this chapter and the last two parts in Chapter 11.

The cycle begins in the lower left portion of the figure after "student needs are identified." These needs are the data-informed student learning needs each action team has decided to address in Step 1 and listed in their action plans in Step 2. At the start of a learning and inquiry cycle, each team selects, by consensus, *one* student need to focus on for their students for the cycle. Each team's cycle of inquiry begins with "clarify focus" and continues through "plan next cycle"—to start a new cycle but continue working with the same need or to start a new cycle working on a new need.

The first part of the learning and inquiry cycle is the part with the number *1* in the figure and has three tasks—clarify the focus, determine current student performance, and set targets. These three tasks build the foundation for the rest of the work in the cycle. *Clarify the focus* means that the team has to reach agreement about what the student learning need means for them and their students—what skills and concepts students must master and what students need to do to demonstrate proficiency with this need. The team may need to learn more about their need to find this information.

The next task, *determine current student performance,* means assessing how much their target students know about the selected need at the beginning of the learning and inquiry cycle. If team members do not have current performance data on the need for their students from school, district, or state benchmark assessments, the team will need to develop their own assessment tasks for students and a scoring rubric to score the tasks and identify levels of performance. After the team identifies or creates its assessment tasks for the selected need, they decide how they will administer the assessment, give it, score the resulting student work, and calculate the number and percentage of students in each subgroup, if applicable, at each performance level. They also examine samples of student work from students at each performance level to identify areas of strength and weakness to help them decide what specific skills and concepts to address in their interventions. Then, they meet again to review the results and *set targets,* the third task, for the changes each member expects at each performance level for his or her students by the end of the cycle.

The second part of the learning and inquiry cycle is the part with the number *2* in the figure and has three tasks—identify content and best practices, acquire appropriate learning and develop expertise, and plan and practice interventions. This is a major learning part of the learning and inquiry cycle.

First, team members need to learn about their students—who scored in each performance level on the beginning assessment and why. This examination and discussion of student work leads to decisions about what specific skills and concepts need to be addressed during the learning and inquiry cycle.

Next, each team identifies the content and best practices or best instructional strategies they can use to reinforce student strengths and address student weaknesses. The team may need to learn more about content and best practices related to their need to find this information. But identifying appropriate content and best practices is not the same as being proficient in using them with students. This leads to the second task in this part of the cycle, acquire appropriate learning and develop expertise. Team members plan their own individual and collaborative learning activities to learn new content and new instructional strategies. These activities may involve sharing resources, book study, observing other teachers, attending workshops, or inviting content area specialists and instructional coaches to meet with their teams. The third task, plan and practice interventions, takes place in team meetings as members decide what content and strategies to use with which groups of students, how to introduce and teach the new content and strategies, and how to assess for changes in student learning and engagement, and then, practice with each other what they will do in their classrooms with their students.

The third part of the learning and inquiry cycle is the part with the number 3 in the figure and has five tasks—implement interventions, examine student work, assess impact, reflect on lessons learned, and plan next steps. This is the action and inquiry part of the learning and inquiry cycle. The circular arrows on the right side of the figure illustrate the iterative nature of teachers working to implement interventions and using new practices and content in their classrooms, and then, coming back to their team meetings to (1) share observations about what worked and what didn't, (2) examine student work and data from scoring student work, (3) assess impact of these interventions, (4) reflect on lessons learned, and (5) plan revisions and modifications for the next round of teaching in their classrooms.

The action teams' interventions in their classrooms are analogous to laboratory experiments. To assess the impact of an intervention, a team needs to know, for each member and for each target class or group, what the classroom environment and the intervention were and how student mastery of specific concepts and skills changed from before to after the intervention. They also need to try out the intervention more than once with each class or group to determine whether they can get consistent results with the intervention. By engaging in this work, each team refines a set of effective instructional practices and content tailored to the specific needs of their students. These proven practices are then shared with other action teams.

After trying out interventions with students, examining results, making modifications, and repeating interventions, the team comes to the end of the time frame they have set aside for this learning and inquiry cycle and the fourth part of the cycle. The fourth part of the cycle is the part with the number 4 in the figure and has two main tasks—assess and reflect on end-of-the-cycle results and plan for the next cycle. This is another learning part of the learning and inquiry cycle.

At the end of the cycle, team members assess and reflect on end-of-the-cycle results by readministering the assessment tasks they gave their students at the beginning of the cycle, scoring the work samples with the same scoring rubric, and compiling results. Now is the time for the after-action review when the team reflects on both the effectiveness of their interventions and how well they learned and worked together during the cycle. The action team updates its action plans to indicate the final results, the strategies they implemented, and the resources they used.

Finally, it is time to plan for the next cycle. The team decides whether to continue working on the same need in the next cycle, if students have not achieved the targets set or certain subgroups of students are still struggling, or switch to another student learning need from the team's action plan, if the team is satisfied with the progress they made toward their targets. This is also a time for sharing the results, lessons learned, and best practices with other action teams.

With this overview of the learning and inquiry cycle, we shall now look at the first and second part of the cycle in detail.[1] For each part, we describe the specific tasks within each part and frame questions for action teams to consider while working on a task. We also present for each part a set of recommendations to action teams for improving success, suggestions for documenting and sharing their work on the part, and guidelines for the amount of time to spend on each task within each part. In a separate section, we alert leaders to the obstacles and opportunities within each part and provide practical advice to them about how to guide and support action teams through each part of the learning and inquiry cycle.

Part 1: Clarify the Focus, Determine Current Student Performance, and Set Targets

There are three tasks in this part—clarify the focus, determine current student performance, and set targets. These are important first steps in learning and inquiry because they help teachers define exactly what they should focus on as they research and design classroom interventions to improve student performance. Schmuck (2006) refers to inquiry that begins with data as "responsive action research," responding to the needs identified in the data (p. 32).

Clarify the Focus

Once an action team has decided which of its student learning needs to address first, the team's next task is to analyze the student need to determine the skills, knowledge, and attitudes students must have to demonstrate proficiency with regard to the need. For schools in the United States that are implementing the Common Core standards, this means teams analyze the relevant standards and the expected performance tasks.

Some questions to consider are the following:

- What are the content skills and knowledge required to demonstrate proficiency for the need?
- What should students be able to do with the skills and knowledge, and what are the performance tasks that demonstrate understanding?
- What is the level of quality that students should reach to demonstrate proficiency, and how do we assess student work for each performance task?

---

[1]Text about these parts of the learning and inquiry cycle is adapted from *Schoolwide Action Research for Professional Learning Communities* (pp. 58–68), by K. H. Clauset, D. W. Lick, and C. U. Murphy, 2008, Thousand Oaks, CA: Corwin. Adapted with permission.

Determine Current Student Performance

The next action team task is to determine for their students where they currently are with regard to the skills, knowledge, and attitudes that they must have to demonstrate proficiency. Setting realistic targets and measuring actual changes in student performance relative to specific student-learning needs depends on knowing where students are *now* on each of these needs. This is establishing a baseline or giving a pre-test.

Learning Forward (2011) emphasizes the importance of using data about student learning to guide the work of learning communities when they state "thorough analysis and ongoing use are essential for data to inform decisions about professional learning" (p. 36).

Usually, schools identify student-learning needs based on district or state assessment results for all of the students in the school. These data might be disaggregated, though, for groups of students identified by grade level, gender, income, ethnicity, English language proficiency, or special needs. However, these data are usually not organized by specific class or specific learning need, so teachers who have formed an action team around a set of student-learning needs identified with schoolwide data often don't have detailed information about how students in their classes this year perform relative to the student needs they have chosen to address. This is why it is important for action teams to have multiple sets of data and why Learning Forward (2011) states that

> data from multiple sources enrich decisions about professional learning that leads to increased results for every student. Multiple sources include both quantitative and qualitative data, such as common formative and summative assessments, performance assessments, observations, work samples, performance metrics, portfolios, and self-reports. The use of multiple sources of data offers a balanced and more comprehensive analysis of student . . . performance than any single type or source of data can. (p. 36)

As Learning Forward (2011) notes, data include student work samples. This is another reason for taking time to collect data on student performance relative to the chosen student needs—teachers may not have samples of student work directly related to the need.

Collecting current data on student performance involves developing or identifying an assessment task, creating a scoring checklist or rubric, deciding which students to assess, administering the task to students, evaluating student responses for levels of proficiency and areas of strength and weakness, and summarizing results. After the data are collected, the team updates page 2 of its action plan with the current student performance data for each member's students.

Action teams create two products when they conduct this initial assessment. The first product is the *quantitative data on levels of student proficiency.* Teams use these data to set improvement targets to achieve by the end of the grading period, semester, or year. The second product is the *qualitative data on areas of strength and areas of weakness* with regard to students' skills, knowledge, attitudes, and behaviors related to the learning need. Teams use these data in Part 2 to decide what to change in content and pedagogy to improve student performance.

Sometimes action teams discover in their analysis of current student performance that their students are more proficient in the selected student learning need than they thought they were. In this case, the team needs to decide whether to continue working with this need or to switch to a different need.

Some questions to consider in analyzing data on current student performance are the following:

- Which skills and concepts do they understand and how well?
- Which skills and concepts do they not understand and why?
- Are there different levels of understanding for different groups of students, and if so, why?
- Who are the students at each of our performance levels?
- How can we display and chart our students' performance throughout the learning and inquiry cycle?

Set Targets

After collecting and analyzing data on current student performance, the next action team task is to establish a target date and performance targets for expected improvements in student skills, knowledge, and attitudes relative to the student-learning need. This is an important task for action teams, because establishing targets for students in their classes gives action teams a clear goal for their work together and it connects action team goals for improving student performance to schoolwide and district performance goals. As noted earlier, Learning Forward (2011) expects learning communities to identify "shared goals for student and educator learning" in their cycles of improvement (p. 24). Our action team targets are the learning communities' shared goals.

Action teams often pick target dates that coincide with the end of grading periods, allowing sufficient time between the time they collect initial data and the target date for trying out interventions in classes and assessing their effectiveness. Action team targets are SMART learning goals—specific, measurable, attainable (but challenging), relevant, and time-bound (Conzemius & O'Neil, 2002). Team members set growth targets for their target students—who needs to move to a higher performance level and who needs to make measurable growth within a performance level? After each team member sets his or her target goals, the team updates page 2 of its action plan with the targets by performance level for each member's students.

Some questions to consider in setting performance targets are the following:

- As a result of our action team work, what improvements in student performance do we want to see for students at each performance level by the end of this learning and inquiry cycle?
- Who are the students we need to move from one performance level to another?
- Who are the students who need to show measurable growth within their current performance level?

Improving Success

We find that action teams are the most successful with this part of the learning and inquiry cycle—clarify the focus, determine current student performance, and set targets—when they do the following:

- **Work on one student need at a time.** Often action teams have identified several student-learning needs as a focus for their team's work. We strongly recommend that action teams start with one specific learning need and go through each part of the learning and inquiry cycle with that need before turning to a second need. Working on one need makes it much easier to stay focused and enables the team to see success within a reasonable amount of time.

- **Clearly define a student-learning need to specify the skills, knowledge, and attitudes students must be able to apply to demonstrate proficiency in the need.** This may require an action team to use external resources that define the skills and knowledge embedded within a need. Sometimes action teams are not sure which specific need is the most appropriate starting point for their students. In this situation, action teams can design an initial assessment to collect data on several related needs and use the results to help them decide where to focus.

For example, an action team has decided to focus on improving reading comprehension but is not sure with which aspect of reading comprehension students are having greater difficulty, identifying the meaning of unfamiliar words, or drawing inferences, or whether both are problems, but for different groups of students. The team could design a baseline assessment task that provides a reading passage with questions to answer. Some questions would relate to identifying the meaning of unfamiliar words, and others would address drawing inferences. For each student, the team would have two scores, an unfamiliar word score and an inference score. The team analyzes the scores for each teacher's class and decides which specific need to address first and which students to target. The data from the assessment becomes their current data.

- **Find or create a classroom assessment task and scoring rubric everyone in the team can use, even if teachers teach different content or grade levels.** One strategy is to model assessment tasks after state or district assessments. Many action teams create or use assessment tools and tasks modeled after the district or state assessments so that students are introduced to tools and tasks they will encounter on these assessments. Performance tasks are now being developed and published for the Common Core standards. For example, the Literacy Design Collaborative (2011) has developed a set of twenty-nine performance task templates and scoring rubrics for argumentative, narrative, or explanatory writing in English language arts (ELA), science, and social studies for teachers in Grades 6–12 that are aligned with the Common Core anchor standards in reading and writing and could be used to assess students' current proficiency with these tasks and their growth over time.

However, many current state and district assessments rely on multiple-choice questions, which are useful to determine levels of proficiency and the percentage of correct answers, but provide no information on what students were thinking about or understanding as they chose answers. We encourage action teams to supplement multiple-choice questions with other questions that ask students to explain orally or in writing why they chose one response over others. For instance, a math problem-solving team modified the instructions they gave students to ask them to explain the word *problem* before solving the problem to check on reading comprehension.

Don't reinvent the wheel! There are lots of websites with assessment tools, tasks, and rubrics available on the Internet. Check the materials in instructional programs used in your school or district in each content area for performance tasks and assessment rubrics. Tap into knowledgeable people in your action team, school, or district. Invite them to come to an action team meeting to share their expertise and resources. Many districts have content-area specialists who have resource materials that teachers can use to adapt or locate assessment tasks and rubrics.

- **Design the assessment task, instructions, and scoring guide so that they can distinguish different levels of performance, such as proficient, almost proficient, and struggling, and can elicit what students were thinking and understanding as they completed the task.** The power of action teams comes from the collaborative work. The best assessment tasks have a limited number of questions or prompts and require students to demonstrate their thinking and understanding. Since calculating class averages on an assessment task reveals little about differences in levels of student performance within a class, we recommend that action teams identify students by level of proficiency and by subgroup in schools with achievement gaps between student subgroups. From examining the resultant student work, action team members can both determine each student's level of proficiency and gain insights into why students are having problems with the need.

- **Use the same assessment tasks during the cycle to assess student progress.** Once a team creates an assessment task, the task can be used periodically, during the period the team is working on the need, to assess the effectiveness of interventions the team tries and, at the end, to determine whether students achieved their performance targets. Don't worry. Students won't memorize the assessment.

- **Set targets for improved student performance for students at each level of proficiency.** Performance targets should be in the same format as the baseline data. If the action team specifies levels of proficiency in the baseline data, then the team should set targets for students at each level. Create charts showing baseline student performance by proficiency level and relevant student subgroups for each teacher's class; then, create a composite chart for the action team and transfer information to the action team's action plan.

- **Keep for future reference all of the work students produce for the baseline assessment.** New questions often surface as an action team starts working on the need about what students understand, and the team may wish to reexamine the work samples.

Document and Share Work

Action teams document and share their work in this part of the learning and inquiry cycle in a variety of ways. They update their action plan to add their assessment tasks and summarize current student data and targets. They attach copies of assessment tasks, scoring rubrics, and data analyses to the action team log for the meeting in which they were discussed and keep copies in their action team binder or a digital folder. They keep samples of student work from the initial assessment for comparison with student work as the team monitors progress. Action teams share their work on clarifying their focus, determining current student performance, and setting targets in cross-team meetings and in faculty meetings, and data from these assessments and targets can be posted in teachers' classrooms for students to see.

Time Spent

Typical amounts of time to spend on tasks in this part of the learning and inquiry cycle are the following:

Task	Time Required
Analyze the student need for underlying skills, knowledge, and attitudes.	Part of one action team meeting (before the meeting, the team may need to identify resources that define the skills and knowledge embedded in the need)
Decide on an assessment task, instructions to students, scoring rubric, and data collection procedures.	Part of one action team meeting (if members search for tasks and rubrics between meetings)
Analyze data from initial assessment, both performance levels and strengths/weaknesses, and set performance targets by performance level.	One action team meeting (if data is organized before the meeting)

Part 2: Identify Content and Best Practices, Acquire Appropriate Learning, Develop Expertise, and Plan and Practice Interventions

This part has four tasks—identify content and best practices, acquire appropriate learning, develop expertise, and plan and practice interventions. This part directly relates to two Learning Forward (2011) characteristics of cycles of continuous improvement stated earlier, "professional learning to extend educators' knowledge of content, content-specific pedagogy, how students learn, and management of classroom environments" and "selection and implementation of appropriate evidence-based strategies to achieve student and educator learning goals" (p. 24).

Identify Content and Best Practices

After identifying in Part 1 students' current levels of proficiency with the learning need and analyzing their work to determine the problems students are having with the need, the team first has to identify the content skills and knowledge and instructional practices they will need to address the specific problems their students are having.

The question to consider is, "What do we need to change or strengthen about what we teach (the content) and how we teach (instruction and assessment strategies) to improve student performance relative to the specific student need we have identified?"

The beginning point for *identifying content and best practices* to use lies in digging deeper into the data about current student performance. Is students' lack of skill or knowledge due to students not being taught or students not remembering or not mastering the skill or knowledge?

For example, an action team has determined that their students are weak in identifying the meaning of unfamiliar words in a reading passage. In examining samples of student work, they realize that students are not recognizing prefixes and suffixes or compound words and are not using context clues to determine meaning.

The team might first ask their students whether their lack of ability in identifying the meaning of unfamiliar words was because they and former teachers hadn't taught students to recognize prefixes and suffixes or compound words and use context clues, or because students had been taught and either did not remember or could not apply what they had learned. The responses the team receives from students will help them to decide whether they need to teach new content or teach previously taught content in new ways for student mastery. They may even decide they need new ways to teach new content.

Action teams naturally share their own content knowledge, instructional practices, and experiences with students, but this is not the end to researching content and best practices. We expect every action team to increase its collective expertise regarding its student needs by seeking outside resources.

In the reading example, the team would seek resources to answer these questions: What do reading specialists and the research literature say are the different skills and knowledge that proficient readers use to find the meaning of unfamiliar words? What instructional practices have proved effective in helping students similar to our students become proficient with these skills?

There are many different kinds of resources teachers can use to build expertise. Resources can be the teachers' guides for instructional programs the school is implementing, or for materials connected with school and district initiatives, such as a writing initiative and ongoing professional development on differentiated instruction or quality teaching and learning. Resources can be found at state departments of education, professional associations, and on the Internet.

And resources are people, other staff in the school and district, or in other districts. Many districts have content and instructional specialists who can help action teams quickly identify content and effective practices. Teams can invite "expert voices" to an action team meeting to share their knowledge and skills. With each resource, the guiding question is, "How can this resource help us better teach our students in the areas where they need to improve?"

Some questions to consider in identifying content and best practices are the following:

- What are our strengths in addressing this need—what do we know we do that works?
- What are others already doing, or what resources already exist to address these needs?

Many schools and districts have multiyear initiatives to strengthen faculty knowledge of pedagogy and content related to student learning needs. Action teams can select specific student learning needs for which they can apply the strategies and knowledge they are already learning.

In the Hawthorn School District in Vernon Hills, Illinois, the district has invested heavily in building teacher expertise in six-traits writing and the Writer's Workshop. In the two middle schools, teachers formed several action teams to address student-writing needs and apply what they had been learning in their professional development.

This is an example of linking ongoing professional learning and action teams with improving student achievement, just as Joyce and Showers recommended in their 2002 book, *Student Achievement Through Staff Development.*

The point to keep in mind is that time set aside for ongoing professional learning can be used to support the need of action teams to develop expertise without having to add more time for action team meetings.

Acquire Appropriate Learning and Develop Expertise

Once the team has identified the specific content and instructional strategies that address the student problems, the members need to learn about and develop their expertise with the new content and strategies. This is job-embedded, targeted professional learning. The action team system is built around the assumption that student learning will not improve significantly if team members keep doing what they regularly do with students. Teachers in action teams focus on improving what they teach and how they teach. As we stated in Chapter 3 with the Universal Change Principle, improvement requires learning.

In schools implementing the Common Core standards or striving to prepare all students to be college and career ready, educators will have to change the way they teach to ensure that students master the new standards (Sawchuk, 2012, p. S12). Findings from the Measures of Effective Teaching Project illustrate the challenges (Kane and Stager, 2012, pp. 16–25).

In analyses of videotapes of 7,491 lessons or lesson segments from classroom teaching by 1,333 Grade 4 through 8 ELA and math teachers from six urban districts participating in the Measures of Effective Teaching Project, the findings indicate that less than half of the lessons were scored at the proficient or higher performance levels for teaching competencies in mathematics that required engaging students in rigorous instruction, using questioning strategies or an investigation/problem-based approach, and "student participation in meaning making and reasoning." Similarly in ELA, most lessons were not scored proficient or higher in competencies such as "intellectual challenge and classroom discourse" and "explicit strategy use and instruction and modeling." Across both content areas, teachers struggled with competencies such as "analysis and problem solving, regard for student perspectives, quality of feedback, instructional dialogue, content understanding," and "using assessments in instruction."

The implications of these findings are that action teams addressing student learning needs connected to Common Core standards will need significant opportunities for high-quality professional learning that teaches and models the expected teaching behaviors. Thomas Guskey is quoted in the *Education Week* special report (Sawchuk, 2012, p. S15) as stating, "The PD will have to model very clearly the kinds of activities we want teachers to carry forward and use in their classrooms." Guskey's expectation for professional development is consistent with the Learning Forward standards for professional learning.

Learning Forward insists on designing and implementing high-quality job-embedded learning experiences by, with, and for learning communities. In their learning designs standard they state the following:

- Educators are responsible for taking an active role in selecting and constructing learning designs that facilitate their own and others' learning.
- Through active engagement, educators construct personal meaning of their learning, are more committed to its success, and identify authentic applications for their learning.
- Learning designs that occur during the workday and engage peers in learning facilitate ongoing communication about learning, develop a collaborative culture with peer accountability, foster professionalism, and support transfer of the learning to practice.
- Effective designs for professional learning assist educators in moving beyond comprehension of the surface features of a new idea or practice to developing a more complete understanding of its purposes, critical attributes, meaning, and connection to other approaches. (Learning Forward, 2011, pp. 41–42)

Proactive action teams plan for their own professional learning and get help as needed. One strategy that action teams use to acquire appropriate learning is to see instructional practices in action, rather than just reading about them. The team arranges to visit another teacher who is successfully implementing the practice to watch her or him use the practice. Another is to model practices in action team meetings by teaching the practice to colleagues before deciding whether to try the practice out on students. But the kinds of changes in teaching that the Common Core standards will require is more than what individual action teams may accomplish on their own. School, district, and state leaders must be proactive in planning high-quality professional learning opportunities for action teams so that they can improve student learning on the Common Core standards.

Developing expertise in new content or a new instructional strategy comes with only practice—first within the action team meeting and then with students. So the task of developing expertise blends into the next task, *plan and practice interventions.*

Some questions to consider in acquiring learning and developing expertise are the following:

- In which areas do we need to develop our expertise?
- What do we need to do to develop our expertise?
- What resources or support do we need to help us acquire appropriate learning and develop our expertise?

Plan and Practice Interventions

The central part of the learning and inquiry cycle is the intervention—what teachers and other action team members try out with students to help improve student understanding and learning. A classroom intervention could be introducing new content knowledge and skills or an instructional strategy, such as mnemonics or graphic organizers, to help students learn important concepts. An intervention could be for part of a class period or for a week or more. In action team meetings, members help each other think through and plan interventions.

Planning an intervention builds on lesson and unit planning. As in planning lessons or units, an action team planning an intervention has to think about and articulate what they expect students to think and do during the intervention, and as a result of the intervention, what they will do before, during, and after the intervention, what resources they will need, and how they will assess changes in student learning as a result of the intervention.

If the team is using a new strategy with students, they need to practice in team meetings to develop their proficiency with the strategy. The action team provides a safe environment for teachers to practice skills, design lessons together using the skills, observe each other, and feel support in determining why some lessons go well and others do not. To ensure skill development at a level that gives teachers the confidence to appropriately and effectively use the skill in the classroom, action team members may need to develop a plan that will include several training components. A plan for skill development includes (a) the theory that explains and supports the importance of the skill, (b) demonstrations of the skill for participants, (c) opportunities to practice the skill to a reasonable competency level, and (d) peer coaching to solve implementation challenges (Joyce & Showers, 2002, pp. 73–74).

Assessing changes in student learning means comparing student performance before and after an intervention—a pre-test and a post-test. For example, to assess how well students can compare and contrast before and after introducing Venn diagrams, an action team would ask students to complete and compare and contrast task before the intervention and after, making sure that the content and vocabulary in both tasks were of similar levels of difficulty. If the group has just collected data on student performance, the initial data might be used as the pre-test data.

Action teams are also concerned about assessing the effectiveness of the interventions they try with students—Is this an effective intervention for improving student performance? This extra dimension means that teams first need to pay attention to how the intervention is actually implemented and how students actually respond during the intervention. Then, the team compares what actually happened with what they planned to determine what changed and how these changes may have affected results with students.

A second approach to assessing the effectiveness of an intervention focuses on students learning, interest, and engagement. In teaching students to use a new strategy, like a graphic organizer, teachers want students to develop proficiency in using the strategy and improve their performance on the need, such as writing, by using the strategy independently, without teacher prompting, and proficiently. Improved learning encompasses both of these elements. The effects an intervention has on student interest and engagement can only be observed while the intervention is taking place.

If the team is using a new intervention with students, its members need to practice in team meetings to develop their proficiency with the new content or strategy in the intervention. The team can also videotape, field-testing the new intervention with students, or visit each other's classrooms when the intervention is first being introduced. At follow-up team meetings members share what they observe and plan how to improve the intervention. We encourage action teams to tell their students about their action team work and their interventions. Teams discover that students appreciate their teachers and efforts to improve teaching and learning.

Some questions to consider in planning and practicing interventions are the following:

- What will we do in our classrooms with students to improve their performance?
- If we are adapting or using a strategy that others have used, how do we need to modify it to reflect the characteristics/needs of our students?
- What do we expect students to think and do during this intervention?
- What changes do we expect to see in samples of student work?
- How will we monitor what happens during the intervention—what we do and what students do?
- How will we assess the effectiveness of the intervention—on student understanding and on student interest and engagement?

Improving Success

We find that action teams are the most successful with this part of the learning and inquiry cycle—identify content and best practices, acquire appropriate learning, develop expertise, and plan and practice interventions—when they do the following:

For "Identify Content and Best Practices"

- Have a clear understanding of their students' strengths and weaknesses regarding the student learning need

- Identify instructional strategies that can be used with students across content areas and grade levels

For "Acquire Appropriate Learning and Develop Expertise"

- Seek expert voices outside of their action team to increase their expertise in the identified student learning need
- Focus on just-in-time professional learning. Successful action teams resist the urge to spend the entire year identifying new content and best practices and developing expertise and begin using new learning in classrooms so that students benefit. Rather than trying to learn everything they can about a need, they limit the scope of research and learning and plan to learn more in the next action cycle. For example, a reading action team might limit its focus to just teaching decoding in its first action cycle.
- Recognize different levels of expertise. Many action teams have members who teach different grades and subjects and have different levels of expertise about the content and best practices related to the need the team is addressing. Different members of the team may need different levels or types of professional development to develop their expertise around the group's need. Some members may need additional support or need to watch another member teach the strategy before they feel comfortable enough to try the strategy in their classroom. The school's instructional specialist can be a helpful resource.
- Use protocols. When members bring articles or other written resources into action team meetings to share, members can use text-based discussion protocols to structure the discussion, such as the Jigsaw protocol developed by Aronson (Aronson & Patnoe, 1997) or the Final Word protocol, developed by Averette and Baron (n.d.).

For "Plan and Practice Interventions"

- Keep the interventions manageable. Start with a simple intervention to keep the work reasonable and to build confidence in executing the parts of the learning and inquiry cycle.
- Use backwards planning. First, define what you want students to think and do to demonstrate their improvement with regard to the learning need after you have tried the new intervention; then, build the intervention activities to accomplish this. This is the *backwards design process* introduced by Wiggins and McTighe (1998).
- Create the assessment tasks, tools, and scoring rubrics—and try them out on each other—before starting the intervention.
- Select assessment tasks for the intervention that are similar to the assessments used to collect initial data. This will help you determine whether students have improved since the initial assessment at the beginning of the cycle.
- Plan to teach the intervention more than once to see if students respond differently the second or third time.

- Let students know that you are engaged in learning and inquiry to help them and involve them as coresearchers by developing strategies to capture their reactions and thinking as they participate in the intervention.
- Plan to use other action team members or a video camera to observe the intervention with students. It is hard to watch students carefully when one is trying out a new intervention and remember all the mid-course corrections one makes in teaching in new ways. Action team members help each other by observing students during an intervention. Teachers also may set up a video recorder to tape student activity during the intervention and review the tape later, either individually or in the next action team meeting.

Document and Share Work

Action teams document and share their work in identifying content and best practices and acquiring learning in a variety of ways. They let their principal and other action teams know that they are looking for resources. They list sources for content and instructional best practices in the resource section of the action plan and keep copies of materials found in action team binders or digital folders with logs of the meetings in which the materials were shared and discussed. They invite other action teams to join them at learning sessions they have arranged, share copies of research and best practices with action teams working on similar needs and at faculty meetings or cross-team meetings, put copies in the school's resource center in the faculty room or library, and post copies and web links to the school's action team website or electronic portfolio.

Action teams document their work with interventions by attaching copies of lesson plans, assessment tasks, scoring rubrics and observation tools they create for the intervention to the logs of the meetings in which these items were developed or discussed and save copies of these documents in their action team binders or in digital folders. They share these materials with colleagues at cross-team meetings, grade-level or content-area meetings, and faculty meetings. They also place copies in the school's resource center or post them on the school's website.

Time Spent

Typical amounts of time to spend on tasks in this part of the learning and inquiry cycle are the following:

Task	Time Required
Decide in what content and practices members need to build their expertise and plan how to acquire it.	One action team meeting
Share resources and discuss implications for students.	One to two action team meetings, depending on the scope of inquiry
Develop expertise in content and promising practices.	One to two action team meetings plus visits with teachers using the practice
Plan and practice the intervention.	One to two action team meetings, including modeling the practice
Plan assessment and observation.	One action team meeting

SUPPORTING LEARNING AND INQUIRY CYCLES FOR INNOVATION AND STUDENT LEARNING

A key question is, "How do principals, school leadership teams, and district staff support implementing learning and inquiry cycles for innovation and student learning?"

The purpose of these cycles of learning and inquiry is to produce, as Learning Forward describes in its implementation standard, "changes in educator practice and increases in student learning." They go on to say, and we firmly agree, that "this is a process that occurs over time and requires support for implementation to embed the new learning into practices" (Learning Forward, 2011, p. 44).

What does this support entail? As schools move to Step 3 in the Decision-Making Cycle, implement learning and inquiry cycles, they are engaged over most of the school year in the work of the action teams to improve teaching and learning in their work with students. In this "after-the-launch phase," a guiding coalition or school leadership team needs to continue to communicate the vision of the Change Creation system and action teams, empower others to act on the vision, and eliminate obstacles to change (Kotter, 1998). They also need to begin working on other Kotter principles, such as planning and creating response to short-term wins, and consolidate improvements and produce more changes. In this section, we will elaborate on specific ways leaders can guide and support action teams as they move through the first two parts of the learning and inquiry cycle by focusing on obstacles and opportunities for change. In Chapter 11, we will focus on how leaders can guide and support action teams as they move through the third and fourth part of the learning and inquiry cycle.

Part 1: Clarify the Focus, Determine Current Student Performance, and Set Targets

Each of the three tasks in this part of the learning and inquiry cycle presents potential obstacles to action teams, as well as opportunities for new learning.

Clarify the focus of their selected student learning need is the same conversation that teachers have when they try to figure out what a new district, state, or Common Core standard means for what students need to know and do to demonstrate proficiency. ELA and mathematics teachers may be more familiar with this process than teachers in other content areas because of the prevalence of standards-based assessments in ELA and mathematics. Leaders may need to assist action teams by providing resources that help teams better understand the content behind the student learning needs they have selected and by modeling a process for analyzing a need for its knowledge, skill, and performance requirements.

A big obstacle for many action teams is creating common formative assessments to use to *determine current student performance* with the selected need at the beginning of the learning and inquiry cycle. Teams may spend many weeks trying to create or locate the "perfect" assessment tool. We strongly encourage action teams to keep it simple and experiment and revise rather than spending extended time perfecting an assessment.

To collect data on students' level of proficiency with the need, areas of strength and weakness, and their thinking processes, the action team needs to give students in their classroom a task to perform that requires students to use the facts, skills, and concepts required by the need. At each step in designing the task, an action team makes choices that affect the nature and quality of the data collected. Choices include such things as the reading level, vocabulary, and content of the prompt, the types of questions asked, and the work that students do. Teams do not have to create totally new assessment tasks. They can copy and modify passages and questions from textbooks, supplementary materials, Internet resources, or state and district tests.

One challenge we find in schools is that teachers often rely on multiple-choice questions to assess student proficiency. While multiple-choice questions can be easily used to compute the number of right and wrong responses, they don't help teachers understand why students chose the answers they did. We encourage teams to ask students to explain their thinking and to show which parts of the prompt they used to formulate their answer. As a consequence, we recommend having fewer items on the assessment but with more detail.

Another challenge to creating common assessments arises if members of a team are working on the same need but teach different subjects or grade levels. We recommend that teams create a common template for the assessment, such as prompt to read and types of questions to answer, and then modify the reading level and the content of the prompt to reflect the appropriate grade or subject.

To help teams create common assessments, some districts have established item-banks with assessment questions that teachers can access, and schools offer "clinics" for teams during team meeting times. Schools also convene cross-team meetings so that teams may share assessment tools and get feedback from other teams.

We have found two obstacles with action teams in *analyzing student performance data and setting targets*—superficial analysis and either forgetting to set targets or setting targets too low. There is a tendency in teams to want to move quickly to identify and implement new strategies without carefully analyzing the data and student work samples from collecting current student performance data. In moving from assessment to action, it is important for action team members to attach student names to the students at each performance level:

- Who are our proficient students, and what do we need to do to help them maintain and improve their proficiency?
- Who are our students who are almost proficient, and what do we need to do to help them reach proficiency?
- Who are our struggling students, and what do we need to do to help them reach proficiency?

Leaders can guard against teams moving too quickly to action by introducing protocols for data analysis and asking teams to share their analyses of their data before moving to Part 2. Learning Forward (2011) explicitly calls for leaders to provide "support in the effective analysis and use of data" (p. 36).

Some teams, in the eagerness for action, either forget to set targets for gains in student learning by the end of the learning and inquiry cycle or set targets too low. Challenging, but attainable, targets are important because they provide a focus for the team's work, a sense of urgency, and they signal that the team has to learn new content and strategies, build expertise, and go beyond "business as usual" to achieve them. To set performance targets, each member of a team has to think about each of her students at each performance level and decide who needs to move to a higher level and who needs to grow within the level. Leaders can support this goal setting by providing data templates that help team members organize their data and set targets and by encouraging teams to display their current data and targets in their classrooms for students to see. We find that making data public is a good motivator for students.

Part 2: Identify Content and Best Practices, Acquire Appropriate Learning, Develop Expertise, and Plan and Practice Interventions

Support for action teams in this part of the learning and inquiry cycle focuses on empowering teams to act on the vision and planning for and creating short-term wins. The main focus of this part of the cycle is learning, and school and district leaders must guide and support that team learning. Launching action teams creates "demand-driven" professional learning—the learning that action teams need to acquire to be able to engage proficiently in cycles of inquiry and to strengthen their practice regarding the student learning needs they are addressing.

Most teachers in action teams are comfortable sharing with each other content, instructional strategies, and resources that they have already used. But some action teams have difficulty *identifying content and best practices*, particularly if they are working in a cross-discipline action team. Members may know through data analysis that a need is important for their students, but may not have had training or experience in the content, pedagogy, and assessment strategies related to the need. Even if the team is skillful at searching the Internet, they may still need advice and recommendations from content area and/or instructional specialists to help them identify key knowledge and effective strategies from the research literature and acquire useful human and material resources. Teams get bogged down and discouraged if they can't find good resources quickly. Helping action teams build their capacity to locate and select appropriate content and best practices is empowering for team members and a short-term win that builds enthusiasm for the work ahead.

Finding resources to support professional learning in action teams is a key role for school and district leaders. With the shift to Common Core standards in many states, it is imperative that school, district, and state leaders help action teams find the resources they need to build their own expertise with the standards and the teaching strategies these standards require.

Learning Forward (2011) makes this point in its resources standard:

> Technology and material resources for professional learning create opportunities to access information that enriches practice. Use of high-speed broadband, web-based and other technologies, professional journals and books, software, and a comprehensive learning management system is essential to support individual and collaborative professional learning. Access to just-in-time learning resources and participation in local or global communities or networks available to individuals or teams of educators during their workday expand opportunities for job-embedded professional learning. (p. 33)

Once teams have identified content and best practices that fit their student learning need, leaders at the school and district level can further empower teams by helping teams to *acquire appropriate learning and develop expertise.* One way to accomplish this is to allocate funds to support professional learning opportunities for action teams through the work of in-school coaches and specialists, book study, participating in workshops, courses, and webinars, and accessing online professional development (PD) resources such as PD 360 from the School Improvement Network or PD In Focus from ASCD. Another strategy that many schools and districts use is to identify excellence and expertise within the school or district and support visits to other teams or to teachers in other schools by arranging substitutes or covering classes.

The challenge for leaders is to ensure that team learning leads to team action and action this year, not some time in the future. Learning Forward (2011) in its leadership standard states, "leaders hold themselves and others accountable for the quality and results of professional learning" (p. 29). As Guskey (2000) reminds us, professional learning adds value when the learning is applied by educators in their work with students and leads to improvements in student learning.

This happens for action teams when they *plan and practice interventions* in their action team meetings. Leaders support the application of professional learning by making expectations clear, providing support to teams in planning interventions, and looking for evidence of interventions in classroom walkthroughs.

SUMMARY

This chapter has described and illustrated the first two parts of the learning and inquiry cycle in which action teams engage as they address student learning needs.

Part 1: Clarify the focus, determine current student performance, and set targets.

Part 2: Identify content and best practices, acquire learning and develop expertise, and plan and practice interventions.

For each part, we explained why the part is important, described what action teams need to do to implement the part successfully and document and share their work, and suggested time allocations that action teams might consider. We also described the kinds of obstacles action teams might encounter as they engage in these two parts of the learning and inquiry cycle and how school and district leaders can guide and support action teams.

The focus for action teams in these first two parts of the learning and inquiry cycle is on learning and planning. Action teams learn about the content and pedagogy associated with their selected student learning need. By giving students tasks to do, they learn about their students' current performance with the learning need, both in terms of their level of proficiency and their strengths and weaknesses. Action teams learn about the resources available to improve student proficiency with the need and develop their expertise with content and instructional strategies so that they can use that expertise with students. And action teams plan and practice interventions that they will use in their classrooms.

For each of these tasks, action teams will need active, timely, and differentiated guidance and support from school and district leaders. The Change Creation system requires demand-driven professional learning, learning that is directly linked to the goals of each action team and to the learning needs of each member of the team. The transition to Common Core standards in the United States and the associated demands for significant changes in what and how teachers teach increases the importance and urgency for ensuring that every action team is a learning team.

The next chapter, Chapter 11, focuses on the third and fourth part of the learning and inquiry cycle:

Part 3: Implement interventions, examine student work, assess impact, reflect on lessons learned, and plan next steps.

Part 4: Assess and reflect on end-of-the-cycle results and plan for the next cycle.

Implementing Learning and Inquiry Cycles for Innovation and Improving Student Learning

11

Parts 3 and 4

This chapter continues to address Step 3 in the Action Teams Decision-Making Cycle, implement learning and inquiry cycles to change practices and improve student learning. It examines in detail Parts 3 and 4 of the learning and inquiry cycle, and it focuses on what teams need to do for each of these parts of the cycle and how the principal and the school leadership team can ensure that the work of action teams in their learning and inquiry cycles leads to learning and innovation.

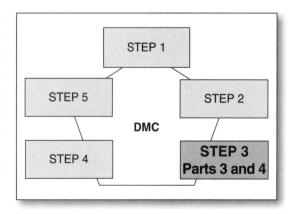

IMPLEMENTING LEARNING AND INQUIRY CYCLES

Step 3 is the cycle of learn-plan-act-reflect and the heart of the learning and inquiry cycle that action teams follow. It is the *action* in action teams.

Working independently, each action team implements learning and inquiry cycles by engaging in the following tasks, organized in four parts:

Part 1: Clarify the focus, determine current student performance, and set targets.

Part 2: Identify content and best practices, develop expertise, and plan and practice interventions.

Part 3: Implement interventions, examine student work, assess impact, reflect on lessons learned, and plan next steps.

Part 4: Assess and reflect on end of the cycle results and plan for the next cycle.

In Chapter 10, we described and illustrated how action teams move through each part of the learning and inquiry cycle (see Figure 10.1 on page 155). We also explained the first two parts in detail and highlighted for leaders the obstacles inherent in these first two parts and the opportunities for empowering action teams to learn and innovate.

In this chapter, we focus on Parts 3 and 4.[1] We describe the specific tasks and frame questions for action teams to consider while working on each task. We also present recommendations to action teams for improving success, suggestions for documenting and sharing their work, and guidelines for the amount of time to spend on each task. Finally, we alert leaders to the obstacles and opportunities and provide practical advice about how to guide and support action teams through each part.

Part 3: Implement Interventions, Examine Student Work, Assess Impact, Reflect on Lessons Learned, and Plan Next Steps

This part is the *action and reflection component* of the learning and inquiry cycle—implement interventions, examine student work, assess impact, reflect on lessons learned, and plan next steps.

Implement Interventions

The first task in this part, implementing interventions with students, is the *action* in action teams. While implementing interventions, team members keep track of what they do and the adjustments they make, either through a journal or by videotaping an intervention, such as a lesson. They collect student work samples and monitor students' interest and engagement in activities. Results of what and how teachers teach are mirrored in what students do. Students give back to us, in some way, what we have given them or led them to do, or what they have discovered. It is this work that guides the teacher's work. Teacher action is grounded in student action that is grounded in teacher action. This process is an

---

[1]Text about these parts of the learning and inquiry cycle in the following sections is adapted from *School-wide Action Research for Professional Learning Communities* (pp. 70–81), by K. H. Clauset, D. W. Lick, and C. U. Murphy, 2008, Thousand Oaks, CA: Corwin. Adapted with permission.

iterative cycle. As we mentioned in Chapter 10, Learning Forward (2011) also emphasizes action and reflection by learning communities when they apply "their learning . . . at the work site" and use "evidence to monitor and refine implementation" (p. 24).

To assess the impact of an intervention, an action team needs to know, for each member and for each class or group, what the classroom environment and the intervention were and how student mastery of specific concepts and skills changed from before to after the intervention. They also need to implement the intervention more than once with each class or group to determine whether they can get consistent results with the intervention. This is the heart of the inquiry process that action teams follow—*learn-plan-act-reflect*—learning about research-based content, pedagogy, and assessment for their selected student learning need, planning interventions in their action team meetings, acting on the plans with students in their classrooms, and then reflecting on the results and planning next steps back in their action team meetings. While Parts 1 and 2 of the learning and inquiry cycle emphasize the *learn* and *plan* actions, Parts 3 and 4 emphasize the *act* and *reflect* actions. Action teams also learn and plan as they experiment with interventions in Part 3 and examine student work, assess impact, and plan next steps. Figure 11.1 illustrates this iterative cycle.

Two techniques that action team members use to document the classroom environment during an intervention and the actual implementation of the intervention are to videotape the intervention or invite another action team member to observe and document.

Figure 11.1 The Action Team Learn-Plan-Act-Reflect Cycle

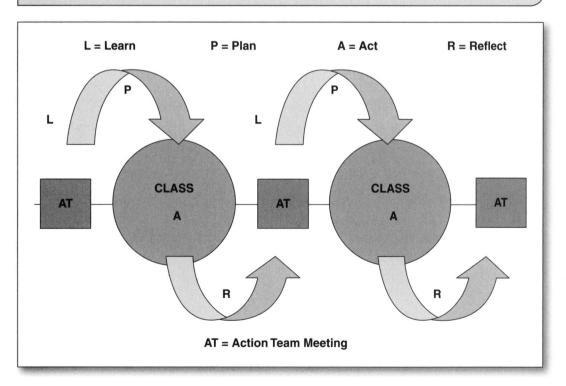

L = Learn   P = Plan   A = Act   R = Reflect

AT = Action Team Meeting

To assess changes in student mastery of skills and concepts, action team members use pre-tests and post-tests. They also assess the quality of work products produced during the intervention. Learning Forward (2011) reinforces this expectation in the data standard,

> at the classroom level, teachers use student data to assess the effectiveness of the application of their new learning. When teachers, for example, design assessments and scoring guides and engage in collaborative analysis of student work, they gain crucial information about the effect of their learning on students. (p. 37)

Pre-tests and post-tests enable action team members to determine if there are any changes in student mastery after an intervention. Both tests should be similar in design and should assess the specific skill(s) and concept(s) addressed in the intervention. Depending on the skills and concepts addressed, pre-tests/post-tests may be the same as the initial assessment task used in Part 1 of the learning and inquiry cycle, a part of the task, or an entirely different assessment.

Some questions to consider about implementing interventions are the following:

- How well are we implementing this intervention, and what can we do to improve our proficiency with this intervention?
- What adjustments did we make in the intervention as we implemented it, and why did we make these adjustments?
- What effects are the interventions having on student interest and engagement?
- How might we improve this intervention when we use it again?

Examine Student Work, Assess Impact, Plan Next Steps

After the interventions, the action team meets to reflect on their interventions, examine student work, look at student performance data obtained from assessment tasks, assess what changed and why, and plan next steps. Looking at data and work samples helps the action team identify in which areas students are improving and where students are still struggling. The advantage of collaboratively looking at student work and student performance data is that each action team member brings different perspectives to the data and work samples.

Looking at samples of student work collaboratively as a team is a basic strategy that all action teams should use. One key precept of looking at student work collaboratively is that less is more. In a 45- to 60-minute action team meeting, the team might examine only a small number of samples of student work, such as all members examining one student's work or each member examining work from a different student on the same assignment. The work samples have no names and no grades or teacher marks on them to influence the team's conversation about the work. Teachers look at student work for evidence of critical thinking, knowing skills, facts and concepts and being able to apply them, and misconceptions and patterns in errors. They also look for evidence that the student understood the assignment task and instructions. The recorder summarizes the insights gained from examining student work either on the team meeting log or a separate form, such as the one shown in the online Resource T.

A second key precept is the use of protocols to guide the examination of student work and structure the team's conversation. Murphy and Lick (2005) state that

> A protocol consists of agreed-upon guidelines for a conversation and it is this structure that permits a certain kind of conversation to occur. . . . A protocol creates a structure that makes it safe to ask challenging questions of each other; it also ensures that there is some equity and parity in terms of consideration of each person's issues. (p. 145)

There are a number of different protocols for looking at student work. See, for example, McDonald, Mohr, Dichter, and McDonald (2003) and the Looking at Student Work website by the National School Reform Faculty (www.lasw .org/protocols.html). Action teams decide at the preceding meeting what work will be examined, how many samples, which protocol to use, and who will be the presenting teacher, facilitator, recorder, and timekeeper.

Some questions to consider in examining student work are the following:

- What does this work tell us about what students are thinking, and what questions does it raise?
- What does this work tell us about students' understanding of important skills, concepts, and attitudes, and what questions does it raise?
- What does this work tell us about the performance task we asked students to do or our teaching, and what questions does it raise?
- What does this work tell us about students' interest and engagement in the task, and what questions does it raise?
- What are the implications of what we see, or of the questions we raise, for our next steps?
- Are the interventions we are trying out in our classrooms helping students build and demonstrate understanding?

In an action team meeting, teachers assess the impact of interventions both by examining student work samples and by sharing the data on student performance that they have from pre- and post-assessment tasks given to students in relation to a specific intervention. They also share copies of the assessment task and the scoring guide or rubric used to evaluate the student products. Teachers format and label data so that they are easy to understand and, wherever possible, disaggregate the data by importance or relevant student subgroups and present data by proficiency levels rather than letter grades.

In analyzing the data, the action team first focuses on what they see in the data (e.g., patterns, trends, and outliers) and for similarities within and among groups of students. Then, they shift to discussing what might be the causes behind significant patterns, trends, and differences or similarities in the data, in terms of what and how the intervention was implemented and what students were and were not doing and understanding.

Even if there are changes in learning from the pre-test to the post-test, these changes may not be the result of the intervention. To rule out this possibility, study-group members assess the quality of the work students do during the intervention. For example, if the intervention involves using a graphic organizer, the teacher reviews students' completed graphic organizers, assesses how well each student mastered the use of the graphic organizer, and compares these results with the changes in the student's learning between the pre-tests and post-tests.

Some questions to consider when examining data about student work before and after the intervention are the following:

- Did the intervention improve student understanding and performance?
- Was the intervention more or less effective in improving student performance than other practices or strategies?
- Are all of our students improving at the same rate?
- Why are some students improving more slowly or more rapidly than others?
- What changes do we need to implement to help students who are still lagging?

Reflecting on lessons learned answers the "so what" question: What have we learned, and what further improvements do we need to make during this learning and inquiry cycle?

This is a logical extension of the preceding tasks, examining student work and assessing impact. It begins with summarizing what happened—whether or not there were changes in student learning, interest, and engagement as a result of the intervention.

Next, the action team uses the information gathered from teacher observations and from looking at student work samples and performance results to develop explanations for why the changes did or did not occur and for why the intervention may have yielded different effects for different students. In this task, the action team is revising or updating its understanding about why students had problems with this need in their initial assessment.

Finally, the team plans next steps. If the intervention was unsuccessful or partially successful in improving student learning, the team could decide to modify and improve the intervention and try it again with students, perhaps focusing on students who did not improve. They can also decide to keep working on the same need but try a different intervention now that they have a better understanding of their students' needs.

If they decide the intervention was successful and they have met their student performance targets, the team may be ready to set higher targets and continue working on the same need.

If the team meets its performance targets in one need, it can choose to move on to the next learning need and start a new action inquiry cycle.

Regardless of what the action team decides to do next, the team should plan strategies for helping students maintain and use the proficiencies they have developed.

Some questions to consider in reflecting on lessons learned and planning next steps are the following:

- As a result of this intervention, in what areas have students improved and why?
- In what areas have students not improved and why?
- Which students are improving and in which areas and why?
- Which students are not improving and in which areas and why?
- How have the results from this intervention changed our thinking about our students' strengths and weaknesses?
- What improvements should we make in this intervention?
- How can we become more proficient in this intervention?
- Is this intervention effective enough to share with other teachers?

Improving Success

We find that action teams are the most successful with this part of the learning and inquiry cycle—implement interventions, examine student work, assess impact, reflect on lessons learned, and plan next steps—when they do the following:

For Implement Interventions

- Assess student learning and understanding before and after each intervention.
- Document the adjustments each teacher makes to the intervention as they implement it. Like any good researcher, teachers need to document what really happens in classrooms, both by the teacher and students, when trying out an intervention. Some teachers use two-column notes with the left-hand column for notes taken during or immediately after the intervention and the right-hand column for reflections, analyses, and connections. Others videotape the intervention to analyze in team meetings.
- Involve students in the learning experiments. Involving students as participant-observers as teachers try out interventions in classes encourages them to be more conscious of, and reflective about, their own learning and provides the action team with more information about how interventions are affecting students.
- Teach the intervention more than once to see if students respond differently the second or third time.
- Observe each other teaching the intervention and debrief and refine the intervention.
- Monitor student interest and engagement, as well as their work, using colleagues or a video camera to help capture and observe student reactions.

For Examine Student Work and Assess Impact

- Plan in advance for a meeting on looking at student work or looking at student data so everyone knows the purpose of the meeting and has the materials they need to be productive.
- Use protocols for looking at student work samples and examining data from pre- and post-intervention assessments.
- Since detailed data analysis for an entire class takes time, select a sample of students, representing different subgroups and proficiency levels, and limit the detailed data analysis to this sample of students.
- Compare the findings from looking at data derived from scoring student work to the findings from looking at student work.
- Take time in their discussions of student work and performance data to summarize key findings and implications before ending the meeting.
- Look at student work over time. Instead of trying to look at student work from an entire class of students, monitor student work over time from a representative sample of students, such as a higher-performing student, a student approaching proficiency, and a struggling student. Create portfolios for each student being tracked with work samples, data, and reflections from students and the action team about their work.
- Create charts to track students' performance over time on the learning need.

For Reflect on Lessons Learned and Plan Next Steps

- Use lessons learned to revise interventions and plan to test the revised interventions with students.
- Identify and record lessons learned and next steps from one intervention before starting on another intervention.

Document and Share Work

Action teams document their implementation of interventions for two purposes—to bring information back to their action team meetings to help the team assess the effectiveness of the intervention and, if the intervention is effective, to be able to share detailed information and teaching tips with other teachers. Teachers keep their observations and notes in a journal or in field notes in their action team binder.

In addition to their own observations, teachers collect student-work samples and students' performances on the assessment tasks. Teachers will want to bring back to their action teams both data about student performance and samples of student work for the next step in the action inquiry cycle, looking at student work and data.

Action team members attach data about student performance on assessment tasks and samples of student work to the action team log for the meeting in which the work and data were discussed, and they place copies in their action team binders. The action team logs provide space for summarizing action team conversations about looking at student data or looking at student work and decisions regarding next steps.

Action teams share the interventions they used and their findings with other action teams at cross-team meetings, grade-level or content-area meetings, and faculty meetings. Many schools have processes for sharing among all staff effective practices identified and tested by individual action teams and for incorporating these practices into the school's improvement plan.

Time Spent

Typical amounts of time to spend on tasks in this part of the learning and inquiry cycle are the following:

Task	Time Required
Implement interventions.	Implementing and monitoring interventions takes place in classrooms with students, not in action team meetings. Therefore, interventions occur between action team meetings. However, the team may want to schedule a meeting to revise an intervention, based on the reactions to students while members are using the intervention and results from looking at student work and performance data.
Look at student work.	One action team meeting for in-depth conversations about one to three samples of student work. In a longer time block, members could examine several sets of work samples. Action team members should decide at the preceding meeting who will bring work and whether a protocol will be used.
Look at student data.	One-half to one action team meeting to analyze student performance data from assessment tasks. Action team members should decide at the preceding meeting who will bring the data and whether a protocol will be used.
Reflect on lessons learned and plan next steps.	This discussion could either be included in a meeting focused on looking at student work samples or data, or scheduled at a follow-up meeting.

Part 4: Assess and Reflect on End-of-the-Cycle Results and Plan for the Next Cycle

This part, *assess and reflect on end-of-the-cycle results and plan for the next cycle,* is a new part that we have added to the learning and inquiry cycle to emphasize the importance of reflection and planning at the end of each cycle of learning and inquiry, not just at the end of the year. Reflection after action is an integral part of team learning and is essential for improving team effectiveness. This is also the last task in the Learning Forward cycle of continuous improvement, evaluate results and plan the next cycle (Learning Forward, 2011, p. 24).

Assess and Reflect on Results and Plan for the Next Cycle

At the end of the cycle, team members assess and reflect on end-of-the-cycle results by readministering the assessment tasks they gave their students at the beginning of the cycle, scoring the work samples with the same scoring rubric, and compiling results. This is the time for the after-action review when the team reflects on both the effectiveness of their interventions and how well they learned and worked together during the cycle. They update their action plans to indicate the final results, the strategies they implemented, and the resources they used. Finally, it is time to plan for the next cycle. The team decides whether to continue working on the same need in the next cycle, if students have not achieved the targets set or certain subgroups of students are still struggling, or switch to another student learning need from the team's action plan, if the team is satisfied with the progress they made toward their targets.

This is also a time for sharing the results, lessons learned, and best practices with other action teams. At the end of the year, teams typically discuss whether they want to stay together for the following year or disband to become members of new teams.

Some questions to consider in assessing and reflecting on end-of-the-cycle results and planning for the next cycle are the following:

- How has our work with students changed as a result of the expertise we have developed with this student learning need?
- What impact have we had on student learning, and why did we have this impact?
- Which interventions are best practices that should be shared with other teams?
- If we repeated this cycle, what would we do differently to get better results?
- How have our processes for working together as a team improved over this cycle?
- What are the implications of our work this cycle for our next cycle, both in terms of the student need we address, and how we work together?
- What are our lessons learned from this cycle that we can share with other action teams?

Improving Success

We find that action teams are the most successful with this part of the learning and inquiry cycle—assess and reflect on end-of-the-cycle results and plan for the next cycle—when they

- Reflect on what has changed and the reasons why with regard to team processes, members' work with students, and student learning
- Schedule a separate meeting for an end-of-cycle review and use a protocol to guide their review
- Present their results, best practices, and lessons learned to other teams

Document and Share Work

Action teams document their end-of-cycle results on student learning in their action plan and update their action plans to reflect resources and instructional strategies used in the cycle. They document their reflections, lessons learned, and plans for the next cycle in their action team meeting log.

Some schools organize an end-of-cycle sharing by action teams at a cross-team meeting or a faculty meeting. For example, each action team prepares a trifold display that describes the team's student learning need, interventions used, results, lessons learned, and next steps.

Time Spent

Typical amounts of time to spend on tasks in this part of the learning and inquiry cycle are the following:

Task	Time Required
Assess and reflect on end-of-the-cycle results.	One action team meeting
Plan for the next cycle.	Part of the action team meeting to assess and reflect on results from the cycle
Prepare to present results, best practices, and lessons learned.	One action team meeting

SUPPORTING LEARNING AND INQUIRY CYCLES FOR INNOVATION AND STUDENT LEARNING

A key question is, "How do principals, school leadership teams, and district staff support implementing learning and inquiry cycles for innovation and student learning?"

In this section, we will elaborate on specific ways leaders can guide and support action teams as they move through the third and fourth part of the learning and inquiry cycle by focusing on obstacles and opportunities for change.

Part 3: Implement Interventions, Examine Student Work, Assess Impact, Reflect on Lessons Learned, and Plan Next Steps

Teams are eager to try out new content and strategies with students. The challenge lies in how they *implement interventions* and what they learn from the interventions. It is easy to be superficial in planning and implementing interventions and the impact on student learning is often disappointing. As we stated earlier, action teams are conducting experiments when they implement interventions with students, and they should pay attention to and document both what they do and how students respond. Many teams use video cameras or other team members in their classrooms to document an intervention so that they can discuss and analyze the intervention back in a team meeting. Leaders should expect to see evidence of these analyses in the team meeting logs and the artifacts teams collect. The other key components of any intervention are the assessments and scoring guides that team members use to collect evidence of student learning during the intervention. Leaders should review assessment tasks and scoring guides and provide timely constructive feedback to teams. Helping teams implement quality interventions through just-in-time training, feedback, and support creates short-term wins and empowers teams.

Action teams are expected to *examine student work* collaboratively, regularly, and rigorously as they engage in interventions with students in order to assess the impact of these interventions on students' engagement, thinking, and mastery. Yet many teams lack the skills to do this and do not see the value of looking at student work together. This is a key area of professional learning for action teams, and school leaders need to assess faculty expertise and provide training, modeling, and guided practice to strengthen teams' capacity to use protocols proficiently to examine student work and to identify and act on the implications both for improving the interventions and for providing follow-up support for students. This speaks to one of the Learning Forward outcomes for professional learning—to "model and engage educators in practices they are expected to implement within their classrooms and workplaces" (Learning Forward, 2011, p. 50).

Teams often forget that making time for reflection during and after implementing interventions with students is *action*. Teams cannot become more effective if they do not reflect on their work. This is why we ask action teams to discuss, after looking at student work or analyzing data, "what have we learned?" and "now what are we going to do based on this learning?" Leaders must teach, model, inspect for, and celebrate making time for reflection and planning next steps both during learning and inquiry cycles and at their end. It is, as Donald Schön said in his 1983 book, becoming the reflective practitioner.

Leaders also recognize that reflecting on team accomplishments and experiencing success at achieving team goals help to build full and genuine acceptance of the Change Creation system of action teams as an effective vehicle for improving practice and increasing student learning. As team members see that their collective learning and action lead to desired changes, their sense of efficacy increases, and they are less likely to resist involvement in action teams. In Chapter 3, we discussed resistance to change and pointed out that the proof of the value of the change initiative lies in seeing results.

Part 4: Assess and Reflect on End-of-the-Cycle Results and Plan for the Next Cycle

Just as making time for reflection is a challenge for action teams during learning and inquiry cycles, it is also a challenge at the end of the cycle. Educators are accustomed in their work with students to moving from one marking period to the next without even pausing. The best strategy for leaders to use to ensure that action teams take the time to *assess and reflect on end-of-the-cycle results and plan for the next cycle* is to create a calendar for action team meetings that explicitly designates end-of-cycle reflection and planning meetings. Coupled with arranging time for reflection, leaders should remind action teams that they expect to see action teams update their action plans and describe their reflections and planning decisions in their meeting logs.

The end of each cycle is a time to share and celebrate short-term wins. Many schools set aside time at the end of each learning and inquiry cycle to share and celebrate the work of action teams—their results, lessons learned, and best practices. They also put information about action team accomplishments in faculty and parent newsletters.

SUMMARY

This chapter has described and illustrated the third and fourth part of the learning and inquiry cycle in which action teams engage as they address student learning needs.

Part 3: Implement interventions, examine student work, assess impact, reflect on lessons learned, and plan next steps.

Part 4: Assess and reflect on end-of-the-cycle results and plan for the next cycle.

For each part, we explained why the part is important, described what action teams need to do to implement the part successfully and document and share their work, and suggested time allocations that action teams might consider. We also described the kinds of obstacles action teams might encounter as they engage in these two parts of the learning and inquiry cycle and how school and district leaders can guide and support action teams.

The focus for action teams in these last two parts of the learning and inquiry cycle is on action and reflection that leads to more learning and planning. Action team members act in their classrooms or work settings with students to implement the interventions they planned and practiced in their team meetings. They act to assess the impact of their interventions on students' learning, interest, and engagement. They act to document how interventions are implemented and the context for the intervention. They reflect on the information they collect about their interventions. They examine samples of student work and reflect on the impact of the interventions on student work and the implications for next steps. They analyze data about student performance, interest, and engagement and reflect on the results and implications for the next round of interventions. At the end of a cycle, the team reflects on what they have learned and accomplished and makes plans for the next cycle— whether to continue working on the same student learning need with the same students or to shift focus to another need with the same target students or different students.

The challenge for leaders in guiding and supporting action teams in these parts of the learning and inquiry cycle lies in the quality of action teams' work in documenting, assessing, and reflecting on interventions. The key to disciplined inquiry by action teams to improve student learning isn't simply "doing" the intervention. It is about determining whether interventions are effective in improving student learning, what conditions enhance or inhibit success, and how to replicate the intervention both by the same action team and by other teams. This is why it is so important for action teams to document, assess, and reflect. But teams are not skilled in this disciplined inquiry. They will need active guidance, feedback, and support from their leaders to develop their capacity to do these tasks and to persevere.

The time action teams spend in learning and inquiry cycles is most of the school year. It is during this time that action teams become true learning teams and the school becomes a learning community.

The next chapter, Chapter 12, focuses on the last two steps in the Action Teams Decision-Making Cycle—Step 4, assess the impact of action teams' work on teacher practice and student learning, and Step 5, share results and best practices and apply lessons learned.

Assessing the Impact of Action Teams and Sharing Results and Best Practices

12

This chapter addresses the last two steps in the Action Teams Decision-Making Cycle (DMC)—Step 4, assessing the impact of action teams on teacher practice and student learning, and Step 5, share results and best practices and apply lessons learned. It focuses on what each team needs to do to assess its own impact on teacher practice and student learning and how the principal and the school leadership team can assess schoolwide impact on teacher practice and student learning. It also focuses on the importance of sharing results and best practices at the end of learning and inquiry cycles and at the end

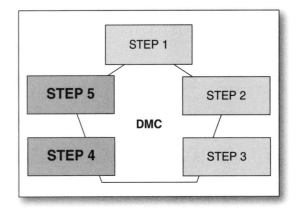

of the year, as well as creating mechanisms to ensure that teams learn from each other and that lessons learned are applied throughout the school. Both of these steps are crucial for the school if it is to become a genuine learning community.

In the end-of-the-year review process, teams look back on their work for the year to ask, "So what have we learned and accomplished?" In addition, the school assesses how well the system of action teams has functioned during the year and answers the "So what?" question about the collective work of all the action teams. The assessment and reflection in Step 4 of the DMC is the "so what" that leads directly to the "now what" of Step 5—share results and best practices and apply lessons learned.

ASSESSING THE IMPACT OF ACTION TEAMS ON TEACHER PRACTICE AND STUDENT LEARNING

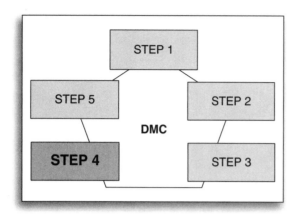

Action teams cannot improve the quality of their work and their impact on their practice and on student learning without assessing and reflecting on the work they have done. We expect action teams to assess and reflect at the end of each learning and inquiry cycle, and we expect teams to conduct an end-of-the-year review.

Our expectations for action teams link closely with the two Learning Forward Standards for Professional Learning that focus on data and outcomes. As we stated in Chapter 7, the purpose for creating action teams is to improve educator practice and student learning through cycles of professional learning and inquiry. The Learning Forward standard on outcomes states "with student learning outcomes as the focus, professional learning deepens educators' content knowledge, pedagogical content knowledge, and understanding of how students learn the specific discipline" and "learning for educators that focuses on student learning outcomes has a positive effect on changing educator practice and increasing student achievement" (Learning Forward, 2011, pp. 49–50).

Neither individual action teams nor the school as a whole can assess whether they are making progress in improving educator practice and student learning without using data. The Learning Forward data standard emphasizes using data to evaluate professional learning and indicates, "at the school level, leadership teams use data to monitor implementation of professional learning and its effects on educator practice and student learning" (Learning Forward, 2011, p. 37). And, the Learning Forward standard on data echoes Kotter's statements about the importance of short-term wins that demonstrate success, "evidence of ongoing increases in student learning is a powerful motivator for teachers during the inevitable setbacks that accompany complex change efforts" and "ongoing data collection, analysis, and use, especially when done in teams, provide stakeholders with information that sustains momentum and informs continuous improvement" (Learning Forward, 2011, p. 37).

As we described in Chapter 11, at the end of each learning and inquiry cycle, team members assess and reflect on end-of-the-cycle results by readministering the assessment tasks they gave their students at the beginning of the cycle, scoring the work samples with the same scoring rubric, and compiling results. This is the time for the after-action review when the action team reflects on both the effectiveness of their interventions and how well team members learned and worked together during the cycle. They update their action plans to indicate the final results, the strategies they implemented, and the resources they used. Finally, it is time to plan for the next cycle. The action team decides whether to continue working on the same need in the next cycle, if students have not achieved the targets set or certain subgroups of students are still struggling, or switch to another student learning need from the action team's action plan, if it is satisfied with the progress it has made toward its targets.

In the end-of-the-year review, action teams reflect on what they have learned and accomplished during the year. We also expect the whole faculty to assess how well the system of action teams has functioned during the year. These actions provide the "so what" that leads directly to the "now what" of Step 5—share results and best practices and apply lessons learned.

The above reflection is guided by a set of questions for individual action teams and the whole school.

For individual action teams:

> **Questions for End-of-the-Year Reflection**

- How has our students' performance improved in the specific student learning needs we addressed?
- How did our teaching practice improve as a result of our action team work?
- Does our action plan, with revisions, accurately reflect what we did this year?
- What have we learned from other teams?
- How have we improved our strategies for acquiring professional learning?
- How have we improved our ability to implement cycles of learning and inquiry?
- Has the quality and synergy (i.e., teamwork) of our work together improved?
- Are our meetings more effective and productive?
- What should we improve if we continue together next year?

For the school:

- Has student performance on state, district, and schoolwide assessments improved as a result of our action teams' work?
- Has teacher practice improved as a result of our action teams' work?
- How well were action teams supported in developing their action plans and implementing their inquiry cycles?
- How well did we as a school do in following the action team guidelines?
- How effectively have we shared the work of our action teams among teams and with students, parents, and other schools?
- How effective were our strategies for supporting professional learning by action teams and their application of that learning?
- Have we provided effective time and resources for action teams?
- What should we improve for next year's action teams?

Assessing the Impact of Individual Action Teams

Individual action teams are asked to assess and report on the types of activities the team engaged in, the perceived benefits of the action team's work to its members and to students, changes in student learning on the needs it addressed, changes in teacher and team practice, and how well it has implemented the action team process guidelines (see Resource U for a sample set of forms). Action teams also review and update their action plans to ensure that the plans accurately reflect their work during the school year.

Some schools use online survey tools, such as Survey Monkey, www.surveymonkey.com, to electronically collect and compile data from teams. These tools reduce the amount of time leaders need to send in compiling and transcribing reflections and survey responses from action teams.

Assessment data from individual action teams is aggregated and shared with the entire staff and discussed at a cross-team meeting or faculty meeting. Data from action teams on student performance on specific student learning needs are used at the beginning of the next school year as schools begin the DMC anew with Step 1, identify student learning needs and form action teams.

Connecting Changes in Classroom Student Performance to Changes on School, District, and State Assessments

Action teams use classroom assessments as their primary vehicle to monitor changes in student learning. But, it is important to ask whether the impact of action team work on student learning can be seen in student-performance results on schoolwide, district, and state assessments. This question is linked to the larger research issue about demonstrating the impact of classroom practices on student achievement. Examples of this research are the meta-analyses referenced in *Classroom Instruction That Works* (Dean, Hubbell, Pitler, & Stone, 2012) and *Visible Learning* (Hattie, 2009) and the findings from the Measures of Effective Teaching (Kane & Stager, 2012) discussed in Chapter 10.

Questions for Linking Action Team Results to School, District, and State Assessments

The short answer to whether action team results can be seen in school, district, and state assessments is, "Yes, but it can be difficult." The questions that determine whether results seen in classroom assessments can be directly linked to student performance on school, district, or state assessments are the following:

- Is the student learning need addressed by an action team also addressed in school, district, and state assessments at the same level of specificity?
- If the action team has members who teach at different grade levels but all work on the same student need (e.g., a team of Grades 2, 3, and 4 teachers working on "making inferences"), is the student need addressed in school, district, and state assessments at the same level of specificity for the different grade levels represented in the action team?
- Is the classroom assessment task used by the action team to gauge changes in student learning similar to the assessment task used in school, district, and state assessments?
- For the student learning need, are there at least three or four assessment items in the assessments so that a student's proficiency with the need is based on more than one question?
- Did the students assessed by the action team also take the school, district, or state assessments?

- Did the students assessed by the action team also take the school, district, or state assessments *after* the action team completed a learning and inquiry cycle on the need?
- Can data on individual student performance on individual assessment items be retrieved from the school, district, and state assessments?
- Can data on individual student performance on individual assessment items from the school, district, and state assessments be linked with their teachers in the action team?

If the answers to the questions above are all "Yes," then it is possible to compare an action team's student performance data from their classroom assessments with data on school, district, or state assessments.

The challenges are illustrated in a 2006 study of thirteen teams in two elementary schools in Franklin County Public Schools, located in central North Carolina (Clauset, Lick, & Murphy, 2008, pp. 126–135). Clauset found that none of the six cross-grade teams had district benchmark data on specific reading skills for all of their classes because different skills were assessed at each grade level. Three of the six cross-grade teams had data for at least one member of the team, but one of these teams only had data on one question for one class. Three of the seven grade-level teams had data for all their classes, but the other four grade-level teams had no district data because the skill was not assessed at their grade level. The number of assessment items for a specific skill on the district assessment varied from one to ten items, so even if a teacher had district data there may not have been enough items to gauge proficiency. Despite these challenges, Clauset did find that teams' results for student learning on classroom assessments were comparable to results on the grade level district benchmark assessments where benchmark items matched teams' selected student needs.

It was impossible to link classroom data on student performance from any team with performance data on the North Carolina End of Grade Reading Tests because North Carolina only reported data by broad concept strands,[1] such as cognition (sequence events, main idea, context clues, author's purpose), interpretation (make inferences, draw conclusions), and critical stance (compare and contrast). Each strand (North Carolina Department of Public Instruction, 2005) also provided assessment items that ask students to demonstrate other reading skills (p. 6). Therefore, student performance on a strand encompasses more than the needs addressed by an action team. During this period, the state did not provide, as other states do, release items, item analyses, or performance on specific North Carolina Learning Standards.

Hopefully, as the use of data warehouses increases, action teams as well as individual teachers can use data from school and district benchmark assessments to improve student learning. Many districts are introducing reading, writing, and math benchmark assessments that are aligned with state standards, administered two or three time a year, and return diagnostic

---

[1]The North Carolina Department of Public Instruction has since modified the categories it uses to report performance in reading to align them with the Standard Course of Study, but they are still broader than the learning needs action teams address.

data to teachers within weeks instead of months. Action teams can use the benchmark data to compare student performance with the results from their classroom assessments.

Assessing the Schoolwide Impact of Action Teams

Three sets of data support schoolwide evaluation of the action team system: (1) data from individual action teams, (2) staff feedback on implementation of the system, and (3) status on the Action Teams Rubric. In online Resources U, V, and W, we have provided tools school leadership teams might use to collect these data. These tools are examples of one of the expectations contained in Learning Forward's standard for the implementation of professional learning, "Individuals, peers, coaches, and leaders use tools and metrics to gather evidence to monitor and assess implementation" (Learning Forward, 2011, p. 44).

As mentioned in the preceding section, the first set of data is assessment data from individual action teams on team activities, the perceived benefits of the action team work to its members and to students, changes in student learning, changes in teacher and team practice, and implementation of the action team process guidelines is aggregated and shared with the entire staff and discussed at a cross-team meeting or faculty meeting.

Staff feedback on implementation of the system is the second set of data for evaluating the system. Periodically evaluating the system of action teams and acting on the recommendations build faculty confidence in the system, as is emphasized in the Learning Forward standard on implementation—"Leaders create and maintain a culture of support by encouraging stakeholders to use data to identify implementation challenges and engage them in identifying and recommending ongoing refinements to increase results" (Learning Forward, 2011, pp. 44–45).

One source of feedback on implementation is the feedback to readers during the year on the quality of their feedback and support for action teams. A second source is the feedback on issues and concerns voiced at cross-team or at faculty meetings. A third source is a year-end survey that asks staff to provide feedback on various aspects of the system, including support from the district and external organizations (see online Resource W for an example). This survey can also be used at midyear to collect interim data. The survey, in addition, can be administered using an online survey tool, such as Survey Monkey.

Status on the Action Team Rubric (see online Resource V) is a third set of data for evaluating the system. The primary purpose of the Action Teams Rubric is for action teams to use it to determine the degree to which the action team is meeting expectations. The rubric tells everyone what the system looks like in action, when fully implemented.

A rubric is similar to an Innovation Configuration (Hall & Loucks, 1981; Hall & Hord, 2001). Both identify and describe, in operation, the major components and the practices within each component of the innovation. Both represent the patterns of innovation use, usually on a scale using specific descriptors of behavior, and are ways to precisely define quality and measure fidelity.

Rubrics are often more associated with classrooms, measuring the performance level of students and, therefore, seemingly more evaluative. The Action

Teams Rubric is not an evaluation instrument. Even so, we will use the term *rubric* because teachers more commonly use the word and it does not require an explanation. The Action Teams Rubric measures the fidelity of action team members to the desired behaviors. The ideal description of an implementation behavior, Advanced Implementation, is to the left on the rubric. Increasingly less desirable behaviors, under the columns Developing Implementation, Beginning Implementation, and Not Yet, are along the continuum to the right. For example, one desirable action team practice is for members to use effective meeting processes, including norms, rotating roles, equality of members, agendas, and logs. The least desirable indicators of that practice are for the same person to lead the action team all the time, the team has no norms or ignores them, some members dominate the meetings, and no agendas or logs for meetings. The Action Teams Rubric will determine to what degree action teams are using the proven practices that, when authentically applied, have resulted in higher student achievement.

Schools have used different strategies for completing the rubric. Some schools ask each action team to rate themselves on the indicators using a copy of the rubric. Then, the school's leadership team aggregates the results to develop a schoolwide picture. Other schools enlarge the rubric pages, post them on a wall, and ask each action team to place a colored sticky dot on each indicator to mark where they think their team or the school is currently. The position of the sticky dots provides a visual image of where teams are.

Several schools in Cherokee County, Georgia, used the rubric for an exercise to demonstrate the status or level of implementation of the desired practices. With all of the teachers in the cafeteria, signs were posted on the four walls. One wall had "Not Yet" on it, one had "Beginning," one had "Developing," and one had "Advanced." The leader asked one person from each action team to stand. The leader read a best practice or level of implementation, telling the representatives to go stand beside the sign that best described the behaviors of their action team. After all the representatives were standing by a sign, the leader asked the representatives questions. For example, to one of the representatives standing by "Beginning," the leader asked, "What will facilitate the team's movement to 'Developing'?" The activity reinforced expectations. In the weeks after the activity with the rubric, the principal commented on the number of teams that seemed more focused on doing the right things to get the desired results—higher levels of student learning. When using the rubric, faculties have to be reminded over and over that the desired practices are proven practices.

The Action Teams Rubric was initially developed in 2002 as the Whole-Faculty Study Groups (WFSG) Rubric after years of experimentation with what works best. This version is a substantial revision to the 2002 rubric. The desired outcomes on the rubric have been proven in practice in many schools with very different demographics and at all levels.

For schools in the first year of implementing the action team system, the level of implementation, from "Not Yet" to "Advanced," on each indicator becomes the school's baseline data. Schools in later years of implementation can compare their progress from year to year and use the rubric to target specific areas for improvement that are then incorporated into the school improvement plan.

SHARING RESULTS AND BEST PRACTICES AND APPLYING LESSONS LEARNED

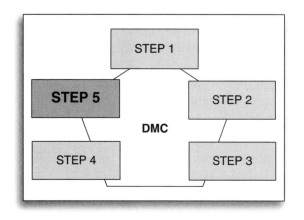

As we stated in Chapter 5, most schools have a school improvement plan (SIP) that the district expects them to implement. The SIP is an operational plan for achieving the school's multiyear goals that are embedded in its school vision, strategic plan, or instructional focus.

In Change Creation schools, action teams *drive* the SIP. Action teams are the *vehicle* for the faculty to work together collaboratively to address the goals in the SIP. The specific learning needs that action teams address are aligned with these performance goals. Through sharing results and best practices from individual action teams and embedding these best practices and lessons learned into next year's SIP and the work of next year's action teams, the school as a whole builds on, and learns from, the action teams.

This step in the DMC connects closely with one of the action team guidelines (see online Resource I): Establish a variety of communication networks and strategies to share the work and results of action teams. It encompasses three related tasks: (1) sharing results and best practices, (2) ensuring that teams learn from each other and that lessons learned are applied throughout the school, and (3) embedding best practices and lessons learned in next year's SIP.

Sharing Results and Best Practices

Sharing action team results and best practices is not just a one-time end-of-the-year event. Rather, it is an ongoing process that occurs throughout the school year.

Communication among action teams and with other groups in the school, including staff, students, and parents, is even more important today than it was when we first developed the WFSG design. It is more important now because of the increased urgency for improving student learning for all students, closing achievement gaps, and preparing students to be college and career ready. Schools cannot become learning communities if faculty members are not learning from each other throughout the school year. Boards of education and district leaders will not provide the time for action teams to meet if they do not see evidence that the work of action teams leads to more effective practice and improved student learning.

Students must be told what is taking place in action teams. Teachers should be encouraged to tell students about their action teams and that a particular strategy or activity they are using in class is a strategy the teachers learned in their action team. This type of sharing has great influence on students and parents because it is important for them to see teachers as learners and understand that learning is a lifelong process.

Right from the beginning, faculty, students, and the community need to know who is in each group and what needs they are addressing. During the learning and inquiry cycles it is important to share resources that action teams may use and progress reports on what is working and what is not working. At the end of each cycle and at the end of the school year, teams share results, lessons learned, and effective strategies.

Effective sharing of the work of action teams requires a variety of communication strategies. Even if action team plans and logs are posted electronically in a shared server, most people will not regularly search and read the documents.

One of the best ways of sharing the work of action teams is face-to-face. Teachers usually participate in other teams besides their action team. On agendas for grade-level, department, and other meetings, it is important to include time for members of different action teams to share what their teams are doing. The other teachers then give their colleague feedback, which could be shared with the original action team. This creates a powerful feedback and input loop for all action teams. Teachers do not have to wait for a whole-faculty sharing time to benefit from what other teams are doing.

As communication expert Judith Glaser (2011) reminds us in her blog, *Navigational Listening—the Racer's Edge,* "Getting to the next level of greatness depends on the quality of the culture, which depends on the quality of relationships, which depends on the quality of conversations. Everything happens through conversations!" (p. 3).

Face-to-face sharing can also occur in cross-team meetings when representatives from each action team meet every four to six weeks to share the work of the teams. We have found that this sharing is more productive when groups prepare in advance for sharing and bring materials to give to those present.

In large schools with more than twenty action teams, it is impossible for twenty or more action teams to have time to share within a 60–90 minute meeting, even if each team only sends one representative. These schools often cluster action teams in groups of three to five teams so that sharing takes place in the smaller clusters and provides more time for each team's representative to share and receive feedback.

Sharing can also take place during faculty meetings. A whole-faculty meeting could be devoted to sharing from a number of teams or each meeting could spotlight one or two teams.

In many schools, teachers and students create electronic multimedia portfolios of their work with artifacts, journals, data, and videos of performances, classes, and other events. Action teams can also create multimedia portfolios to document and share their work together. These electronic portfolios are the richest and most useful when teams begin compiling their portfolios at the beginning of the school year when they start to work together and add to them during each learning and inquiry cycle and during their end-of-the year reflection and sharing.

Action teams can also share resources. Teachers have lots of resources in their classrooms and at home that they may not be using currently. If everyone in a school knows what student needs other teams are addressing, people can loan or give relevant resources to other teams. Some schools set up a resource area for action teams in the school media center or teacher workroom with bins for each team. Then faculty members can leave resources for other teams.

Even with the advances in technology that enable staff to share and access electronic copies of action team work, many schools still post paper copies of action team action plans and logs in a public place in the school for students, parents, staff, and community members to see. They do this because one of the guiding principles in the action team design is that the work is public, and parents, students, and community members often do not have access to the computer networks where electronic copies are kept.

Schools typically put up the team action plans after draft plans have been completed and revised based on feedback from the principal and other action teams. Some schools post the action plan for each action team above the clipboard or plastic pocket for action team logs and put up labels identifying each team's name or category of student needs. Many schools display action team work in the lobby of the school or entrance hallway so that parents and community members can see the work. Others choose to display the work in the teacher workroom or main office.

In most schools, there is also a whole-faculty sharing and celebration time at least twice a year—midyear and the end of the school year. Celebrations are very important. These are special times for leaders to let teachers know that they appreciate and recognize the work action teams are doing. These are special communication times for teams to have fun and do creative things to inspire others and raise the status of learning at the school.

In many schools, principals send a weekly e-mail newsletter to all faculty previewing the week ahead. These newsletters are an excellent vehicle for sharing news about resources and best practices that action teams are using and the results they are getting in with students. Newsletters, blogs, videos, bulletin boards, displays at events such as parent-teacher association meetings, and even Facebook pages and Twitter are also tools for sharing the work of action teams with faculty and with parents.

Ensuring Teams Learn From Each Other and Share Lessons Learned

Just because a school has scheduled opportunities for cross-team sharing about the work of action teams, including best practices, results, and lessons learned, there is no guarantee that teams are learning from each other and that lessons learned are being applied throughout the school.

Good teachers are always looking for new resources, ideas, strategies, and assessment tools to use in their classes and often informally acquire new things to use from other teachers. The challenge for school leaders is how to make peer-to-peer learning more intentional and to expand peer-to-peer learning from individuals to action teams.

We expect every action team to be a learning team. Over the course of a school year, every action team is expected to engage in professional learning to become more knowledgeable and skillful about the student learning needs the team addresses and more productive and effective as a team. Every team needs a variety of "expert voices" to support its members' learning but sometimes it seems easier to look outside of the school for expert voices than to look within. However, schools become sustainable professional learning communities through, as much as possible, identifying and using their own expert voices.

> **Strategies for Using Within-School Expert Voices**

One strategy for using within-school expert voices is purposeful cross-pollination. The instructional coaches and leaders who are reading action team logs and action plans and visiting classrooms of action team members know what resources and strategies their teams are using and what results they are achieving. As they provide feedback and support to action teams during the learning and inquiry cycles, they can tell teams about strategies and resources that other teams working on similar student learning needs are using, and they can encourage and facilitate team members visiting other teachers' classrooms to see best practices in action. They can suggest and facilitate periodic joint meetings among teams working on similar student learning needs or instructional strategies. They can cross-pollinate by inserting information about strategies and resources from different teams into their weekly or monthly staff bulletins. Teams are more likely to explore new strategies and resources that have been recommended by people they trust and respect.

A second strategy for using within-school expert voices is to build cross-team learning into the school's ongoing professional learning program. For example, at meetings or on professional learning days, action teams can hold workshops to teach other teachers successful strategies they have used. They can also invite other teachers to come visit their classrooms to see the strategies in action.

A third strategy for reinforcing the use of within-school expert voices is to ask teams to show evidence of cross-team learning in their action plans, meeting logs, and in their reflections at the end of a learning and inquiry cycle and at the end of the school year. But exhortations to learn from others require actions by leaders to follow up over time with teams to look for, recognize, celebrate, remind, and apply pressure.

Embedding Best Practices and Lessons Learned

In the first part of this chapter, we described how action teams reflect on their own work as a team and with students and how this information is compiled and shared with faculty. We also described a process for conducting an end-of-the-year review of how well the system of action teams is functioning and sharing that information with the faculty. The central question is how is all this information going to be used to consolidate gains, improve schoolwide practice, and institutional new approaches in the next school year.

The information will not be used unless there is a process to ensure that best practices and lessons learned are identified and embedded in next year's SIP and a commitment made by the faculty and the school leadership team to implement that plan. We suggest a three-stage process for embedding practices and lessons learned into next year's SIP: (1) identifying possibilities, (2) prioritizing and selecting possibilities, and (3) planning for implementation.

Here is an example of one school's process.

> At Clarke Middle School in Athens, Georgia, every WFSG study group was asked in March to identify successful practices for improving student learning and to submit them for whole-faculty consideration for inclusion into the SIP for the following year (Murphy & Lick, 2005, pp. 291–295). For each nomination, a team had to briefly describe the practice or idea, indicate whether it had been implemented or tried out, and what the results were. The faculty then met together in April in mixed groups to review the thirty nominations to make sure that every team's recommendations were included, discuss the recommendations, and prioritize them. The school leadership team compiled all of the priority lists and shared the information with the faculty. At a follow-up faculty meeting in May, they developed mini action plans for each high priority recommendation that indicated which person, group, or action team would be responsible for leading or completing the recommended action, the timeline for completing the action, resources required, and action steps. The school leadership team reviewed the mini plans and integrated them into the SIP. They also monitored implementation the following year and provided support to individuals and groups leading the work on different recommendations.

REPEATING THE DECISION-MAKING CYCLE EACH YEAR

At the end of a school year, all action teams complete Step 5 on the DMC. At the beginning of the next school year, all action teams return to Step 1 to examine new data on student learning, identify student learning needs, and re-form action teams. It does not matter if action teams are continuing from the year before or if they have reconfigured; all action teams return to the data for guidance as to what action teams will do.

SUPPORTING ASSESSING THE IMPACT OF ACTION TEAMS AND SHARING RESULTS AND BEST PRACTICES

A key question is, "How do principals, school leadership teams, and district staff support assessing the impact of action teams and sharing results and best practices?"

In Chapters 3 and 5, we introduced and briefly discussed the seven principles from John Kotter (1998) for leaders to follow to ensure success in transforming organizations. The applications of the first four of these principles were covered in Chapters 5, 6, and 10. The last three of these principles, listed below, are especially relevant now for action teams as they move into this step of the Action Teams DMC:

- Empower others to act on the vision and eliminate obstacles to change.
- Consolidate improvements and produce more changes.
- Institutionalize new approaches

We weave these three principles for leading change into our discussion of the supports school and district leaders provide for action teams.

Supporting Assessing the Impact of Action Teams

At the end of a school year, everyone is stressed and there are often a whirlwind of activities. Creating time in the school calendar and protocols for individual action team reflection on the impact of their work and schoolwide reflection on the collective accomplishments of action teams and on the system of action teams is a way for leaders to enact the Kotter (1998) principle, *empower others to act on the vision and eliminate obstacles to change* and ensure that the short-term wins experienced by action teams during the year are documented and lead to consolidating improvements and institutionalizing new approaches.

Time and data are the biggest obstacles. The calendar for action team meetings should set aside one whole action team meeting for individual action team reflection on their work and their impact on their teaching practice and student learning and to complete the survey about the action team system. In addition, the school calendar should include time for a faculty or cross-team meeting to share and discuss the compiled results from all surveys and all action team reflections and to complete the Action Teams Rubric.

Between the reflection meetings by individual action teams and the meeting to share and discuss the results, school leaders should compile the data and organize it into a user-friendly format for action teams to review and discuss. As noted earlier, some schools are using online survey tools such as Survey Monkey to collect data from teams and compile the data. These tools also allow schools to easily compare data from one year to the next.

The larger data question that school and district leaders should address is whether the results of the work of action teams with students can easily be seen in data from schoolwide, district, and state assessments. As the use of data warehouses increases at the district and state levels, leaders should design these warehouses to ensure that action teams as well as individual teachers can use data from school, district, and state assessments to improve student learning.

The final caution for leaders about supporting action teams in Step 4 of the DMC is that there is no point in asking teams to take time to reflect if the data are not shared *and* if the data are not used to celebrate successes and to plan for further improvements.

Supporting Sharing Results and Best Practices

A key question is, "How do principals, school leadership teams, and district staff support (1) sharing results and best practices, (2) ensuring that teams learn from each other and that lessons learned are applied throughout the school, and (3) embedding best practices and lessons learned in next year's SIP?"

Sharing results and best practices

George Bernard Shaw relates that "The single biggest problem in communication is the illusion that it has taken place" (as quoted in Caroselli, 2000, p. 71). While sharing among action teams does take place informally in schools, it is often neither purposeful and widespread nor likely to lead to significant learning by others without conscious continual effort by school leaders. This work is about, as Kotter (1996, 1998) says, *consolidate improvements and produce more changes.*

Implementing the Change Creation system of action teams in schools is a major change initiative that will change the culture of the school. Relentless and continual communication that relates to the vision is essential for the successful implementation. Kotter and Cohen (2002) speak to the importance of communicating change visions and strategies effectively so as to create both understanding and a gut-level buy-in (p. 101). Faculty members develop understanding and buy-in for action teams through learning about what action teams do and the impact they have on students. The Learning Forward standard on implementation emphasizes, as we do, that leaders "engender community support for implementation by communicating incremental successes, reiterating goals, and honestly discussing the complexities of deep change" (Learning Forward, 2011, p. 45). Communication about the value of action teams as a vehicle for professional learning in the Learning Forward leadership standard: "Leaders engage with all stakeholders—those within the education workforce, students, public officials who oversee—schools, parent and community organizations, and the business community—to communicate the importance of professional learning" (Learning Forward, 2011, p. 30).

Establishing a variety of communication networks and strategies to share the work and results of action teams, one of the action team guidelines, needs to proceed concurrently with the creation of action teams and the start of cycles of learning and inquiry. This is a key responsibility for the principal and the school leadership team.

Some of Kotter's (1996) key ideas about successfully communicating include the following:

- Simplicity: All jargon and technobabble must be eliminated.
- Metaphor, analogy, and example: A verbal picture is worth a thousand words.
- Multiple forums: Big meetings and small, memos and newspapers, formal and informal interaction—all are effective for spreading the word.
- Repetition: Ideas sink in deeply only after they have been heard many times.

- Leadership by example: Behavior from important people that is inconsistent with the vision overwhelms other forms of communication.
- Explanation of seeming inconsistencies: Unaddressed inconsistencies undermine the credibility of all communication.
- Give-and-take: Two-way communication is always more powerful than one-way communication. (p. 90)

One of the biggest problems is that communications about really important things, like the work of action teams, get lost in the deluge of information that bombards teachers on a daily basis. So school leaders must make sure that they are both relentlessly communicating about the work of action teams through multiple channels and that they are, as Kotter and Cohen (2002) explain "ridding communication channels of junk so that important messages can go through" (p. 101).

Another challenge that Kotter and Cohen emphasize in the bullets above is leadership by example. If school leaders are communicating messages about the importance of action teams and their results and best practices in meetings and through newsletters but are not following what each action team is doing and giving each action team regular, frequent feedback and support, then faculty members will perceive that leaders aren't walking the talk, and this will undermine their support for the initiative.

During the school year, leaders share different information at different times as follows.

Sharing during the start-up phase

- Who is in each action team and the needs each team is addressing
- Who will be providing feedback and support for action teams
- Expectations for action teams, including attendance, norms, and documentation requirements and procedures
- Calendar for action team meetings, professional learning activities to support action teams, opportunities for cross-team sharing, end of cycle reflection and planning, and end of the year activities

Sharing during and after each cycle of learning and inquiry

- Student learning needs being addressed by each team
- Resource requests and resources used
- Instructional strategies/interventions being used
- Qualitative and quantitative data on changes in student learning
- Best practices identified and lessons learned
- Feedback from action teams on how the system is working and modifications being made

Sharing at the end of the year

- Qualitative and quantitative data on changes in student learning
- Best practices identified and lessons learned
- Feedback from action teams on how the system is working and modifications being made for next year

Ensuring Teams Learn From Other Teams and Lessons Learned Are Applied

Ensuring that teams learn from each other is a strategy to ensure that improvements made by some teams spread to others and is another example of the Kotter (1996, 1998) principle: *consolidate improvements and produce more changes.* This is also about another Kotter principle: *institutionalize new approaches* since applying best practices from action teams schoolwide leads to institutionalizing the approach.

Ensuring that teams learn from each other can occur in a variety of ways and requires encouragement, support, and celebrations of examples of cross-team learning. One way to encourage teams working on similar student needs or using the same resources or instructional strategy to learn from each other is to help them arrange joint meetings or to cover classes so that teachers can observe in each other's classrooms. Teams may also invite members from other teams to be expert voices to attend one or more of their meetings to share strategies and work in progress.

Another way to promote cross-team learning is to use protocols such as "Give One, Get One" to structure cross-team sharing meetings. These require teams to prepare materials to share, with guides for using them, and include time during the meeting for teams to reflect on the new ideas and materials and then choose at least one idea to "commit to try." Each team's exit ticket from the session is its "commit to try."

Some schools, such as Laurel Mill Elementary School in Franklin County, North Carolina, schedule in-school workshops where teams teach other teams how to use an instructional strategy that the team found to be successful. Such workshops can be scheduled in lieu of faculty meetings, before or after school, or on professional learning days.

Many school leadership teams have established the practice of regular instructional walkthroughs or learning walks to visit a number of classrooms for three to ten minutes each while looking for specific instructional strategies. These could be broadened to include other teachers and to focus on seeing action team interventions in classrooms. As with any learning walk, the school would decide in advance where to go and what to look for and would build in time during the learning walk to synthesize observations, plan what to share with the faculty about the learning walk, and discuss next steps.

Leaders can also promote learning from other teams through the feedback they give to action teams on their logs and action plan. In their feedback, they can suggest expert voices, resources or strategies that other teams are using, propose visitations, and recommend joint meetings.

Cross-team learning happens when school leaders are both the advocates and cheerleaders and the facilitators and enablers. Whether best practices and lessons learned get applied schoolwide depends on embedding them into next year's SIP.

Embedding Best Practices and Lessons Learned

This task is about the last Kotter (1998) principle: *institutionalize new approaches* since embedding best practices from action teams in the SIP for schoolwide implementation leads to institutionalizing the approach. Embedding best practices and lessons learned in next year's SIP requires planning by school leaders and engaging the entire faculty over several months. Gone are the days of a few administrators over a weekend putting together next year's plan.

Earlier in this chapter, we suggested three stages to the planning process—(1) identifying possibilities, (2) prioritizing and selecting possibilities, and (3) planning for implementation—and illustrated the process with the work done at the Clarke Middle School in Athens, Georgia. We repeat these three stages here and suggest some guiding questions to consider as you plan each stage:

1. Identifying possibilities

   - What are the best practices, ideas, and lessons learned from this year's work in action teams that should be used or implemented more widely next year?

   > **Guiding Questions for Embedding Best Practices and Lessons Learned**

   - Which aspects of our system for action teams do we want to strengthen, modify, or eliminate to improve the system next year?
   - What is the best way to get input from all action teams?

2. Prioritizing and selecting possibilities

   - Which recommendations will have the greatest positive impact on student learning? On improving educator practice? On enhancing the work of action teams? On strengthening of our culture of collaboration, learning, and action?
   - How do we make decisions about priorities and selection that values everyone's input?

3. Planning for implementation

   - How do we organize the faculty to get broad involvement in planning for implementation?
   - How do we engage families in the development of next year's plan?
   - What is our strategy for building expertise among our faculty in the few best practice initiatives identified, recognizing that members have different levels of understanding and use of the initiative?
   - What is our strategy for ensuring that professional learning about the best practices initiatives leads to changes in practice?
   - What is our strategy for monitoring changes in student performance (without waiting for the results from external assessments) and for using the data to improve instruction?
   - What is our strategy for communicating relentlessly, monitoring, evaluating, and improving our plan and its implementation?
   - How do we get the information we need for each selected recommendation, such as

     o Which person, group, or team should lead or complete implementation?
     o By when do we want this recommendation completed or in place?
     o What resources will it require?

o What are the action steps and timelines required?

o Who will monitor and support the people working on this recommendation?

• How do we review the specific action plans for recommendations and integrate them into our SIP?

• What are we going to stop doing or streamline or reduce to free up time, energy, and resources to support these new recommendations?

The goal with this type of planning process is to create a school plan that is by the faculty and for the faculty—a plan that is less about compliance and more about what the school has decided to work on to improve teaching and learning in every classroom for every student. Most importantly, it is a plan that describes a small set of goals and actions that members of the school community will hold themselves accountable for achieving. The plan is also a brief, easy to read work in progress that the school, led by the school leadership team, will use and modify throughout the year, as appropriate.

SUMMARY

With this chapter, we have completed Part II of this book, where we outlined and unfolded the process for the Change Creation system through the five steps in the DMC and described the nature of action teams.

The first part of this chapter addresses Step 4 in the Action Teams DMC—assessing the impact of action teams on teacher practice and student learning. It focused on what each team needs to do to assess its own impact on teacher practice and student learning; the challenges of linking action team results on classroom assessments to results on school, district, and state tests; and how the principal and the school leadership team can assess schoolwide impact on teacher practice and student learning.

The second part of this chapter addresses Step 5 in the Action Teams DMC—share results and best practices and apply lessons learned. It focused on three related tasks: (1) sharing results and best practices, (2) ensuring that teams learn from each other and that lessons learned are applied throughout the school, and (3) embedding best practices and lessons learned in next year's SIP. These three tasks move the school toward becoming a true professional learning community, as we described in Chapter 4.

In order to accomplish the tasks in these last two steps of the DMC, leaders need to set aside time for reflection, planning, and celebration; provide protocols for reflection and planning; compile and share results and reflections throughout the school community; and incorporate best practices and lessons learned into the SIP for the following year. Without this active, ongoing guidance and support from the principal, the school leadership team, and district staff, the tasks in these last two steps of the DMC will not be accomplished with the quality and thoroughness required for the work of action teams throughout the year to have any lasting impact on the school's culture and on student learning.

A brief epilogue by Carlene Murphy, the founder of the WFSG system, follows this chapter and concludes the book.

Epilogue

This book represents thirty years of proven practice in how teachers work together to take action in their classrooms to increase student learning. Working cooperatively with colleagues is not new to teaching. Teachers have long been eager to share with anyone who will listen. Teaching is a profession of shared experiences. Teachers feel a deep sense of satisfaction in the success of their students and camaraderie with their peers. Teachers have a profound sense of devotion to their work. So, what is different about how we propose in this book that teachers work and learn together? The reader now knows the answer. In the Change Creation system, in small teams we call action teams, teachers learn, plan, act, and reflect in cycles of learning and inquiry. They show or demonstrate how they do what they do with students. Talk is focused. Action is the norm. One teacher demonstrates how he or she teaches a specific skill or piece of information and follows the demonstration with student work or other forms of data for colleagues to further diagnose actions taken in the classroom. Simply put, teachers move from "show and tell" to "watch me teach," from "read and discuss" to "read and translate into classroom use."

How does such a seemingly simple shift in focus create change in a whole school? The synergy or collective energy generated in the teams and classrooms push everyone in the school to a higher level of performance. Have I oversimplified a very complex chain of events? The steps in the system are straightforward and simply stated. The complexity is in the doing, week after week and year after year. Complexity is in the relationships among individual teachers and among teams. Complexity is in the leadership behaviors of leaders in the school and district. Complexity is in the faculty's knowledge of content, pedagogy, and assessment and ability to use appropriately a repertoire of effective teaching models, strategies, or practices. For most faculties, complexity also lies in the bundle of interconnected innovations that encompass the Change Creation system.

When explaining the system to a faculty in a presentation, as one usually does when there is interest in beginning the process, you will hear, "That doesn't sound so bad." Six months later you will hear, "This is hard!" Hard comes in the routine of meetings, following established norms, bringing real work, being authentic, telling what did not work, and keeping records. For insecure teachers, the process is threatening, the fear of being exposed as a less than adequate teacher is real. The key to leading the change creation process and making the complexity less complicated and threatening is a principal who either understands the system or who is willing to work at understanding the system. The principal's role is the cog around which the system turns.

As the faculty learns and experiences the Change Creation process, results are evident. Results are first seen in interactions among the faculty and their appreciation for what each individual does. A sixth-grade teacher in Kentucky who was in a group with a kindergarten teacher told me, "I spent my weekend looking for materials Mary Jane (K teacher) could use in introducing fractions." In Seattle, a music teacher and a physical education teacher incorporated measurement into their teaching plans to support a math teacher in their group. In Augusta, Georgia, we began working with three faculties at the beginning of the school year. By mid-year, the schools felt different. Teachers were talking about instruction in the faculty lounge, teachers were calling each other by their first names, which had not been a common practice, the halls displayed more student work, and discipline referrals were markedly down. The schools were more open. Their climates were shifting. The schools were changing. Each had a long way yet to go, but they were moving. By the end of the year, student performance was noticeably and measurably improving.

Data from schools throughout the country collected by researchers from major universities have proven that schools can change. We have shared descriptions of schools that changed from low performing to high performing. Teachers in schools can become more effective teachers and more responsive to student needs. The evidence is in this book. As individual teachers become more skilled in teaching, the whole faculty becomes more skilled, changing expectations from mediocrity to excellence. Schools can change as the whole faculty generates the synergy to turn the wheel of change.

Changing schools is hard work on everyone's part. And the hard part is that it does not get easier. There are always hills to climb, students to push up the hill, parents who don't cooperate, and new teachers and administrators to orient. Every year it takes energy to restart the process. While repetition is boring, student results are the motivation. Celebrating student results keeps the focus on the target. Building refinements and novelty into the process keeps boredom at bay. The process is integrated into the school's standard practices, the steps become invisible, there is fluidness in teams moving into different patterns, student data drive decision making, and the school changes as these things happen.

If we know schools can change to better meet the needs of students and teachers, why don't all schools choose a path to make their schools more effective at meeting state and national standards? In my opinion, it's politics. My opinion is based on more than fifty years of work in schools. I have seen proven improvement programs lose continued funding because of politics within the district. I have seen ineffective teachers and administrators remain in schools because of politics. I have seen proven leaders leave schools and districts for more prestigious positions. I have seen politically connected teachers who do not want to work as hard as is required for their school to change to use their connections to stop progress. In Seymour Sarason's (1993) book, *The Predictable Failure of Educational Reform: Can We Change Course Before It's Too Late,* he challenges educators to understand that to continue to struggle for "power over" rather than "power with" will doom meaningful change. I have seen politics and power struggles within schools, districts, regional offices, and state departments stop meaningful change. This fact is common knowledge among all levels of education. However, most people are afraid of losing their current status or feel helpless in seeking a remedy.

In the foreword, I asked, "What will be the next revolution in our profession?" I hope it will be a rebellion against territorial wars and power struggles at all levels of education that result in schools being left without physical and financial support to continue major school improvement programs. I hope individuals in schools that have documented increases in student performance will rebel in a public way when politics stop the improvement process. Can we imagine teachers championing the continuation of a specific schoolwide improvement effort as vigorously as they politic for salary and benefits issues? Such action would truly be a revolution.

Schools can change to be more effective schools for all students. We know what to do. But where are the school, district, state leaders, and the teachers with the will and the skill to do it? Why isn't every leader and every teacher in schools across the United States doing what has been proven to work? Books giving roadmaps are no good if educators are not going to follow the maps. Some do. More don't. The Change Creation system can be one road map for real change. The question becomes threefold: What must happen for schools to sustain over time proven, meaningful change? What must happen for all leaders in all state education agencies, districts, and schools and for all teachers to step up to the plate and do what is needed? What must *each of us* do to ensure that every student is career and college ready? The future of public education hinges on the answers.

Carlene U. Murphy

References

Alger, G. (2012, Winter). Transformational leadership practices of teacher leaders. *Academic Leadership: The Online Journal, 10*(1). Retrieved from http://www.academicleadership.org/article/transformational-leadership-practices-of-teacher-leaders

Aronson, E., & Patnoe, S. (1997). *The jigsaw classroom: Building cooperation in the classroom* (2nd ed.). New York, NY: Longman.

Asimov, I. (n.d.). Asimov on science fiction. Retrieved from http://www.goodreads.com/quotes/show/110684

Averette, P., & Baron, D. (n.d.). *The final word protocol.* Retrieved from http://www.turningpts.org/pdf/FinalWordProtocol.pdf

Barker, J. (1991). Discovering the future series: The power of vision [Video]. Retrieved from http://www.starthrower.com/power_of_vision.htm

Barna, G. (1992). *Power of vision.* Ventura, CA: Regal Books.

Barth, R. (2006). Improving relationships inside the schoolhouse. *Educational Leadership, 63*(6), 13.

Beaudoin, M. F. (2007). Institutional leadership. In M. G. Moore (Ed.), *Handbook of distance education* (pp. 391–402). Mahwah, NJ: Lawrence Erlbaum Associations.

Beyerlein, M. M. (1997a). Why do teams fail? Let me count the ways: The macro level. *Center for the Study of Work Team Newsletter, 7*(2), 3–4.

Beyerlein, M. M. (1997b). Why do teams fail? Let me count the ways: The micro level. *Center for the Study of Work Teams Newsletter, 7*(2), 12–13.

Beyerlein, M. M. (2003). A tool approach to forgotten team competencies. In M. M. Beyerlein, C. McGee, G. D. Klein, J. E. Nemiro, & L. Broedling, *The collaborative work systems fieldbook: Strategies, tools, and techniques* (pp. 581–594). San Francisco, CA: Jossey-Bass/Pfeiffer.

Birmbaum, R. (1988). *How colleges work: The cybernetics of academic organization and leadership.* San Francisco, CA: Jossey-Bass.

Blanchard, K., Carew, D., & Parisi-Carew, E. (2000). *The one-minute manager builds high performing teams.* Escondido, CA: Blanchard Training and Development.

Blanchard, K. (2011, April 4). *Full steam ahead! Unleash the power of vision in your company and life* (2nd ed.). San Francisco, CA: Berrett-Koehler.

Blythe, T., Allen, D., & Powell, B. S., (2008). *Looking together at student work* (2nd ed.). New York, NY: Teachers College Press.

Bolstad, R., & Hamlett, M. (n.d.). *The ecology of business.* Retrieved from http://www.transformations.net.nz/trancescript/the-ecology-of-business.html

Burkett, H. (2006, January). *The school improvement planning process* [Slide 24]. The Center for Comprehensive Reform and Improvement. Retrieved from http://www.centerforcsri.org/files/presentations/SchImpPlanningProcess.pdf

Burton, R. A. (2009). *On being certain: Believing you are right even when you're not.* New York, NY: St. Martin's Griffin.

Caroselli, M. (2000). *Leadership skills for managers.* New York, NY: McGraw-Hill.

Clark, T. (2011, February 14). The power of vision provides organizations with direction, inspiration. *Deseret News.* Retrieved from http://www.deseretnews.com/article/705366518/The-power-of-vision-provides-organizations-with-direction-inspiration.html

Clauset, K. H., Lick, D. W., & Murphy, C. U. (2008). *Schoolwide action research for professional learning communities: Improving student learning through the whole-faculty study groups approach.* Thousand Oaks, CA: Corwin.

Collins, J. (2001). *Good to great.* New York, NY: HarperBusiness.

Collins, J. (2001, January). Level 5 Leadership: The triumph of humility and fierce resolve. *Harvard Business Review, 5.*

Collins, J. (2005). *Good to great and the social sectors.* New York, NY: HarperCollins.

Conner, D. (2006). *Managing at the speed of change.* New York, NY: Random House.

Conzemius, A., & O'Neil, J. (2002). *The handbook for SMART school teams.* Bloomington, ID: National Educational Service.

Covey, S. (1990). *The seven habits of highly effective people.* New York, NY: Fireside.

Creighton, T. (2003). *The principal as technology leader.* Retrieved from http://cnx.org/content/m19197/latest

Danielson, C. (2007). *Enhancing professional practice: A framework for teaching.* Alexandria, VA: ASCD.

Darling-Hammond, L. (2010, May 20). Restoring our schools. *The Nation.*

Dean, C., Hubbell, E., Pitler, H., and Stone, B. (2012). *Classroom instruction that works: Research-based strategies for increasing student achievement* (2nd ed.). Alexandria, VA: ASCD.

Diedrich, W. F. (2007, February 10). A culture of discipline. *Ezine.* Retrieved from http://ezinearticles.com/?A-Culture-of-Discipline&id=455166

Drucker, P. (1985). *Innovation and entrepreneurship: Practices and principles.* New York, NY: Harper & Row.

DuFour, R. (2003, Summer). Leading edge: Ask for more, but focus on doing better with what's at hand. *Journal of Staff Development, 24*(3), 67–68.

DuFour, R., & Eaker, R. (1998). *Professional learning communities at work: Best practices for enhancing student achievement.* Alexandria, VA: ASCD.

DuFour, R., DuFour, R., & Eaker, R. (2008). *Revisiting professional learning communities at work: New insights for improving schools.* Bloomington, IN: Solution Tree Press.

Eastwood, K., & Louis, K. (1992). Restructuring that lasts: Managing the performance dip. *Journal of School Leadership, 2*(2), 215.

Educational Leadership Policy Standards: ISLLC 2008, The Council of Chief State School Officers. Retrieved from http://www.ccsso.org/Resources/Publications/Educational_Leadership_Policy_Standards_ISLLC_2008_as_Adopted_by_the_National_Policy_Board_for_Educational_Administration.html

Epstein, M., Atkins, M., Cullinan, D., Kutash, K., & Weaver, R. (2008). *Reducing behavior problems in the elementary school classroom: A practice guide* (NCEE #2008–012). Retrieved from http://ies.ed.gov/ncee/wwc/publications/practiceguides

Farhi, P. (2011, May 20). Five myths about America's schools. *Washington Post.*

Fletcher, A. (2002). *FireStarter Youth Power Curriculum: Participant Guidebook.* Olympia, WA: Freechild Project. Retrieved 11/28/11 from http://www.freechild.org/Firestarter/Fist2Five.htm

Fullan, M. (1991). *The new meaning of education change* (2nd ed.). New York, NY: Teachers College Press.

Fullan, M. (1993). *Change forces: Probing the depths of educational reform.* London, UK: Falmer Press.

Fullan, M. (2001). *Leading in a culture of change.* San Francisco, CA: Jossey-Bass.

Gallo, C. (2011, January 18). Steve Jobs and the power of vision. *Forbes.* Retrieved from http://www.forbes.com/sites/carminegallo/2011/01/18/steve-jobs-and-the -power-of-vision/

Glaser, J. E. (2011, December 9). Navigational Listening—the Racer's Edge [Web log post]. Retrieved from http://juditheglaser.blogspot.com/

Good, T. (2010, November 1). *School reform: Yesterday, today, and tomorrow, 2010.* Dean's Symposium, Florida State University, Tallahassee, FL.

Guide to transformational leadership. (n.d.). Retrieved from http://www.legacee.com/ Info/Leadership/LeaderResources.html

Guskey, T. (2000). *Evaluating professional development.* Thousand Oaks, CA: Corwin.

Hackman, J. R. (2002). *Leading teams: Setting the stage for great performances.* Boston, MA: Harvard Business School Press.

Hall, G. E., & Hord, S. M. (2001). *Implementing change: Patterns, principles, and potholes.* Boston, MA: Allyn & Bacon.

Hall, G. E., & Loucks, S. F. (1981). Program definition and adaptation: Implications for inservice. *Journal of Research and Development in Education, 14*(2), 46–58.

Hattie, J. (2009). *Visible learning: A synthesis of over 800 meta-analyses relating to achievement.* New York, NY: Routledge.

Hawaiian Avenue Elementary School. (n.d.). School vision. Retrieved from http:// hawaiian-lausd-ca.schoolloop.com/vision

Heathfield, S. M. (n.d.). Build an organization based on values: Why values, what values? Retrieved from http://humanresources.about.com/od/strategicplanning1/a/organiz values_2.htm

Hord, S., Rutherford, W., Huling-Austin, L., & Hall, G. (1987). *Taking charge of change.* Alexandria VA: ASCD.

Hord, S. M., & Sommers, W. A. (2008). *Leading professional communities: Voices from research and practice.* Joint Publication of Corwin, National Association of Secondary Principals, and the National Staff Development Council.

Joyce, B., & Showers, B. (1983). *Power in staff development through research on training.* Alexandria, VA: ASCD.

Joyce, B., & Showers, B. (2002). *Student achievement through staff development* (3rd ed.). Alexandria, VA: ASCD.

Joyce, B., & Weil. M. (1986). *Models of teaching* (3rd ed.). Englewood Cliffs, NJ: Prentice-Hall.

Joyce, B., Weil, M., & Calhoun, E. (2008). *Models of teaching* (8th ed.). Boston, MA: Allyn & Bacon.

Kane, T., & Stager, D. (2012). *Gathering feedback for teaching: Combining high-quality observations with student surveys and achievement gains.* Research paper from the Measures of Effective Teaching Project, Bill & Melinda Gates Foundation. Retrieved from http:// www.metproject.org/downloads/MET_Gathering_Feedback_Research_Paper.pdf

Kanter, R. M. (2001, February). *Evolve: Succeeding in the digital culture of tomorrow.* Boston, MA: Harvard University Press.

Kissinger, A. (2007). Strengthening school improvement plans through district sponsorship. In D. W. Lick & C. U. Murphy (Eds.), *The whole-faculty study groups fieldbook: Lessons learned and best practices from classrooms, districts, and schools.* Thousand Oaks, CA: Corwin.

Klein, J. (2011, June). The failure of America's school. *The Atlantic.*

Knight, J. (2006, April). Instructional coaching: Eight factors for realizing better classroom teaching through support, feedback and intensive, individualized professional learning. *School Administrator.* Retrieved from http://www.findarticles.com/p/articles/mi_m0JSD/is_4_63/ai_n16130545/

Koenigs, A. E. (2004). *The affects of whole-faculty study groups on individuals and organizations.* Unpublished doctoral dissertation, Wichita State University, Kansas.

Koenigs, A. E. (2007). Answering the question: Do professional learning communities really work? In D. W. Lick & C. U. Murphy (Eds.), *The whole-faculty study groups fieldbook: Lessons learned and best practices from classrooms, districts, and schools.* Thousand Oaks, CA: Corwin.

Kotter, J. P. (1995, March/April). Leading change: Why transformational efforts fail. *Harvard Business Review,* 1–3. Retrieved from http://www.power-projects.com/LeadingChange.pdf

Kotter, J. P. (1996). *Leading change.* Boston, MA: Harvard Business School Press.

Kotter, J. P. (1998, Fall). Winning at change. *Leader to Leader, 10,* 27–33.

Kotter, J. P., & Cohen, D. S. (2002). *The heart of change: Real life stories of how people change their organizations.* Boston, MA: Harvard Business School Press.

Leach, D. J., Rogelberg, S. G., Warr, P. B, & Burnfield, J. L. (2009). Perceived meeting effectiveness: The role of design characteristics. *The Journal of Business and Psychology, 24,* 65–76.

Leana, C. R. (2011, August 16). The missing link in school reform, *Stanford Social Innovation Review.*

Learning Forward (2011). *Standards for professional learning.* Oxford, OH: Author.

Lemov, D. (2010). *Teach like a champion: 49 techniques that put students on the path to college.* San Francisco, CA: Jossey-Bass.

Lick, D. W. (1999). Proactive comentoring relationships: Enhancing the effectiveness through synergy. In C. A. Mullen & D. W. Lick (Eds.), *New directions in mentoring: Creating a culture of synergy.* London, UK: Falmer Press.

Lick, D. W. (2000, Winter). Whole-faculty study groups: Facilitating mentoring for schoolwide change. *Theory Into Practice, 39*(1), 43–48.

Lick, D. W. (2006). A new perspective on organizational learning: Creating learning teams. *Journal of Evaluation and Program Planning, 29,* 88–96.

Lick, D. W. (2007, July 10). *Status of technology in the learning process: How effective is it and how can its effectiveness be improved significantly?* The 11th World Multi-Conference on Systemics, Cybernetics and Informatics, Orlando, FL.

Lick, D. W., & Kaufman, R. (2000). Change creation: The rest of the story. In J. Boettcher, M. Doyle, & R. Jensen (Eds.), *Theory-driven planning: Principles to practice.* Ann Arbor, MI: Society for College and University Planning.

Lick, D. W., & Murphy, C. U. (2007). *The whole-faculty study groups fieldbook: Improving schools and enhancing student learning.* Thousand Oaks, CA: Corwin.

Literacy Design Collaborative (2011). Template Task Collection I. Retrieved from http://www.mygroupgenius.org/files/static_pages/LDC_Template_Tasks_November_2011.pdf

Lulee, S.-T. (2011, March 13). Transformational leadership: Leadership for education [Web log post]. Retrieved from http://www.educause.edu/blog/susanlulee/TransformationalLeadershipLead/225662

Marzano, R. J., Pickering, D. J., & Pollock, J. E. (2001). *Classroom instruction that works: Research-based strategies for increasing student achievement.* Alexandria, VA: ASCD.

McDonald, J. P., Mohr, N., Dichter, A., & McDonald, E. C. (2003). *The Power of protocols: An educator's guide to better practice.* New York, NY: Teachers College Press.

Meadows, D. (2011, February 2). Donella Meadows: The power of vision. Retrieved from http://www.peopleandplace.net/media_library/video/2011/2/2/donella_meadows_the_power_of_vision

Mehta, J. (2011, June 6). Four paths for the future, *Education Week* blog on the futures of school reform. [Web log post]. Retrieved from http://blogs.edweek.org/edweek/futures_of_reform/2011/06/four_paths_forward.html

Mosley, L. (1986). *The real Walt Disney.* London, UK: Grafton.

Murphy, C. U. (1992). Study groups foster school-wide learning. *Educational Leadership, 50*(3), 71–74.

Murphy, C. U. (2012). Rebel with a cause: A pioneer in the field reflects on the evolution of professional learning communities. *JSD, 33*(3), 43–52.

Murphy, C. U., & Lick, D. W. (1998). *Whole-faculty study groups: A powerful way to change schools and enhance learning.* Thousand Oaks, CA: Corwin.

Murphy, C. U., & Lick, D. W. (2001). *Whole-faculty study groups: Creating student-based professional development.* Thousand Oaks, CA: Corwin.

Murphy, C. U., & Lick, D. W. (2005). *Whole-faculty study groups: Creating professional learning communities that target student learning.* Thousand Oaks, CA: Corwin.

Nadeau, A., & Leighton, M. S. (1996, July). *The role of leadership in sustaining school reform: Voices from the field.* U. S. Department of Education, Office of the Deputy Secretary (Contract EA 9478001).

National Board for Professional Teaching Standards. (2002). National Board Certified Teachers. Retrieved from http://www.nbpts.org/the_standards/standards_by_cert

National School Reform Faculty (n.d.). Looking at student work web site. Retrieved from http://www.lasw.org/index.html

Newmann, F., & Wehlage, G. (1995). *Successful school restructuring: A report to the public and educators by the center for restructuring schools.* Madison: University of Wisconsin Press, 37–38.

NGA Center (National Governors Association Center for Best Practices) and CCSSO (Council of Chief State School Officers). (2012). *English language arts standards.* Retrieved from http://www.corestandards.org/the-standards/english-language-arts-standards

North Carolina Department of Public Instruction (NCDPI), Division of Accountability Services/North Carolina Testing Program. (2005, Spring). Grade 4 reading comprehension sample selections and items, test information document. Retrieved from http://www.ncpublicschools.org/accountability/testing/eog/reading/

Pellowe, J. (2000). Leadership: The motivating power of vision. *Leader Values.* Retrieved from http://www.leader-values.com/article.php?aid=311

Perkins-Gough, D. (2010, Summer). MetLife survey: Collaboration improves job satisfaction. *Educational Leadership, 67.* Retrieved from http://www.ascd.org/publications/educational-leadership/summer10/vol67/num09/MetLife-Survey@-Collaboration-Improves-Job-Satisfaction.aspx

Richardson, J. (1999). Norms put the "Golden Rule" into practice for groups. *Tools for Schools.* Oxford, OH: National Staff Development Council.

Richardson, J. (1996, October). School culture: A key to improved student learning. *The School Team Innovator, 1*(4).

Richardson, J. (2001, August/September). Learning teams: When teachers work together, knowledge and rapport grow. *Tools for Schools,* National Staff Development Council.

Retrieved from http://www.boces.com/cms/lib3/NY26000031/Centricity/Domain/9/Learning_Teams.pdf

Rogers, E. (2003), *Diffusion of innovations* (5th ed.). New York, NY: Simon & Schuster. Retrieved from http://steveapplegate.com/consultant/adopter/index.htm

Rosenholtz, S. (1989). Teacher's workplace: The social organization of schools. New York, NY: Longman.

Roy, P., & Hord, S. (2003). Moving NSDC's staff development standards into practice: Innovation configurations. Oxford, OH: National Staff Development Council.

Rumelt, R. (2011). The perils of bad strategy. *McKinsey Quarterly, 1,* 30–39. Retrieved from https://www.mckinseyquarterly.com/The_perils_of_bad_strategy_2826

Saphier, J., & King, M. (1985, March). Good seed grow in strong cultures. *Education Leadership, 42*(6), 67–74.

Sarason, S. (1993). *The predictable failure of educational reform: Can we change course before it's too late.* San Francisco, CA: Jossey-Bass.

Sawchuk, S. (2012). Many teachers not ready for the common core: Special report on the Common Core State Standards. *Education Week, 31*(29), S12–15.

Schein, E. (2004). *Organizational culture and leadership.* San Francisco, CA: Jossey-Bass. Retrieved from http://www.thinktransition.com/articles/four-elements-for-sustainable-culture-change/

Schmuck, R. (2006). *Practical action research for change* (2nd ed.). Thousand Oaks, CA: Corwin.

Schön, D. A. (1983). *The reflective practitioner: How professionals think in action.* New York, NY: Basic Books.

Senge, P. (1990). *The art and practice of the learning organization.* New York, NY: Doubleday-Currency.

Senge, P., Kleiner, A., Roberts, C., Ross, R., Roth, G., & Smith, B. (1999). *Dance of change.* New York, NY: Doubleday.

Springfield Public Schools. (2011, September). SPS learning model: Summary and update. Unpublished.

Sugai, G., Horner, R. H., Algozzine, R., Barrett, S., Lewis, T., Anderson, . . . Simonsen, B. (2010). *School-wide positive behavior support: Implementers' blueprint and self-assessment.* Eugene: University of Oregon. Retrieved from http://www.pbis.org/common/pbis-resources/publications/SWPBS_ImplementationBlueprint_vSep_23_2010.pdf

Thompson, M., & Thompson, J. (2003). *Learning-focused strategies notebook.* Boone, NC: Learning-Focused.

Transformational leadership. (n.d.). In *Wikipedia.* Retrieved from http://en.wikipedia.org/wiki/Transformational_leadership

Troen, V., & Boles, K. (2011, November/December). Rating your teacher team. *Harvard Education Letter, 27*(6), 1–2. Retrieved from http://www.hepg.org/hel/printarticle/519

Vanzant, L. (1980). *Achievement motivation, sex-role acceptance, and mentor relationships of professional females.* Unpublished doctoral dissertation, East Texas State University.

Vescio, V., Ross, D., & Adams, A. (2008). A review of research on the impact of professional learning communities on teaching practice and student learning. *Teaching and Teacher Education, 24,* 80–91.

Waters, J. T., & Marzano, R. J. (2006). *School district leadership that works: The effect of superintendent leadership on student achievement.* Denver, CO: Mid-continent Research for Education and Learning. Retrieved from http://www.mcrel.org/products-and-services/products/product-listing/01_99/product-90

Waters, J. T., Marzano, R. J., & McNulty, B. A. (2003). *Balanced leadership: What 30 years of research tells us about the effect of leadership on student achievement.* Aurora, CO: Mid-continent Research for Education and Learning, *4*, 9–12. Retrieved from http://www.mcrel.org/products-and-services/products/product-listing/01_99/product-82

Wienholt, G. (2010). Discipline of thought. Retrieved from https://docs.google.com/viewer?a=v&q=cache:9-zOUvijTysJ:www.franchisespeakers.com/wp-content/uploads/2010/01/Gerry-Wienholt-Discipline-of-Thought.pdf+Discipline+of+thought,+Wienholt,+2010&hl=en&gl=us&pid=bl&srcid=ADGEESivAe650hBaZo6p9olnflUHI-LQS8l8K-lWcC0E9uv9AgQEwwanxns5dsQsfBFGMaevJ6F4aVJy7jMFEKFKelT67DlaABdRGW4bXc1mo21uXhniY_MXPwhKqgl_t0tBIkOi2v9w&sig=AHIEtbTaSE-rIDxGjBoidTPLh7M0B5wzPg

Wiggins, G., & McTighe, J. (1998). *Understanding by design.* Alexandria, VA: ASCD.

Wilson, I. (1996). The practical power of vision. *On the Horizon, 4*(2), 1. Retrieved from http://horizon.unc.edu/projects/seminars/futurizing/practical.html

Index

Action learning, 51
Action teams, 4
  administrator of, 131
  authenticity of, 58
  based on grouping patterns, 97
  based on student learning needs, 96–97
  bundle of changes to deal with, 116–117
  collaboration within, 56–57, 105
  definition of, 103–104
  desired evolution of, 56 (figure)
  developmental stages of, 122–126
  failure and, 63
  feedback for, 121–122
  focus on student learning, 119–120
  impact assessment of individual, 193–194
  meetings for, 98–99, 114–116, 120
  primary purpose of, 106
  principles of, 110–111
  process guidelines for, 111–114
  purposes of, 106–109, 192
  researchers and, 57
  routines for, 120–121
  size of, 98
  standards and, 56–57
  struggling, 127–130
  student expectations of, 104–106
  support for, 119–132
  teachers and, 57–58
  See also Decision Making Cycle (DMC);
    Team action plan
Action Teams Decision Making Cycle (DMC).
  See Decision Making Cycle (DMC)
Action Teams Rubric, 117, 196–197
Administrator action teams, 131
Advocate, change, 43
After-action review, 192–193
Alger, G., 23
Appropriate learning, 51–52
Aristotle, 19
Aronson, E., 169
Asimov, I., 37
Assessment
  action team impact, 193–194
  benchmark, 156, 195–196
  end-of-cycle results, 185–186, 188–189

  impact (*see* Impact assessment)
  student learning needs, 107–108
Assimilation capacity, 40–42, 109
Attempt, attack, abandon cycle, 48
Averette, P., 169

Barker, J., 35, 36
Barna, G., 35–36
Baron, D., 169
Benchmark assessments, 156, 195–196
Best practices, 201–202
  embedding in SIP, 206–208
  sharing of, 204–205
Beyerlein, M. M., 63
Blanchard, K., 35
Burkett, H., 33
Burnfield, J. L., 114–116
Burton, R. A., 47

Calendar, for action team, 101
Celebrations, 200
Change, 37–54
  basics of, 19–20
  change roles, 42–46
  creation of, 20–21, 30
  dealing with overload, 40–42
  potential of, 38
  principles of successful, 39–40
  removing obstacles to, 39–40, 100–102
  resistance to, 46–51, 93
  response to, 37
Change advocate, 43
Change agent, 42–43
Change Creation process, steps in, 9–10
Change Creation system, 7–10
  appropriately changing culture, 7–8
  components of, 77
  critical elements for success in, 38–39
  generating new teaching/learning
    approaches, 8
  goal of, 28, 71–72
  implementation decisions, 88–89
  key elements of, 7–8, 9 (figure)
  learning communities and, 71–75,
    73 (table)

learning community example, 74–75
preparing foundation for, 84–88
roots of, 4–5
Change sponsor. *See* Sponsor
Change target, 43
Clark, T., 36
Clauset, K. H., 112, 195
Cohen, D. S., 204
Collaboration, 21–22, 30
Collaborative culture, 22
Collaborative teams, 4
   See also Action teams
Collins, J., 5, 6, 17
Comentoring, 63–64, 67
Common Core standards, 94, 97, 106,
   107, 158, 161, 165, 166
Conner, D., 19, 44–45, 47, 58, 59
Continuous Classroom
   Improvement (CCI), 75
Covey, S. R., 19, 46
Creativity, 27–28
Creighton, T., 50–51
Cross-pollination, 201
Cross-team learning, 206
Cultural change, 28–29
Cultural shifts, 16–17
Culture
   of change creation, 19–21
   of discipline, 5, 17–19, 30
   of relationships and collaboration,
      21–22, 30
   of transformational leadership, 22–28
   school (*see* School culture)

Danielson, C., 107
Darling-Hammond, L., 3
Data standards, 94, 111–112, 159,
   173, 180, 192
Data warehouses, 195, 203
Decision Making Cycle (DMC), 79–90
   as multiyear effort, 79–80 (figure), 84, 202
   Change Creation system preparation
      for, 84–90
   overview of steps in, 81 (figure)–83
   school improvement plan and,
      84, 85 (figure)
Developmental stages of action teams,
   122–126
   as circular, 126
   consequence stage, 125–126
   forming stage, 122–123
   grumbling stage, 124
   time spent in each stage, 126
   willingness stage, 125
Dichter, A., 181
Disney, W., 31–32
Districtwide impact assessment, 194–196
Districtwide interventions, 107
Drucker, P., 20
DuFour, R., 21, 72

DuFour, R., 72
Dysfunctional behavior, 41

Eaker, R., 72
Early Adopters, 48, 49
Early Majority, 48, 49
Educational Leadership Policy Standards, 7
Electronic portfolios, 199–200
Empowerment, 25, 39–40, 59, 99–100,
   102, 203
End-of-cycle results, assessing/reflecting on,
   185–186, 188–189
End-of-year review, 192–193
Expertise, 167, 169, 174, 201

Farhi, P., 2–3
Feedback, for action teams, 121–122
Final Word protocol, 169
First-order change, 21
Five Core Propositions, 7
Fullan, M., 28, 43, 69, 116

Gallo, C., 33
Glaser, J., 199
Good, T., 2
Grade level/content area teams, 95
Gretzky, W., 37
Grouping patterns, action teams
   based on, 97
Guiding coalition, 39, 86–87, 90, 171
Gusky, T., 166

Hall, G. E., 37
Heathfield, S., 33
Hord, S. M., 37
Huling-Austin, L., 37

Impact assessment
   at district level, 194–196
   at schoolwide level, 194–195, 196–197
   at state level, 194–195
   of individual action teams, 193–194
   of interventions, 181–182, 184, 188
   of teacher practice and student learning,
      83, 192–197
   supporting, 203
Implementation standards,
   111–112, 171, 206
Incentive system, 8, 24, 28
Innovation Configuration, 196
Innovators, 48–49
Instructional programs/practices,
   improving, 108
Integrity, 26
Interventions
   assessing impact of, 181–182, 184, 188
   districtwide, 107
   implementing, 178–180, 183, 187–188
   planning and practicing, 167–168,
      169–170

Jigsaw protocol, 169
Jolly, A., 65
Joyce, B., 107, 165

Kanter, R. M., 50
Kaufman, R., 20
King, K., 74
King, M., 29
Kissinger, A., 4
Klein, J., 3
Knight, J., 48
Koenigs, A. E., 61, 72
Kotter, J., 38, 39–40, 84–85, 86, 87,
    192, 203, 204–205, 206–207

Laggards, 48, 49–50
Late Majority, 48, 49
Leach, D. J., 114–116
Leadership standards, 53, 87, 174, 206
Leana, C. R., 69
Learning and inquiry cycle tasks
    acquire appropriate learning, 165–166,
        169, 174
    assess and reflect on end-of-cycle results,
        185–186, 188–189
    assess impact of interventions,
        181–182, 184, 188
    clarify focus, 158, 171
    determine current student performance,
        159–160, 171–172
    develop expertise, 167, 169, 174
    document and share work, 163, 170,
        184–185, 186–187
    examine student work, 180–181,
        184, 188
    identify content and best practices,
        163–165, 168–169, 173–174
    implementation, 82–83, 153–190
    implement interventions, 178–180,
        183, 187–188
    overview of, 155 (figure)–158
    plan and practice interventions, 167–168,
        169–170, 174
    plan for next steps, 182–183, 184, 188
    reflect on lessons learned, 182, 184, 188
    support for innovation and student
        learning, 187–189
    support tasks, 171–174
    target-setting, 160, 172–173
    time spent on, 163, 170, 185, 187
    tips for success, 161–162, 168–170,
        183–184, 186
Learning capacities, 38
Learning community standards, 45, 86, 96,
    104, 160, 179
Learning design standards, 111–112, 166
Learning Forward standards
    action teams, 56–57
    data, 94, 111–112, 159, 173, 180, 192
    implementation, 111–112, 171, 206

leadership, 53, 87, 174, 206
learning communities, 45, 86, 96,
    104, 131, 160, 179
learning designs, 111–112, 166
outcomes, 192
professional learning, 188
resources, 174
sponsorship, 45
support, 173
overview of, 6–7
Learning needs, student, 81–82, 91–95
    action teams based on, 96–97
    assessment and, 107–108
    identification of, 93–95
    needs to be addressed, 92–93, 99
    support for identification of,
        93–95, 99–102
    targeting schoolwide, 108–109
Learning teams, 27, 64–68
    building of, 65–68
    capacities of, 64–65 (figure)
    fostering comentoring in, 67
    Foundational Phase of, 66–67, 81
    Learning and Inquiry Cycle Phase of,
        67–68, 81
    Recheck Phase of, 68, 81
Learning walk, 206
Learn-plan-act-reflect cycle, 68, 72,
    177, 179 (figure)
Leighton, M. S., 33
Lemov, D., 107
Lessons learned
    applying, 83, 200–201
    embedding in SIP, 201–202, 206–208
    reflecting on, 182, 184, 188
Lick, D., 20, 24, 25, 98, 181
Literacy Design Collaborative, 161
Little, A. D., 38
Logs, action team, 114, 121
    feedback on, 151
    template for, 147 (figure)
Lulee, S.-T., 23

Marzano, R. J., 20–21, 25, 28, 107
McDonald, E. C., 181
McDonald, J. P., 181
McNulty, B. A., 25
McTighe, J., 169
Meadows, D., 35
Meetings, for action teams
    agenda for, 114
    chairperson/leader for, 115–116
    facilities for, 115
    for reflection, 203
    log template, 147 (figure)
    minutes/logs for, 114, 121
    punctuality and, 115
    team action plan and, 146–148, 151
    times for, 98–99
    times for, protecting, 120

Mehta, J., 3
Microsoft, 34–35
Mohr, N., 181
Mosley, L., 31–32
Murphy, C., 48, 80, 98, 112, 181

Nadeau, A., 33
National Board Certified Teachers (NBCTs), 7
National Board for Professional Teaching
    Standards (NBPTS), 7

Online professional development, 174
Outcomes standards, 192

PD 360, 174
PD In Focus, 174
Pellow, J., 34–35
Pickering, D. J., 107
Planning process, stages in, 207–208
Pollock, J. E., 107
Portfolios, electronic, 199–200
Positive Behavioral Interventions and
    Support (PBIS), 92
Positive Behavior Support (PBS), 92
Post-tests, 180, 182, 184
Practical learning-team design
    process, 71–72
Pre-tests, 180, 182, 184
Principal
    administrator action teams and, 131
    as change advocate, 43
    as change agent, 42–43
    as change sponsor, 42, 44, 45
    as chief leader of learning, 26, 53
    as transformational leader, 25–28, 30
    communication of work and results of
        action teams by, 200, 204–205
    feedback by, 121–122, 145, 146, 148,
        149, 151, 200
    fluidity of change roles of, 43
    identification of student learning needs
        and, 91, 102
    implementation of Change Creation
        system and, 88
    resistance to change and, 52
    review of action plans and logs,
        124, 125, 129
    role in action teams, 72, 73 (table)
    role in formation of action team, 122–123
    role in guiding coalition, 86–87
    routines and, 120–121
    school vision and, 33, 34, 87, 88
    struggling teams and, 127
    support of action teams by, 129
Professional learning communities (PLCs),
    69–75
    Change Creation system and,
        71–75, 73 (table)
    definition of, 69–71
Professional learning standards, 188
Protocols, 169, 181

Relationships and collaboration, 21–22, 30
Resistance to change, 46–51
    control issues, 50, 93
    dealing with resistance, 49–50
    Early Adopters and, 48, 49
    Early Majority and, 48, 49
    general resistance, 47–50
    human nature and, 46–47
    Innovators and, 48–49
    Laggards and, 48, 49–50
    Late Majority and, 48, 49
    other reasons for, 50–51
    quick fixes and, 48
Resources, 139–140, 200
Resource standards, 174
Respect, 8, 24, 25–26, 27, 29, 92, 141, 201
Results
    end-of-cycle, 185–186, 188–189
    sharing, 83, 130–131, 198–200,
        204–205, 206–208
Reward and incentive system, 8, 24, 28
Risk taking, 27–28
Rogelberg, S. G., 114–116
Rogers, E., 48
Rosenholtz, S., 127
Rutherford, W., 37

Saphier, J., 29
Sarason, S., 210–211
Schein, E., 47
Schön, D., 188
School change leader, principal as, 26
School culture, 14–17, 29
    assumptions in, 15–16, 17
    behaviors and, 15, 16, 17
    beliefs and, 15, 16, 17
    building blocks of, 7–8, 15–16, 26, 58
    definition of, 15
    norms of, 29
    role of principal in creating, 26
    shifts in, 16–17
School improvement, expectations for, 1–2
School improvement plan (SIP),
    84, 85 (figure), 198, 202, 206–207
School reform, 2–3
School vision, 32–34
    characteristics of, 32
    definition of, 32
    example of, 33
    format of, 33–34
    perspectives on, 33
Schoolwide impact assessment,
    194–195, 196–197
Second-order change, 21
Senge, P., 38
Shared values, 25
Shared vision, 25, 36
Shaw, G. B., 206
Showers, B., 165
Site Professional Learning Systems, 75
SMART learning goals, 93, 160

Sponsor, 26, 42
  characteristics of strong, 44–45
  dealing with weak, 45–46
Sponsorship standards, 45
Standards for Professional Learning by
    Learning Forward, 6–7
  See also Learning Forward standards
Statewide level impact assessment, 194–195
Struggling action teams, steps for helping,
    127–130
  administrative support, 129
  content area/instruction/district
      support, 129
  feedback from other teams, 127–128
  observations of meetings, 130
  obtaining second opinion, 129
  reassurance, 128–129
  suggestions from designated reader, 129
Student learning, focus on, 119–120
Study groups, 4
Support standards, 173
Survey Monkey, 194, 196, 203
Synergy, 58–63, 209
  checklist for, 61, 62 (figure), 68
  learning teams and, 66–67
  norms for, 60 (figure)
  prerequisites for, 59, 61, 63
  process for creating, 59–61

Target, change, 43
Teacher practice/student learning, assessing
    impact of, 83, 192–197
Team action plan, 82, 133–152
  actual performance in, 142–143
  contextual information in, 140
  current performance in, 142
  data sources/performance levels in, 142
  essential question in, 139
  example of completed,
      137 (figure)–138 (figure)
  feedback on, 149, 151
  feedback on meeting logs, 151
  guidelines for, 148–149
  instructional strategies in, 139
  learning needs/standards in, 134, 139
  norms and, 140–141
  problems with, 150 (table)
  reasons to develop, 133–152
  resource section in, 139–140
  specific student needs in, 141–142
  steps in creating, 144–145
  target performance in, 142–143

target students for, 139
team meeting log and, 146–148
team meeting log template, 147 (figure)
template for, 134–143,
    135 (figure)–136 (figure)
updating, 145
Teams
  comentoring, 63–64
  learning, 27, 64–68
  See also Action teams
Thompson, J., 107
Thompson, M., 107
Transformational leader, 23–24, 30
  key characteristics of, 24 (figure)
  principal as, 25–28
Trust, 7, 8, 22, 24, 25, 26, 29,
    115, 141, 201

Universal Change Principle, 51–54
  appropriate learning and, 51–52
  leadership standard and, 53
  proper application of, 53
Urgency, sense of, 39, 85–86, 90,
    99, 100, 173

Values, shared, 25
Vision, 31–36
  cautions, 35–36
  creating and communicating, 39, 87–88
  meaning of, 32
  power of strong, 34–35
  practical power of, 36
  school, 32–34
  shared, 25, 36
  vignette about, 31–32
Vision Creation, 25
"Vision Killers," 35–36

Walking the talk, 87, 131, 205
Warr, P. B., 114–116
Waters, J. T., 20–21, 25, 28
Weil, M., 107
Welch, J., 32
Whole-Faculty Study Group (WFSG),
    4–5, 10, 72, 80
  action plans, 140
  action teams, 104, 105, 106,
      110, 112, 121
  Action Teams Rubric, 197
  student learning needs, 94–95
Wiggins, G., 169
Wilson, I., 36

CORWIN

A SAGE Company

The Corwin logo—a raven striding across an open book—represents the union of courage and learning. Corwin is committed to improving education for all learners by publishing books and other professional development resources for those serving the field of PreK–12 education. By providing practical, hands-on materials, Corwin continues to carry out the promise of its motto: **"Helping Educators Do Their Work Better."**

Advancing professional learning for student success

Learning Forward (formerly National Staff Development Council) is an international association of learning educators committed to one purpose in K–12 education: Every educator engages in effective professional learning every day so every student achieves.